JOURNEY AFTER DAWN

JOURNEY
AFTER DAWN

by

BILL PEASCOD

CICERONE PRESS
HARMONY HALL, MILNTHORPE, CUMBRIA, ENGLAND

© Bill Peascod 1985

ISBN 0 902 36368 9

First published 1985

Printed in Great Britain by
Butler & Tanner Ltd, Frome and London

For Etsu, Emma and Alan

Contents

Illustrations

Foreword

High is our calling friend. Creative art
Demands the service of a mind and heart
Though sensitive, yet in their weakest part
Heroically fashioned

W. Wordsworth

West Cumberland, though not many miles removed from the rest of England, used nevertheless to be remarkably remote. It was a small mining and industrial community forgotten, and out of place, on the edge of the precious Lake District and surrounded by farming and 'County' communities. In the past, when it was as easy to travel by sea as by land, it had as much connection with Wales as with the rest of England. Even in the nineteen-fifties many West Cumbrians knew the Lake District only from day tours taken while on holiday at Blackpool.

Bill Peascod is a West Cumbrian and his book is not just an account of climbing adventures. It is a story of discovery and growth, of an adventurous and creative mind breaking out into the light. Thus it is more than a climbing book; it is a true romance and its author is a modern romantic, whose questing spirit has not only produced routes which have delighted thousands of climbers, but has also broken new ground in the world of art.

The best romantics have always been the ones with a strong sense of reality, and to climb with Bill Peascod is to be aware of this. For on rock he is a model of practicality, good judgement and common sense. Add to these qualities a high degree of aspiration and you have the man who ventured on, and came safely through, all those first ascents.

About 1950 he tried out his Honister Wall on me by getting me to lead it. This was the first time I was on a rope with him and I remember his delighted laughter as I made my own tentative advances up the climb. We also some time after climbed Zig Zag on Castle Rock. But then to my disappointment he departed for Australia and it was nearly thirty years before we renewed acquaintance. Nowadays, as he moves upwards with authority and a certain ponderous grace, he is just the same in essence as he was in youth, and with the same drive and enthusiasm.

Bill Peascod is a cragsman. No-one deserves that appellation more. He started life wresting a living from rock underground, and in his sixties he is still drawn to the harsh and demanding verticalities of the crags. What is at the root of this life-long love-affair with rock? Read this book and you will perhaps understand.

Tom Price

Acknowledgements

Personal memory alone is not sufficiently accurate to signpost a journey such as this. I have leant heavily on the reminiscences and writings of others. Chief of these have been the excursions I have made into the diaries and recollections of my climbing companion of early days, S. B. Beck. There are many others — Brian Dodson, Brian Blake, Stan Dirkin, George Rushworth, Jack Carswell, Tom Price and more.

In Australia there were Les and Jill, Evan and Mary, Peter and Irene — my close friends from Wollongong and Jamberoo who succoured me when the way became very rough. Neil Lamb in Brisbane and David Oliver who helped me to find the mountains, again.

To Mike and Eileen Sellers who gave unstinting support and encouraged me to write and to Shotei Ibata who led me to Japan.

I owe them all my thanks — most of all, I think, for their friendship — and I extend such in deep sincerity.

More recently, for giving my latter day journey rich and undreamt of excitement there are Bill Birkett, Ronnie Faux and David Craig (who also cast a professional eye over my text). They, too, I thank, with humility, for sharing with me their skills and love of mountains.

For allowing me to browse through and quote from their journals I thank the President and Editor of the Fell and Rock Climbing Club and Walt Unsworth, the Editor of *Climber and Rambler*.

For the effort she has put into correcting and typing my manuscript I owe and extend my sincere thanks to Mrs. Julie Jones.

Finally, to my wife I offer, a deep and grateful thanks — not only for the support she has given me in the recording of this journey but for the valiant efforts she has made in the smoothing of the pathway of the latter years.

Bill Peascod
Melbecks
1985

Prologue

It was one of those magical hours around dawn — the dawn of a beautiful, still, English summer's day. I had just come out of the pit — a lonely teenager; sweaty, grimy, tired. On my old push-bike I cycled home and stopped on Stainburn hill. The birds' morning songs ranged across an infinity of moorland; a cockerel proclaimed its farmyard authority; the last star faded; in the distance a blush of light threw the Cumbrian fells into profile; beside me the bottoms of hedgerows rustled with tiny mysteries.

Reaching home, where my father had arrived a few minutes earlier, we ate our morning (evening?) meal, then bathed in the tin tub in front of the fire. The dirt sloughed away and I returned to thinking about the day outside.

My father went to bed, but the dawn sounds still haunted me. I went outside, took my bike from the passageway between the houses and rode out to meet the morning.

It was probably the most momentous decision I was ever to make. From that instant my life's course was shaped! It was the start of a journey which still continues . . . It led out to the sun and the hills. Along it I discovered friends and assuaged needs. Through the noon time heat into the late afternoon — along fine footpaths and rough hillside, through storms and thunder and again into sunshine.

The road has had its ups and downs and potholes — but I am grateful that I have had the luck and the stamina to make the journey after dawn . . .

1

The Beginnings

Seven days before her twentieth birthday my mother gave birth to
the first of her two sons; the date was May 3, 1920. Like my father
and his father, and doubtless many another of the line before them, I
was called William. Like them, I was never known by this formal
given-name, except in official documents, or by those who didn't
know me. Amongst my family I was known as La'al Billie, to
distinguish me from my father who, after my birth, became Big
Billie. It was as good an arrangement as any, and didn't lead to quite
the same difficulties as were to be found in those large West
Cumbrian families who manage to rear legions of children whilst
using only a minimum of Christian names. I knew of one such family
who had three sons. They were called John, James and Bill. Each of
these had several sons and also included some Johns, James' and
Bills. The second generation was identified as John's John and Bill's
John, or Bill's Bill or James' Bill and so on. It seemed to work well
enough. By the time the third generation came along the War and
the cinema had emancipated the parents and freed them from the
tight strictures of family first-name conventions and the Clints and
Glens (and, inevitably Shirley!) took over — although, for my
money, Clint's Clint doesn't roll off the tongue quite as smoothly as
John's John.

My father was twenty-one when I was born and we lived with my
one remaining grandparent, my grandmother, who was known to
her death as Mother Peascod, in an old cottage in what is officially
referred to as Sharp's Yard, but which we knew as The Fold, in
Ellenborough, a couple of miles east or so of the Solway Coast near
Maryport. As I grew older, in this pleasant little village, events
began to register themselves in my memory. I recall; for instance,
with still some wonder, the old couple who lived in the next cottage to
us in the Fold. They were a brother and sister. He was called

Dumbie, because he was deaf and dumb and she was called Betty, and was blind. I never knew Dumbie's real name — nor how they managed to communicate.

The houses in which we lived were very old — mid seventeenth century (and now being carefully preserved as buildings of 'historic interest').

Cooking was done over an open fire in the only living room — which was known as the Kitchen. Above the fire a hook hung down the chimney and from it was suspended the frying pan or broth pan. There was an oven on the left where bread and scones were baked and which was heated through an arrangement of dampers from the open fireplace. On the right of the fire stood a hob where the cast-iron kettle sat for much of the day and sang its life away.

My grandmother, they used to tell me, once owned a cat; an old grey Tom. It was an inveterate and accomplished thief — and all its cunning was made manifest whenever Betty decided to cook Dumbie a kipper for his tea. Tom had to time his movements carefully if he didn't want either fried paws or a roasted hide or broken ribs. When Betty approached the fire, kipper in pan, Tom had to be ready. Leaping up onto the hob he would neatly hook the kipper out of the pan with one claw and leap away. If he left his run too late he would get burnt either from the pan or the fire. If Betty suspected his presence she would lash out with the poker. If Betty hadn't realised the cat had made its successful strike she would be busily cooking the empty frying pan and only when the time came to turn the elusive kipper with her fork would she realise that Tom had paid a visit. Now Betty may have been blind — but she was not dumb. 'That bloody cat,' she would yell. 'It's been at my frying pan again.' Everyone would be concerned except Tom who would be up at the top of the garden enjoying the fruits of his thieving. In the game of survival, honours were about even between Betty and Tom.

But Tom's days were numbered. My father caught him in the act and put him in my grandmother's oven, but he forgot to release Tom before going out to play. Mother Peascod unwittingly began to stoke up the fire and prepare the oven for baking. It took her some time to find the source of the piteous cries and when she opened its door not only was the oven hot, so was Tom. He went, she told me years afterwards, three times round the kitchen without touching the floor and disappeared up the chimney. He was never seen again.

One day, one of my father's younger sisters, Belle (there were eight brothers and sisters), was wearing a new dress — a great rarity, it should be realised. The dress was covered in pretty little pink flowers. Sitting on a stool in front of the fire Belle had acquired a pair of scissors and was completely involved in the absorbing task of cutting out the tiny flowers from the dress. Had Mother Peascod's hands not been full the matter would have been resolved immediately by Belle receiving a ringing blow across the ear, but her hands were occupied with a tray of hot scones she was drawing from the oven and with these she smote Belle across the top of her head. Belle's hair came out soon afterwards — she never cut pink flowers from her dress anymore!

Life was hard. Solutions to problems were achieved more frequently by the swing of an open palm than by reasoned debate. Yet there was love, affection, loyalty and a warm family spirit between my grandmother and her offsprings.

As I grew up, into the years of memory, we began to move. First from Ellenborough to Maryport, then to Clifton, where my father was working in the mine.

Those childhood years, the ones that I can remember most clearly, had been times of freedom, adventure, discovery — without a real care to trouble my boyhood existence. My father worked hard but did not bring in much money. Mining did not rate, either on the social or industrial scale, anywhere near the level it now commands. There was a story we were told, years later, about a well known society lady who drove past Gate Head, at Clifton, in her chauffeur-driven Rolls. Pointing to some miners she enquired of her chauffeur, 'What are those?' 'They are miners, my lady,' he answered. In a surprised voice she queried, 'What? Do they walk?'

I recall, vaguely, the National Strike in 1926. My father, with others, went up onto the moors and mined 'outcrop' coal in shallow holes dug in the moorland waste; I still remember the colour of the coal — not at all like the stuff we used to get from the 'coal man', or that which I met in greater abundance in later years, but a dirty brown, iron-stained product, small in size, that struggled manfully, but with hardly resounding success, to keep alight in our firegrate.

Life in the village was a fairly routine existence. Nearly all the men with a job worked in the mines. During the week, when not in the pit, they were either at home, sleeping or eating, or trying to eke some entertainment out of life in the Hall, provided from a Miners' Welfare Fund, where there were billiard tables, dominoes and chequer boards, papers and magazines, and bowling rinks. Called the 'Reading Room' it was the cultural centre of the village. Women and children rarely went there.

The woman of the house, in the main, stayed at home. There was much to do. With no gas or electricity in the village the fireplace was the centre of her world. On it she lavished care and attention. On her knees in the hearth she would polish the hobs, the oven door and the 'tidy', which hid the ashes under the fire, with black lead, whilst copper hoods shone until they glistened with pride.

The fender was often enough made of brass, but sometimes of steel, and these too were attacked until they glittered in the fire's warmth. Tongs, poker and shovel, also in brass, rested on the fender ends and two china dogs or cast iron lions sat in the hearth on either side of the fire and leant against the hobs. The mantelshelf, which was often decorated with a moth-eaten velvet drape some six or eight inches deep with an undulating hem adorned by dusty velvet balls, carried the 'tea-caddy' and a pair of brass candlesticks and sometimes the carefully trimmed and polished paraffin lamp.

There was, of course, no T.V., although a few radio amateurs built their own receiving sets and operated them off masses of wet cells, which were taken away periodically for recharge. I never knew anyone in the village who had a telephone or a car, other than the most affluent publican and general storekeeper. I knew of no one who went away for holidays in the twenties and early thirties. But life was not without its moments.

At the weekends the hard core of village bachelordom went to Workington, two miles away, on either Saturday or Sunday evenings — most times as a group, some ten or fifteen strong, dressed in its weekend best. Every working man had a blue serge suit — it served for weddings, christenings and funerals. When the nap was worn off, and the seat and back began to shine, it became 'second best' and was serviceable for general social functions — such as a booze-up in Workington. To complement the blue serge would be a collarless white shirt held closed at the neck by a brass and celluloid stud and set off by a long neckerchief (paisley pattern or red/maroon colours were favourites) which was wrapped round the throat and knotted at the front over the collar stud. The two long ends from the knot were then flattened across the chest, like some socio-religious symbol, and tucked under the braces. On the head a cloth cap would be rakishly set, high up at one side where it was padded with newspaper and low over the ear on the other. On the feet would be sported the inevitable Lankies. (Lancashire clogs, so different from the heavy reinforced pit clogs; fine pieces of craftsmanship with their thin wooden duck-bill shaped soles, brass toe-plate and intricate Art-Deco swirls and scrolls incised into the leather — the whole lot polished with loving care until the leather gleamed like ebony.)

Thus with jacket open, waistcoat left in the wardrobe, hands thrust into trouser pockets and chest thrown proudly forward, flaunting jaunty cap and gleaming clogs, the village lad and his mates embarked on their weekly adventure. Two miles they would walk into town in a balmy summer's evening, the focus of their attention being a favourite pub or a particular barmaid. Then, thirst slaked, back they would walk to the village — not quite so proudly or steadily as they had on their outward venture — with a song or two to serenade the evening star. And at five o'clock in the morning most of them, a bit quieter than they were a few hours previously, wearing much less dashing clothing, smelling a little of stale beer and sweat would be dropping like stones in a dark pit cage to try and squeeze from the earth enough of a livelihood to allow them, next Saturday or Sunday, to walk once more into excitement and forgetfulness.

The women rarely left the village. They were too busy trying to keep up standards or circulating village gossip over a cup of tea in the house next door.

In the village most of the occupants lived in terraced houses. There were areas set aside for allotments where potatoes, cauliflowers, sprouts, peas and carrots were grown — or which housed a few hens and numerous pigeon sheds. Pigeon racing was a very popular pastime and, where a big race was involved (the birds flying from France), there was much excitement throughout the village. This was partly due to the fact that the race involved bird — and man!

The pigeon lofts were spread over a large area in the village and to give everyone a fair chance, the clock on which the birds' times were to be registered was situated at a central check-point. Now the pigeons, of course, would fly back to their own lofts — not to some arbitrarily chosen landing depot. As a bird alighted at its loft its identification ring would be drawn from its leg and the pigeon keeper or his nominee would hare-off as fast as he could go, with the ring, to the recording point where the birds', and the runners', times would be recorded on the carefully guarded recording clock kept for the purpose. It was clear, therefore, that the chances of winning the first prize could be augmented quite considerably if one had a good runner. Jack Coffey, was as renowned for his speed as he was for his bandy legs. To see Jack tearing down Lowther Street, waistcoat flying in the breeze, shirt neck open, head held high and Lanky clogged feet twinkling at the ends of those remarkable legs was a vision of delight for the entire street.

Another rare athlete was Billie Gunson — a man of splendid physique and the rolling confident gait of one who revels in the pitting of his God-given skills in friendly contest with his fellows or nature. Billie, it was said, could jump a five-barred 'yat'. What could he have done with training?

My father, mother and I lived in a place called Denton Square and it was here that my brother was born. Our house could never have been described as a romantic haven or the most desirable residence in the village. It was the only house in a narrow cul-de-sac. No traffic and little light ever came into our cul-de-sac. Our house had one door, with two rooms downstairs and two upstairs, the windows from which took in the same identical view of an enormous, rough-cast wall — a few feet away — the back of a street of houses which faced away from us.

The first room downstairs, a kind of scullery, was decorated (if that is the term) with a damp stained terra cotta coloured distemper of ancient vintage. Our kitchen, the next room, flaunted a dull pucey-green distemper and seemed even darker than the scullery. In one corner steep stairs led up to the two bedrooms. It had a door at the bottom to stop the draught; it was not very effective! I was six years old at the time but remember it perfectly clearly — possibly because on one memorable occasion I did the complete descent of the stairs in one stride, performing a distinctly recalled somersault in the process.

Aunt Liza (my mother's sister), my uncle Wilson and my cousins lived in Lowther Street, a few minutes' walk away. I spent a lot of time there. They had a front door and a back door and the air in summer passed through the house. The back door let in the morning sun and the front window welcomed the evening light. We had no sun in our house — at any time of the day or year!

Lowther Street was typical of the rows of terraced houses in many an industrial town or village — the front doors of each house opening straight onto the street. The back doors of houses along one side of the street opened out into a narrow lane, some three feet wide, whilst those on the other side led onto an open area containing a long building without windows — but many doors. These were the communal earth closets or lavatories shared by the entire street. The need to use one of these toilets could involve quite a walk if you lived on the wrong side of the street!

The houses in the street contained neither lavatory nor bathroom nor laundry. The laundry, always referred to as the 'wash-house', occupied a separate block near the toilets. Bathrooms, like electricity, telephones and television were for the future. We were bathed in a tub in front of the fire — bathrooms were not considered to be necessary even though most of the men in the village were miners; and there were no baths at the mine — at least not for the miners!

On the whole, life went on in Lowther Street pretty much as it did in any other. Front door steps were scrubbed and decorated with a white chalk line with frequent and constant regularity; windows shone; brass door knockers or letter boxes gleamed; curtains hung in carefully placed drapes. Cleaning became almost a fetish.

A fierce pride burned in the wifely breast — not only would the house be clean but it would be seen to be clean, even from the outside. This pride extended to the table and to the children's dress and appearance. She saw almost as a mark of disgrace, the feeding of margarine instead of butter to her family. A flea, should one even dare to enter the house and alight on an occupant, was hunted with ferocity until it met its inevitable death between two thumb nails. Boys' hair was close cropped, except for the 'topping' at the front, which was combed straight downwards in a fringe. Girls' and boys' hair was examined ritually with a fine-toothed comb to check for lice. Cockroaches were sought and poison laid near the outlet from their nests behind the warm stones of the fireplace. The greatest social crime was 'bugs' — those repulsive red, squashy insects that got into the layers of old wallpaper on the bedroom walls or even into the straw mattresses. Should such a misfortune, the finding of a 'bug', ever befall a household the walls would be stripped and the straw mattresses burned.

Occasionally domestic routine would be shattered by the eruption of an inter-family squabble. A 'fratch' as it was known in the dialect (which everyone spoke) would set the street agog.

It would usually start over some simple matter like two of the children of families in the street having cause to afflict injury on each other on the way home from school. Instead of letting the matter rest there one of the mothers would feel it necessary to come to the defence of her offspring and, at the earliest opportunity, would 'have words' with his assumed aggressor to attempt to dissuade him from further molestation of her dearest son. The fact of her intervention would be relayed to the other mother almost in minutes and she in turn would feel it necessary to enter the lists.

A fratch was carried on almost in accordance with some unwritten rules. The combatants rarely came to the physical discomfitting of each other but was more in the nature of a verbal brawl conducted from the rostrum of each of the two protagonists — her front door step. Some of the participants, being more theatrically inclined than others, would come to their doorsteps rolling up their sleeves; one fiercely let down her hair, which was long and black.

After a few opening sentences which dealt more or less specifically with the matter of recent origin the verbal exchange would become more general; this was what the street had been waiting for! Apart from the combatants, each on her doorstep, the street would be empty, except for the little ones like us, who were expressly instructed by those who may have been out of vision of any dramatic action to run back into the house and report such events immediately. The conquistadors on their doorsteps, knowing perfectly well that they were the centre of the village attraction, gave of their best. Ancient scores were re-examined; long buried skeletons were disinterred; the opposition's family honour and legitimacy would be seriously questioned.

In the silent intervening houses and those across the street doors would be eased gently open just a fraction wider and curtains would quiver with excitement. On occasions the husband of one of the gladiators would feel that the matter had gone on long enough and would come to his door and haul his beloved in off her doorstep.

The scene of the action would change immediately. Within seconds the husband, who was probably on his way to the Reading Room (quite possibly with the husband of the other protagonist) and his wife would launch into their own private discussion. This redirection of hostilities would leave the lady on the other doorstep now without an object of attack so, taking the matter philosophically, she would accept the hurried departure of her opponent as a sign of victory and, after sending one last withering blast along the street, would retire to her own hearth, closing her front door with a mighty crash, on a note of defiance and invincibility.

Fratches rarely came to anything. Sometimes the combatants may have ceased to speak to each other, maybe even for years, until long after either of them could remember what it was they were 'not speaking' for! On the other hand the wounds could be healed a couple of days later, over a cup of tea, when, as like as not, the erstwhile enemies had found a third party who was to be seen as a mutual foe — and may even, just possibly, have been the guilty party in the recent fracas!

My brother was born just before the strike and died at the age of ten months. Shortly afterwards my mother found she had T.B. and, as the years went by, became less able to move — wasting, gradually, away — quietly, uncomplaining and alert — to the threshold of death. My mother was twenty-nine when she died; I was nine. I recall the day quite vividly. We were living with my Aunt Eliza at the time, who had moved to a larger house at Carter Garth. It was a Thursday, about eleven in the morning when she asked to see me. I went into the front parlour where her bed had been permanently set up for some months. It was surrounded by silent relatives. She hugged me and said, 'Billie, I'm going a long way and won't be coming back. I want you to be a good boy and to do what you are told . . .' I left her not knowing quite what was happening. She died exactly two hours later. I remember her as a sweet gentle woman of infinite tenderness, with sad eyes and long auburn hair, a characteristic of all her family and of which she, like them, was inordinately proud. She was buried on the Saturday. I didn't go to the funeral; they sent me to the pictures instead. It cost one penny.

After my mother's death I went back to live with my grandmother in Ellenborough. It was here, sheltered by her kindness and care, and that of my two uncles, that the world began to reveal its secrets. With my cousin, Mike, I roamed the countryside, free, untroubled, not a care in the world. We knew where to find which kind of a nest — and called the birds by their dialect names: a chaffinch was a 'scoppy', I remember, and a shrike was a 'shrelty'. We knew exactly which branches would make the best bows and which the arrows. We knew where to find newts and tadpoles. We stole sweet yellow ambers from my great-uncle's garden, thinking that he couldn't see us lying in the long grass under the gooseberry bushes.

Other times we spent 'ratching' around the communal garbage tip or setting fire to grass in the hedges and waste ground to the intense disapproval of our nearest and dearest. At the end of a long summer's evening of wonder and peace we would wind our ways slowly home — diverted by any inconsequential matter that crossed our path.

Before mounting the kitchen doorstep it was necessary to erect our defences; Mike would say, 'Can you smell me?' I would take hold of his jersey and sniff deeply. 'No! Can *you* smell *me*?' I would counter. The performance would be repeated on my outer garment and I would be assured that I, too, was without fault. And we would pass into the kitchen, stinking to the highest heaven of garbage or burnt hay or cow dung or whatever particularly noxious trifle had attracted our recent interest. Aunt Nellie would take one sniff and pounce 'You two have been at it again! Where did you get the matches from . . .?' And we'd be bundled into the wash house to pass through the motions of the practically impossible task of trying to render ourselves fit for human society. We loved to visit Uncle's. (He was actually my father's Uncle Percy.) Apart from the attentions of a particularly vicious and somewhat scruffy Bedlington terrier named Gyp (who preferred to bite first and leave someone else to find out why, later), they were interludes of mystery and delight. Uncle lived in a small, thick-walled cottage of stone and tiny windows, on the edge of the moors, with his wife Martha and his sister, Aunt Annie. We were always just a little afraid of Martha, who disappeared whenever anyone called and, although I suppose she must have done so, never, to my recollection, ever said a single word to either of us.

Aunt Annie we loved. She was tiny, not much taller than Mike or I at ten or eleven years of age, with a deformed spine, due, we were always led to believe, to some accident when a baby. She always dressed in black, in long ankle length skirts, frilled blouse and shawl. A black bonnet and massive carpet bag completed her ensemble. She spoke in a courtly manner, in a precise, well modulated voice, which hinted at 'better times'. We never did know why she was so different — there were vague comments about a shop, and the drink — but our thoughts never dwelt for long on the mysteries of the ancient past. There was far too much happening around us in the present to attract our interest.

Uncle Percy was the exact opposite of his sister. He was strong and bluff and spoke only in the dialect, every noun of which was embellished by at least one descriptive swear-word. Swearing was so natural to him that we ceased to notice it — until the vicar arrived with a new, charming and obviously 'well-brought-up' young wife. Uncle, in the presence of this young lady refrained, with great difficulty, from swearing. The effect on us was dramatic and the carefully laundered speech, delivered for the benefit of the vicar's wife made us far more conscious of Uncle's treatment of the language than ever his more ambitious flow of expletives could have done.

Uncle sold firewood and paraffin from a horse drawn oil cart and his cottage nestled amongst stables, oil sheds and gardens. As well as gooseberry bushes, blackcurrants and strawberry patches, he had a collection of other items that we found of absorbing interest. In one of the stone out-houses he kept several boxes of ferrets, of all sizes. Their little red eyes and sharp teeth were, to me, the epitomy of wickedness — and we watched in never diminishing awe, his handling of these little ambassadors of the devil himself. He also kept several splendid game-cocks and there was occasionally vague talk of cock-fighting. He was skilled too at whippet-slipping — the act of releasing a whippet in a whippet race, where freeing the dog from its collar at the correct instant could make the difference between the animal winning the event or losing it. There was little doubt in my mind, as I grew older, that Uncle was not unacquainted with the lesser known blood sports of long-gone days — whether they were legal or otherwise, although I was never introduced to any of them!

In those days it was necessary to pass an examination to be admitted to either Workington or Cockermouth Grammar Schools. I passed both. I longed to go but had to face reality. My father took me to one side and explained to me quietly that much as he would like me to be admitted he had no money to buy uniforms or books, so I stayed in 'Elementary' school. When I was thirteen my idyllic existence came to an end. My father had remarried and I had to leave my grandmother to live with my new family. My step-mother was only ten years older than me and quite clearly, I see now, as perplexed at being the sudden acquisitor of a thirteen year old son as I was at finding I had to adapt to a totally new regime in another village and at a strange school. But time and understanding on both sides brought respect and a closeness which lasted until her death more than forty years later. Again we moved to Clifton — 'Big' Clifton we called it, to distinguish it from 'La'al' Clifton, though a casual observer would hardly have noted much disparity in size. From our home to school at Chapel Brow was a mile and a half walk through fields and along the main road (now the A66). On this section, some three miles east of Workington we must, every clear day, have noticed the magnificent panorama of the Western fells — surely one of the grandest views in Cumbria — stretching from the little known Binsey in the north across to the sleeping Skiddaw massif, the shy fells of Wythop, the obtuse angled Grisedale Pike, dramatic Hopegill Head and blunt, commanding Grasmoor. The view continues away up the Buttermere valley where Fleetwith Pike's profile is unmistakable and swinging to the right the peaks of the Loweswater and Mockerkin fells fade in outline into those of Western Ennerdale.

When in February or March the wind and weather came from the East and the hills were blanketed in their dazzling white shroud we would comment about 't'snow on t'fells' — obviously struggling, in a bumbling way, to make words that would convey our half formed sense of wonder.

We saw 't'fells' almost every day yet none of us went to visit them. In my last year I went into the 'top' class; my teacher was Gibby Hayton from Keswick. Gibby was very tall and athletic; we boys held him in some hero worship and a little fear. He travelled from Keswick every day, by fast motorbike and just occasionally he would talk to us about the fells and walking and climbing on them. He was the first person I ever met who tried to communicate to me the joy to be found in the hills. I never forgot him.

At fourteen two things happened. I left school and we moved to Workington. Life took on a very different complexion. There were no hedgerows in the town; I had no friends; and most important of all it was time for me to earn my bread. My father didn't want me to go into 'the pit'. And I searched all the avenues I could to find an alternative. In those days, 1934, in West Cumberland, a term like 'Job Satisfaction' had not been invented. Had it been, I'm certain it could not have been applied, except in the negative, to my first job. I was employed in the back shed of a fish and chip shop — cleaning potatoes. I had to fill three large barrels (about seven hundred-weights) with cleaned potatoes every day except Sunday. I started work at eight in the morning and finished around five in the afternoon. For this privilege I was paid five shillings a week. Five shillings, it was felt, was not enough of a wage to permit the luxury of pocket-money — and so I didn't get any! But on most Fridays the employees of the local Post Office would put an order into the fish and chip shop owner — the order to be delivered by me on my way home for lunch. For this service they gave me a tip — usually threepence, sometimes tuppence halfpenny and occasionally a heady fourpence. This was my only source of personal income. If only those wonderful Post Office workers had known what they meant to me in terms of financial independence and self esteem . . . I kept the job until March 1935, by which time the need to have some money of my own in return for my labours became paramount. There was only one place where I could find 'more money' . . .

Thus, whilst still just fourteen years of age, I went to work in the mine at Clifton. Life had taken the same predictable course for me as it had for most of my school mates; from now on all I needed to do was work hard, collect my pay packet, go to the pictures on Saturday night or, as maturity descended upon me, to a selected pub — eventually get married, have a youngster, take care of him well, make sure he had a job in the pit to go to before his school life ended . . . My first pay docket from the mine came to nineteen shillings and eleven pence — almost four times as much as I had received from my job in the back yard of the fish and chip shop.

From this sum I was granted one shilling (five pence) pocket

money with which to launch myself onto an unsuspecting world —
strangely enough my new-found wealth met my immediate needs.

We seldom travelled anywhere. When we did it was on the bus,
pushbike or on foot. There was a fair chance that the limits of our
excursions on any particular day would lie within a radius of five or
six miles of the kitchen fire. To go to places like Carlisle or Keswick
demanded major appraisal; to take the August Monday boat trip
between Workington and the Isle of Man, which I did once, was to
participate in a journey of inter-stellar significance. The war and
television and package tours eventually changed all that — but the
war was still four years away.

At fourteen, then, the hungry maw of the mining industry
swallowed me. For a short while I worked on the surface and then I,
too, went to work below. On my first day underground I descended
in the same cage as my father; I sensed his pride and protective spirit
and hoped I didn't show how much I needed both.

Even for youngsters like myself work was hard. The mine was an
old one; the main underground roadways were low and it was
impossible in many places to walk upright. The coal faces were some
three miles from the bottom of the shafts. There was no mechanical
'man-transport'. To get to where we had to work involved a three
mile walk — and the same back out again at the end of the shift. One
eventually developed skills at being able to walk with a maximum of
conservation of effort — avoiding rails, sleepers, water and rollers on
the floor and wooden bars, steel girders and bare rock with the head,
whilst at the same time keeping an eye open for what was going on in
front and an ear cocked behind one for the sounds of runaway tubs or
horses or falling roof-stone.

In my mid-teens I led a fairly lonely existence. There were few
avenues of escape that I could see. The only way that I did find,
eventually, proved to be so incredibly simple and so totally satisfying
a solution as to be almost ridiculous. I discovered the local library.
As simple as that!

When you've owned only two books in your life, and those two are
a handed down Hans Andersen and a tattered P. G. Wodehouse
(given to me by Gibby Hayton), a library offers a magic carpet of
such colour and design and manoeuvrability as to induce in its
passenger sensations of the gayest abandon and the most
indiscriminate selections of journey. Thus it was that I met *Tess of the
D'Urbervilles*, and *Tarzan of the Apes* — Rider Haggard, T. E.
Lawrence, Jeffrey Farnol, Sabatini, Jerome K. Jerome, Dickens,
Fred Nurk . . . and on and on. The Pandora's Box that opened for me
fed my hunger and thirst for adventure and escape and humour and
pathos and plain sentimentality. At first I changed the books every
two weeks or so. Quickly the borrowing time dropped to a week, then
half a week. Within a short time I was changing my books every

other day . . . when it happened that I borrowed books in the morning and took them back to change them later on the same day, the library staff called a halt. "We haven't had time to get the tickets sorted out!' they complained, good humouredly.

I must have rectified my ways! They never stopped me again. Visions of far away places and glorious healthy existence in the depths of some savage jungle fed my imagination. (Spencer Chapman had not yet written *The Jungle is Neutral* and even if he had it's doubtful, at that time, that I would have believed him.) How much of my next decision was a result of reading, blatant romanticism or intuitive searching, I'll never know, but the effect of a subsequent action was to alter the whole direction and meaning of my life.

I had been on night shift. When I came out of the pit, up into God's real air, the morning was so beautiful I couldn't bear to go to bed. I cycled home, had a meal, then my bath, where my father and I always bathed — in a tub in front of the fire; got dressed and onto my old broken down bike that my father had bought me for five shillings and I set out — towards the sun.

On that day, at seventeen years of age, I discovered Lakeland . . . it was a revelation. All my life I'd lived within fifteen miles of the Buttermere Valley. I had never seen it or thought about it or even considered going to it. Like London or Mars, I knew it existed. But there had never been any point in going to find out where. On this day I worked my way through the lanes of Dean and Ullock and over the Mockerkin fells. As I breasted the hill the whole panorama of the beautiful valley began to unfold. Below me Loweswater and the hazy fells slept in a gentle dawn. From high up on Fangs Brow I could hear the Valley sounds — voices of man and beast — the 'clip-clop' of a draught-horse. Apart from them all was still and totally at peace. After a night spent in the darkness and turmoil, amongst the sweat and stink of stale air, pit ponies and one's own pit shirt, my discovery of Western Lakeland set my senses in a whirl.

From that moment my thoughts and needs took wings. All my spare time was given to extending the limits of my world of discovery on my bike, on foot and in dreams. I explored throughout the summer and the winter. I walked many miles in a day — Workington to the top of Grasmoor and back, a round trip of 30 miles with a near 3000 foot peak half way; Workington to Buttermere across the Floutern Tarn track to Ennerdale and then back home; Cockermouth to Buttermere and then over Honister, to sleep in a quite useless sleeping bag beside the beck at Rosthwaite — all night I listened to the voices in the water and the owls in the trees, frightened by this totally new experience. There was frost on the ground and I was bitterly cold. By dawnlight I was on my way up Langstrath, when I got into Langdale the hordes were just leaving their warm farmhouse beds and their bacon and eggs. Down Langdale and over Red Bank to Grasmere and Dunmail Raise I walked. On reaching Keswick I took a bus back home. My feet were sore and blistered with all the road walking but my spirits were far from quenched. My gear was obviously inadequate and it would be nice to talk to someone, sometimes!

Again the solution was so easy. I was walking back one Sunday from Ennerdale and had just reached Branthwaite when a bus came along. To my surprise it stopped and picked me up. It was under charter to the Workington Rambling Club. I hadn't even guessed that such an organisation existed.

Their approach to fell-walking was totally civilized. The bus was taken to the starting point of the walk. Its occupants then headed up the fell and along the ridge, to the pick up point in the next valley, or did the round of a valley head, as the case may be.

I joined them immediately. We did some splendid ridge walking. It was a far cry from my long, lonely road walks and my first cold eerie tentless bivouac under a Borrowdale night sky. The weekends were idyllic — but there was just that little something missing.

2

Coal Face to Cliff Face

One day my father said to me, 'My mate is leaving. If you want to come with me, as my apprentice, it'll have to be now.' At eighteen years of age, then, I went to work 'on the coal'. The seam was twenty inches thick. The 'face', in the height of the seam, was ninety yards long. There were six pairs of miners on the face each pair with fifteen yards of coal to fill out, or as much of it as they could. On the next shift another six pairs of miners took over, stripping off the remaining coal and blasting down part of the roof so that tubs could be brought right up to the face.

The only machine on the face was the electric coal cutter which undercut the entire ninety yards of face to a depth of four and a half feet. When this had been done we drilled holes into the seam by hand and shot the coal down. We bought our explosives at the mine and in turn were paid only for the coal we filled or the amount of roof stone we shot down and packed away. We weren't paid for drilling holes or for walking to the coal face.

At the face a day's pay usually came to around twelve shillings (sixty new pence) a shift. It could be higher, if things had gone well — adequate supplies of empties, good conditions — or it could have been six shillings and eight pence, the minimum wage we could legally be paid, should things have gone wrong. On the whole we seemed to average one day 'on the mini' per working week — hence a fairly typical take-home pay for six shifts for a miner in our locality would, at the time (1938), be around three pounds ten shillings. It was not a lot of money but for people who did not consider cars, telephones and inter-continental holidays to be either essential or, indeed, attainable, it sufficed.

Most of the miners asked little of life — a pint or two of beer at the weekend, a packet of Woodbines, which came in open packets of five at tuppence a packet (and when things were really bad it was always possible to go to Henrietta's and buy the odd cigarette — or even get one or a packet on the tick!) and threepence on a horse or a football pool.

When one worked at the coal face and when what was earned depended on the amount one filled no further inducement to get to the face was necessary. Indeed, our principal objective was to get down the mine at the earliest possible moment and stay there until the last. In between these two 'riding' times my father and I worked as a team, against time and against the other men on the face, when tubs were short — as they very often were. One rarely stopped to eat, and if one did it was only for as long as it takes to swallow a jam sandwich and a couple of mouthfuls of water.

On the face no quarter was asked and none was given; it was simply a matter of 'every man for himself and if you can't fend for yourself you shouldn't be here.' It was a hard, but thoroughly understandable attitude, forced upon us by the methods of working and system of payment.

Only when disaster struck did the purely mercenary attitude of neighbours on the face break down. If the roof collapsed (and because it was newly exposed every day this was the most likely place for it to do so) or if the coal peeled off the face and a miner was buried, the rush to his aid was immediate. Ours was a camaraderie that defies words. At one moment two men would be fighting each other for possession of a tub, in the next, one would be literally risking his life to drag the recent adversary out from a fall of stone.

Life was hard and fairly merciless. Whatever hellishness I thought I had undergone prior to working on the face, paled into pleasant memory when set against this new experience. But there were compensations in life — and not the least of them was finding a good collection of Cumbriana in the reference section of the library. It was here that I discovered O. G. Jones' *Rock Climbs in the English Lake District,* the Fell and Rock Journals, the climbing books by G. D. Abraham and many other sources of information on the fells.

It was about this time also that I made my first tentative efforts at rock climbing — on boulders and small outcrops.

Walking three miles twice a shift and filling twenty tubs of coal, or swinging them round in a confined space, or drilling and blasting and packing away several tons of stone may not be an ideal form of weight-training but it prepared me well for rock climbing — both psychologically and physically. Barely ten stones in weight and fairly strong in the arm paid off many times in the immediate future.

When I began to solo recognised routes I decided to buy a rope! It was fifty feet of three-quarter weight manilla hemp, containing those magical three red strands plaited into the lay, which indicated a genuine climbing rope. That they *were* magical has to be accepted! I dragged those fifty feet of hemp behind me up several climbs —

(Central Gully on Great End in September 1938 and Sphinx Ridge on the Napes, about the same time, come to mind) and not once did I fall off! Had I done so I'm sure that the rope would have performed some incredible feat of anchorage or maybe would have stiffened into a rigid rod, holding me fast against the rock. With it I felt I was a Climber, without it I was Nought.

But the necessity of companionship became more apparent — not because I wanted to talk but because I felt it would be better if someone *held* the rope!

I had taught myself how to nail boots with proper clinker type climbing nails and coerced my cousin into going rock climbing by offering to provide him with a pair, which I did. My source of supply for boots was the local Army Disposal store. The pattern of nailing I had adopted was clinkers all round the welt and heel. To do this it is necessary to drive the spike of the nail up through the welt then double it down over the front and tuck it behind the pair of wings which are a feature of the outer edge of the nail. When placed close together all round the welt a complete set of clinkers looks like nothing so much as a fractured horse-shoe — and feels like it. Whatever reservations I may have had, and I don't remember any, there was no doubt about the authenticity of the pattern — as could be seen by anyone who cared to look at those superb photographs in Abrahams' photographic shop window in Keswick.

So with loins girt and rope hidden in rucksack we set off for Gatesgarth by bus and made for the only climb I knew of in the area — Stack Ghyll! A harder, wetter, looser, less attractive climb on which to launch a beginner (and this term easily covered both of us) would have been difficult to find. Needless to say we didn't get up. Instead I managed to pull some blocks down onto my fingers and damaged them rather badly. A short time later I developed septicaemia in the arm and was off climbing for a month or two — I still bear the scars!

In fairness to Stack Ghyll I should say that, climbing it much later, with more experience under my belt, I found it to be a good route of some four hundred feet — quite typical of the kind of climbing beloved of the aficionados of the Gully Epoch. It was, incidentally, one of the early aid climbs — climbed on the last day of 1900 by Shaw, Oppenheimer and Craig (three hard men of their time). The team resorted to pushing a doubled rope through a hole behind the chockstone until a loop of it fell down in front; this was then used as a foothold to get over the awkward obstruction.

My retreat from our early attempt on Stack Ghyll was only a temporary set back. It gave me time to read, think and dream — it had also been a useful lesson. The books I was reading, and from which I was learning all I knew up to then about climbing and rope management were, as I've mentioned, those written by Owen

Glynne Jones and George D. Abraham and, whereas Jones and the Abraham brothers must be numbered amongst the finest climbers of their day, it would have to be admitted that the impression one gained from photographs and descriptions of climbs produced thirty or forty years earlier was hardly the technology to equip one for the performances of 1938.

But I got about quite a good deal and kept my eyes open. By watching the experts on Green Gable and the Napes I learned that there were guidebooks to climbing more up to date than George D's *British Mountain Climbs;* that the ropes used were much longer than fifty feet, and that real climbers had a secret weapon called rubbers. These were tennis or gym shoes. One bought the ones without the thick protective rubber pad in front of and over the toes and one or two sizes too small. Colin Kirkus in his delightful book *Let's go Climbing**, published in 1941, said 'these are ordinary plimsolls or gym shoes. Get a pair with rubber soles — not crepe. The cheaper and lighter they are, the better . . . if the soles are too thick you cannot feel the holds so well. Wear them with only one pair of stockings and see they fit very tightly, they are useless if there is a lot of empty space in the toe.' There is so much distilled experience poured into that description.

I preferred to buy the cheap sort from Woolworths. There was one type with a bright yellow gutta percha sole, of which, I'm sure, Kirkus would not have approved. The sole, on dry rocks, stuck like glue — on wet rock it acted like a roller-skate. But as I used to take them off and climb in socks when the rocks were wet, this latter consideration was of secondary importance. The first job, after getting the plimsolls home was to trim the edges with a razor blade. All the excess rubber around the sole was pared away. If the rubbers were too tight above the instep then a little judicious hacking of the stitching at the base of the tongue was necessary — but this was always a rather dicy procedure . . . it let the foot spread out rather more; a hole then rapidly wore through the canvas over the little toe, which in turn eventually allowed the latter to poke straight through the side of the shoe. There is nothing more off-putting, except wet rock!

Most of this I discovered for myself in later years — as I did that ubiquitous device, the sling. In those days the sling consisted of a length of rope just long enough to wrap round the waist and tie into a snap link or karabiner. It was made from hemp, like the rope, and may well have been a length cut off from an old rope. The ends had to be whipped to prevent unravelling or sometimes an eye was spliced into one or both ends, or the rope was spliced into a continuous loop in which case it went round the waist doubled. Later, when manilla hemp was replaced by nylon for climbing ropes the sling cord came in the same material and was of three or four various diameters,

*'Let's go Climbing', C. F. Kirkus, published by Thos. Nelson & Sons, 1941.

rather like today. This was an enormous technical advance in climbing equipment.

The function of the sling was to afford the leader some protection. The nature, thickness and shape of the rope used in the sling made it necessary to have some substantial spike across which to hang it so that the safeguard thus effected would be more positive than psychological.

As well as on rock climbs, slings were used for carrying firewood, wrapping round gear, and (I've no doubt) for pulling cars out of bogs. They were also standard dress on the hills and in the back bar of the Scafell or the O.D.G. Hotels where it was seen as a symbol separating the 'enlightened' from the non-climbing 'dross'! The only trouble with this identification process was that impressive gear did not necessarily equate to high climbing standards — hence it sometimes occurred that those who tended to wear the greatest number of slings in the bar, seemed to be less obvious about actually taking them onto a cliff face . . .

I discovered the guide books in the Workington library. They told me where the climbs were and gave gradings of difficulty.

I learned that the climbs were all classified on a scale of increasing difficulty through six stages. These were: Easy, Moderate, Difficult, Very Difficult, Severe, Very Severe. And I learnt to mouth magical abbreviations like Diff. and V.Diff. and VS and in time I began to know what they meant.

3

Climbing Friends

The climbing world began to open for me early in 1939. A guide book, rubbers, longer rope and two, by now, very good friends were my companions on Grey Crags in Birkness Combe. It was the first time any of us had been to the place.

My friendship with Alan and Gordon Connor began in the mine. I had been cycling home one day, off the morning shift, when I passed a young fellow going in the opposite direction. I thought, 'I've seen you before!' The next day it happened again. On the third I kept my eyes open a little wider and sure enough he passed me by and five minutes later he passed me again. The mystery was solved. They were the most identical twins I have ever seen. Their facial resemblance was so close that, as it happened, few people — very few — could tell which was which. We eventually became very close, almost inseparable, friends. At that time they worked on the surface, on the same job, so identification did not present any difficulty, but when they moved underground, this problem became more acute. As it happened the management, in its wisdom, resolved the problem to everyone's satisfaction — well almost! Alan was sent to the westernmost working of the mine, Gordon to the east. It was quite easy — they were five miles apart. No identification worries; all was well!

To my horror, one day, I arrived at the underground meeting place, miles away in the western workings when I spotted Gordon instead of Alan in the assembled throng. He wore an enormous grin, as much at my consternation, as the total oblivion of those around him. 'What the hell are you doing here?' I whispered. 'We got fed up,' he said, 'so our kid and I swapped jobs. They won't know the bloody difference!' 'They' didn't. I reflected then, as I do now; who would 'they' have buried if he'd got killed?

The twins were a couple of years younger than me, somewhat

taller and slightly heavier built. They had an enormous sense of humour and loyalty. Like many twins they couldn't stand each other at times — but couldn't bear to be separated. They dressed identically, as much for the problems it created, as from habit. When one knew them as I did the differences in character became obvious. Alan was the slightly more dominating personality. He claimed this right — having been born first. Gordon was the more ravenous. Their mother was a widow and a splendid cook who knew her offspring well. Frequently she would bake a plate cake — a large apple tart on an enormous enamel dish. My first experience of Gordon's gustatory prowess — that only hinted at things to come — was with one of these plate cakes. Ma Connor was out when we arrived home one day. 'Would you like a piece of cake?' queried Gordon. And without waiting for my answer began to attack the cake. The first slash was to cut it precisely in two, then one half was neatly divided again. I was presented with a massive quarter of the cake thinking, 'I'll never eat this. It's too big!' Alan was given the other quarter and began to dispose of it rapidly, doubtless thinking that if he hurried he might get a chance at another piece. Silly man! Gordon, took the remaining half of the huge plate cake and had eaten it before either of us had finished.

Although both Alan and Gordon went climbing with me it was the latter who revealed the greater skill and an affinity with rock. He was a strong and graceful climber; he also possessed a most terrible singing voice — a talent which he particularly liked to share when in the most inconsiderate of places. I recall on many occasions my reaction to this!

There I would be, a long way above him, not feeling at all as well as I ought to, while he, comfortably ensconced on a tiny airy ledge (Gordon believed in comfort!) would be roaring out some mangled lament in his most abysmal of tenor voices. I used to get the distinct impression that 'this bloody man doesn't care a stuff about me . . .'

Alan's climbing was steadier, more deliberate and probably more motivated by friendly brotherly rivalry than any other cause.

Oh, those lost days of youth, of joy, of freedom, of living! In 1940 Alan, Gordon and I went to join the R.A.F. They were accepted, I was rejected. Whatever latent skills I may have possessed in respect of the extermination of Nazis it was less important than my proven ability to fill coal. Alan had a really rough war-siege of Malta, Italian campaign and others. Gordon was kept in the U.K. and eventually trained as a rear gunner in Lancasters. Three months after completing his training he got his 'one-way ticket' and never came back from a flight over Germany.

On that day in Birkness Combe the war was still light years away for many of us. The sun was shining, it was warm, we had just done Harrow Buttress (since climbed so very many times!) and the Slabs

Climb, and were standing at the foot of the Oxford and Cambridge Buttress watching with interest a party on the Direct Route, being led by a silver haired gentleman in a black beret who climbed with skill and obvious experience. After they had all completed the climb the elderly gentleman in cultured tones called down, 'Would you care for a rope?' What a question! My first Severe — I leapt at it. Indeed, after I had tied on to his rope I shot up the climb so quickly that he chided me gently, but firmly, for climbing too fast and not savouring the delights of the climb. It was my first contact with G. R. Speaker, President of the Fell and Rock Climbing Club. A gentleman in every sense of the word, we kept up a correspondence until his death on the Napes in 1942. He proposed me for membership of the Club and recognised my hunger for the mountains. He began to send me books and wrote to me at length on his attitude towards mountains and those who climb them. I still treasure those letters. His death on an easy climb was a great shock. (Bentley Beetham and I went up a couple of days later to try to find out why it had occurred.) That day on Grey Crags, in 1939, probably saw the first faint opening of the flood gates. Three weeks after the day with Speaker we were back in Birkness Combe where I was determined to lead the Oxford and Cambridge Direct. Gordon took a photo of me, I recall, on the crux! It revealed all the delicacy and poise of an inebriated crab. But it was climbed — hesitatingly to be sure and not at all with the speed and aplomb of three weeks earlier. It was my first lead of a Severe — and in those days Severes mattered!

Within a year the gates were flung wide — and we were also at War!

The Connor twins and I had many days together. I had been to Brackenclose in Wasdale at Easter, where A. T. and Ruth Hargreaves took me up the Arrowhead Ridge. It was a cold, grey day but the knowledge that I was climbing with such an illustrious pair was warmth enough for me. That same weekend another party took me to Pillar. My first visit — I was bursting with unspoken enthusiasm! This great Rock, the North Climb, the Nose (shades of O. G. J. and the Abrahams) — at last I was to meet them, to climb, to feel. I was so keen it was almost as if the Rock's life span had been determined and that it was soon to be spirited away by some selfish mountain God; I had to get there quickly to climb it before it evaporated before my very eyes.

The party I was with was rather a large party (I regret that I can't remember the names of anyone in it); it was also a slow party. By the time we reached the Rock and the foot of the North Climb I had chewed my finger nails with impatience to the bare flesh. But at last we arrived; ropes were set to one side, rucksacks were opened, a pressure stove was unearthed from one of them. 'Tea, anyone?' said the owner. 'Oh, rather,' was the unanimous (but-one) reply. So tea was dutifully brewed and sipped . . . Another party, even slower than ours had arrived and started up the Climb in front of us. I was near to weeping with frustration. The people who took me to the Rock were clearly so kind and helpful, possibly they didn't climb very much (I never met any of them again) yet our needs were poles apart. What I wanted was rock in my hand and air beneath my boots. What they needed was — tea! Whose need was the greater? Obviously there's no answer; our needs were different.

Late in April 1940 I met Bert Beck.

As Bert was to write later in an amusing personal discourse on our getting together 'Just as Marshall had met Snelgrove and Crosse met Blackwell it was perhaps inevitable that Peascod should meet Beck . . .'

After I had joined the Fell and Rock Climbing Club I was sent its Handbook containing a list of members. I scoured its pages searching for those who lived in Workington; there were very few. His address suggested that he probably was not a miner.

Plucking up courage I knocked at his door and somewhat tongue-tied was ushered, by his landlady, into his presence. I was very conscious of my dialect; Bert had none. He was taller than me, a good three inches, putting him around 5 feet 9, I would say, and was, I found out later, some thirteen years older. Sparingly built he was also long of leg and sinewy rather than muscular. His fair hair was meticulously parted and brushed and his thin moustache carefully trimmed. He offered me afternoon tea; I noticed that his was exceedingly weak. He nibbled at a biscuit; I ate everything in sight. At home we never indulged in afternoon tea — it tended to be a meal.

Bert said he was a teacher (I found out later he was the English master at Workington Grammar School). He had climbed quite a bit, he said, and mentioned climbs on Pillar, Scafell and Gable; he had also been to the Alps — I answered him knowingly when he questioned me about my own activities trying desperately to recall what I'd read of the routes he mentioned and, very much aware of my own woefully limited experience, I dropped what names I could — I had met G. R. Speaker of the Fell and Rock and actually climbed with A. T. and Ruth Hargreaves (to be sure only Arrowhead Ridge and Doctor's Chimney!) I told him. We arranged to climb the following weekend — the day after I celebrated my twentieth birthday. As he showed me to his front door he happened to mention that he tried to keep himself in training — he walked to school every day, he said. I thought quizzically of the few hundred yards or so he lived from the school gates — and my own six miles daily walk underground. As it happened, training or no, I was to find Bert a remarkably good walker. His long legs, rolling gait and slightly turned-in toes gobbled up the miles. We never travelled very fast on the hills (I still don't, but for different reasons!); we preferred, we were to find, the steady plod up Gavel Neese or Brown Tongue (the steep spurs of Gable and Scafell) and laughed a bit superciliously at the young hikers who would rush past us in neat shorts and flimsy shoes on these paths and whom we usually found gasping at the next boulder.

Gordon and I had been out fairly frequently. We had climbed from Buttermere and Borrowdale — wherever public transport or pushbikes could land us. We had even picked up a couple of amiable little new climbs on Round How, that delightful outcrop of compact rough rock on the bog above Warnscale.

Our first climb with Bert was to be on Pillar. The day was beautiful, the beginning of a long warm summer (how the Mountain Gods smiled upon us after all). The opening gambit was the pedestal below the North Face — this had been done some three years earlier by Chorley and Fergus Graham. It turned out to be a most interesting expedition. We were in nailed boots and there was just sufficient drainage water around to give the climb some edge. It was also a good introduction to rock that slopes the wrong way.

To follow Pedestal Wall we selected Rib and Slab, on the West Face of High Man. This climb then, as now, was one of the best to be found anywhere on Pillar — a delightful expedition on rough rock with some splendid situations.

That day on Pillar Rock, was the beginning of an extremely energetic period of rock climbing as well as life-long friendship.

Bert's joining us was most advantageous — he brought to the party maturity of years as well as several seasons of climbing, including one in the Alps. Bert, although he had led some very fine climbs, saw his role as that of second man. It was a role he filled so very splendidly. I had only one ambition, so far as position on the rope was concerned, and that was to be at the 'sharp' end'. The arrangement suited both of us admirably. There was never any argument or indecision, where the pair of us was concerned, we gravitated towards our various responsibilities on the rope with remarkable ease and understanding. We knew exactly where we stood and what was expected of each other. One is very lucky to have such a back-up. And on the only occasion when I did come off, to dangle spinning on the rope, Bert held me superbly. I think we had complete faith in each other. It was a faith that was sustained throughout the years we climbed together — on good days and bad; when the Gods were smiling or when they were putting on a bit of an act.

Not the least of the new team's viability was the Morris Tourer owned by Bert. It was draughty — but it got us there. It was slow — but it never let us down. It had difficulty getting up Honister Pass — but managed it with a little bit of consideration, and a push, from its passengers. Bert nurtured his petrol ration with a concern that would have brought tears to the eye of Scrooge. The car was never used for anything but climbing trips; mileages and petrol usage were carefully worked out and controlled by Bert. He knew exactly how much petrol was needed to get us from A to B and, as a result we got in time to all the, then, major crags in Lakeland.

It was some time in mid 1940 that Bert said to me, 'Bill, have you thought of going to the Tech?' 'What for?' I answered. 'Well as I see it,' he replied, 'You're in mining, you have been all your working life. You may as well make the best of it because you're not likely to get out while the War is on.' And eventually an appointment was made for me to visit the Mining Department of the Cumberland Technical College at Workington to discuss enrolling, which I did in September 1940, in the Mining Course — and that was the beginning of another twelve year relationship.

My only other contact with the College had been in my late teens. I had always been considered fairly competent at drawing and when I discovered that during the winter months there were Art Classes conducted at the Workington Technical College, I enrolled. I was not a good student. I could only attend every second week because of shift work. There were people attending who were so much more able (and noisier) than me that I retracted into a shell of self protection and never spoke to anyone. But the decision to study art was yet another seed.

My weekdays now took on new meaning — but I still lived for the weekend. I was a student at Workington Tech until 1947. At the end of that time I had qualified as a Colliery Manager, been accepted as a member of the Institution of Mining Engineers and eventually was registered as a Chartered Engineer.

4

Eagle Crag, Birkness Combe

The summer of 1940 was unforgettable. Elsewhere the Phoney War had taken a bitter turn. In the Lakes the sun shone. On June the Second of that year the three of us, Bert, Gordon and I were standing in Birkness Combe.

Visually the Buttermere Valley is a most appealing place and, like Ennerdale possesses some splendid hanging valleys on the South Western side. They are Birkness Combe, Bleaberry Combe and Ling Combe. Birkness lies between High Crag and High Stile and Bleaberry between High Stile and Red Pike. Ling Combe, less clearly defined, falls away to the North from Red Pike. Nearly all of the rock climbing in the Buttermere Valley is to be found on the almost continuous range of crag, more like a cloven hoof than a horseshoe, which begins on the left near the entrance to Honister Pass and forms an intermittent escarpment of varied rock quality right round Fleetwith Pike, Warnscale and the Combes to Red Pike.

There is a great deal of rock; some good (some remarkably so) some of it splintery and flaky, some disturbingly loose, and as a consequence, climbing of variable appeal and seriousness is to be found. There are many climbs which can be taken lightly, almost flippantly, and there are those that cannot.

The climb up into Birkness Combe is always a pleasant walk, especially from Gatesgarth.

From the foot of Scarth Gap Pass the way lies up the fellside to the right, gently climbing under a knot of reddish crag, and above a steep little outcrop, surmounted by a rowan tree, which offers a splendid view of the Valley Below and sometimes a pleasant little waterfall. Above the waterfall outcrop and across the fell a wall is reached in time and beyond it the noticeable moraines and boulders of the extinct glacier. This is the floor of Birkness Combe.

Once there the eye is arrested by the great mass of Eagle Crag —

further up and to the left hand side of the Combe. It is a very
impressive pile. At its right hand end it presents the sharp profile of
the so-called Western Buttress and to its left the deep clefts of
Birkness Gully and Birkness Chimney. Cutting the centre of this
great five hundred feet high face is a long, increasingly well defined
crack or gully; this is Central Chimney. On this day in June 1940, the
whole mass of the front of Eagle Crag, from the corner which locates
the Western Buttress Route (now called Pigott's Route, after A. S.
Pigott who led its first ascent in 1925) to Eastern Buttress away to the
left of the main face, was totally unclimbed. It was a vast expanse of
rock — big, steep, impressive. We couldn't understand why this
magnificent face had never been climbed. We were to find out why in
the weeks that lay ahead.

On this June morning the weather was warm and the rocks
appeared to be dry — and the time had come to find out what we and
the great face were made of.

As it transpired, the first essay was not in the centre of the cliff but
on a buttress between Birkness Gully and Birkness Chimney — on
rock which was sound and rough but tending not to run to good
holds. The first and last pitches of the two hundred feet climb were
quite pleasant, but the middle sections were a bit scrappy. We called
it Far East Buttress.

A week later we were back in the Combe again. Still the full-frontal
attack did not take place. This time it was a pincer movement, of
sorts. Well to the left of Far East Buttress and the main crag is
another two-tiered buttress which we called Border Buttress,
obviously because it lies at the eastern extremity of the crag
bordering on the less continuous rock on the open fellside. This
climb, too, turned out to be a pleasant enough ascent of two walls on
clean rock. We graded it as Severe but later comers upgraded it
slightly to mild VS.

Having loosened up on Border Buttress we descended the crag to
the foot of Western Buttress on the western wall of Eagle Crag. This
wall turns back at a sharp angle and round the corner from the main
face, into the fellside, and offered, at the time, three climbs on a steep
flat wall of good clean rock. These were Pigott's Route, already
mentioned and two climbs led by Sid Cross and done almost three
years earlier to the day (on June 19). Half Nelson and Double Cross,
were the intriguing names given to these two routes.

Half Nelson begins some forty feet or so to the right of Pigott's
Route and ascends the steep wall on small holds to a pleasant nook
before sheering off to the left to join Pigott's. Double Cross, graded as
VS and the only climb of such grade in the valley prior to June 1940,
started much further to the right, went up an easy ridge that runs
into the face then traverses left across the face to a ledge below a
splendid chimney, which is then climbed to the top of the wall, where

it too joins Pigott's Route.

Our plans had been formulated. Obviously we needed some kind of look at the main face before launching out on it. Nobody had been there before. All we knew, from having been up both Pigott's Route and Half Nelson previously, was that a big grass ledge which we called the Terrace traversed part way across the front of the face. The walls both below and above the ledge were steep. The ideal solution was to 'girdle' the crag and have a look at things as we went by — the obvious start being Double Cross!

So up Double Cross we went and across to the base of the steep chimney. Now came the first difficulty — getting from Double Cross on to Half Nelson. We knew that not far away, round a steep corner, was the pleasant nook at the top of the first hundred feet of Half Nelson. So, leading off, a step down and a few awkward moves got me round the corner and into the restful stance on Half Nelson. From here to the Terrace and Pigott's Route was easy enough and eventually all three of us, Bert, Gordon Connor and I had assembled there. Beyond here everything was new, unsighted, untried, unclimbed. The one single flaw on the main front of Eagle Crag is the Terrace. This ledge starting off from the western end of the face is quite substantial at first but narrows rapidly until, in fifty feet of horizontal traverse, it merges into a mossy slab with steep walls above and below. It was at this point where the Terrace merged into the steep rock that we began to get the feel of Eagle Crag. Searching for a belay on the small ledge proved to be an almost abortive task. Finally, discovering a block buried in the grass, I gardened round it and found a hole through which I could thread my sling. It was not a good belay — only a small block, held down by grass. When Bert reached me he felt that the block, which was quite loose, needed some improvement. I got him to sit on it!

We surveyed our scene. At this point we could probably have continued eastward and eventually got into Central Chimney or we could explore around a little — our belay wasn't much good (in fact, to be honest with ourselves, no damned good at all). Upward progress to a bracket looked feasible and once there it might be possible to find a better belay. So on I went, up the steep wall and groove, above our laughable belay, and stepping to the right began to recognise how misleading from below this particular crag can be. The ledge from below had appeared to be substantial and commodious. When I reached it I found it sloped badly, as do the holds generally, and the belay I had hoped for turned out to be almost as poor as the one I had left with Bert — but the situation was superb. From my feet the face plunged over three hundred feet to the screes below. Above me and to my left the wall bulged in a most disconcerting fashion. A way seemed possible to the right across steep ribs to a water-worn slab. And when my turn came to move, having got Bert up to my stance, I discovered just how delicate this traverse was and pondered on the sloping nature of the holds and what they would be like in wet weather. As soon as practicable I made my way up the slab to a grassy corner at the foot of a superb crack, which is well seen from the floor of the Combe when the early morning sun hits its right hand bounding wall. We felt by now very much on the home stretch. From the corner a traverse round a series of steep, exposed ribs brought us into Central Chimney, beyond which the way led across to Easter Buttress and up it to the top of the crag.

We had seen what we wanted to see. We knew that the wall above the Terrace was steep but that we could get up it. The final crack, leading upwards to the summit, although we hadn't climbed it, looked feasible enough, so all that remained was to climb the wall from the scree to the Terrace.

The following weekend we didn't go near the place; we went instead to Scafell, to the Pinnacle Face and elsewhere. What drew our attention — or why? Was it to drum up courage? Did we want to savour it more? But the next weekend — June 23, 1940 — we were back. The weather was still fine.

Straight up to the centre point of the foot of the main front face we went. From further down the Combe we had seen the morning light on the summit crack wall and on the flank of Easter Buttress — but the main face was sombre, dark and — flat.

We picked our starting point, at the foot of a rib that came down off the face. And the game was on . . .

The rib of sixty feet went easily enough and landed us at the foot of a steep groove. The next pitch, ninety-five feet in length, proved to be one of the most exacting on the climb. Moving up from the belay I got onto a steep gangway, falling away to the left and overhung on the right. Near its top an awkward bulge caused only a temporary halt, and above the bulge steep slabs swept up to a huge overhang. But relief was at hand and eventually a line of flake handholds allowed me to work out to the right below the overhang, gain a good ledge and a huge belay on the right. Safeguards in the form of slings were generally difficult to arrange on this huge face of Eagle Crag and this pitch was no exception. Our supplies of slings was fairly limited anyway (running only to one each) but I had managed to get one in position on the gangway. It was made of thick rope and it came off before I got to the top of the pitch — the day of the splendid 'tape' runners and wired stoppers was still a long way off. The situation was again breathtaking. We were on ground that no man had ever climbed before. We had ascended a pitch that would be most difficult to descend — and we didn't have enough rope to abseil. From the top of the big belay on the top of pitch two a few awkward moves followed and then the angle eased. I could see the

Terrace above me, we had reached the half-way point. My heart was singing as I climbed onto it!

After this we were on known ground. The bracket above the Eastern end of the Terrace was reached without much trouble (this time the belay was improved by a six inch nail which I had picked up in the mine and which I hammered into a crack behind the stance, with a stone taken along for the purpose). Again I repeated the traverse to the right and up the water-worn slabs, then a short ascent led up to the foot of the big final crack — the only part not yet climbed. Here I found a good belay and brought Bert up to it. Then I set off up the last big sixty foot corner. The final crack looks most spectacular from the floor of the Combe. To my indescribable delight it was loaded with splendid hidden handholds. Up without pause, with a song in my heart, if not in my throat. A short scramble led to the top of the crag where Bert, a few minutes afterwards, joined me. We sat there, together, in the sun. The evening was still; we were completely alone in the Combe — in the world! The War, the pit . . . they didn't exist. We didn't say much. What was there to say? Each of us was drenched in his own emotions, dreaming his own dreams and experiencing that most exquisite of sensations — the elation of success at having climbed something really worthwhile. We called the climb Eagle Front. It was, I discovered many years later, to become regarded as 'a classic'. I can understand why!

After we had done the climb it was necessary to grade it for difficulty — here we ran into a temporary problem!

The grading system used in the Lakes was based upon that promulgated by Owen Glynne Jones forty years or so before in his book *Rock Climbing in the English Lake District* — which had been modified by later comers (as it has been several times since) to meet newer developments.

Even at this time, 1940, the six stage system of Easy through to Very Severe was beginning to become rather unwieldly because of the wide range of difficulty that could exist in any one stage. This was overcome, in part, by having the climbs in each stage graded relative to each other in an ascending order of hardness. Thus one could have a Hard Severe or an Easy Severe, a Hard VS or an Easy VS. It is obvious therefore that the two gradings covered a very considerable span of difficulty and it was the practice of many climbers to work gradually and systematically up through these lists.

My personal problem, and I doubt if wild horses would have dragged the fact out of me at the time, was that in June 1940 I had *never done* a guidebook VS — either as leader or anywhere else on the rope! I hadn't done many Severes either! The bare naked truth was that here we were doing new climbs on a superb piece of rock, grading them as VS, only because we thought they were so much *harder* than anything we had done before, and yet we hadn't actually climbed on a VS together. In fact the first four VS climbs I ever did (and later Border Buttress was elevated to this category) were all new climbs . . .! They were Eagle Front, Eagle Girdle, Far East Buttress, and a new climb in Gillercombe.

It was only through picking off the guidebook classics later (VS and otherwise) that we finally determined that our assessment of the difficulty of the Eagle Crag climbs wasn't so very far wrong!

Someone, some day, will devote a thesis to attitude of mind in climbing and it may help to explain why with supreme confidence a relative newcomer could hurl himself into the challenge of a huge practically unmarked face of rock, without meeting undue difficulty, and yet find himself in trouble on much easier climbs followed from a guidebook description.

The answer may well lie in a comment of Galen Rowell (a fine American mountaineer) who wrote 'it suddenly dawned on me why we had been so scared in the sixties (and to this I might add 'and the forties also') — *we believed the written word . . .*'

Because nobody had been up the front of Eagle Crag nobody was able to tell us it was steep and exposed; that it didn't run to sharp incut holds; that the belays were noticeable more through their absence than their quality; that when it came to using serviceable protection points, one may as well have left the slings and karabiners at home and saved oneself the job of carrying them up the mountain — because useful and positive flakes and threads were not readily available. But nobody was there to tell us — so we just went out and did the climbs.

5

. . . And After

The euphoria of Eagle Front lasted for a week. Alan and Gordon were soon to be in the Forces — and Bert and I climbed very much alone. Occasionally, Frank Monkhouse joined us and we spread our activities wide. The weekend after Eagle Front we spent on Gimmer and Dow Crag — my first visit to both places. On the Saturday we scampered up and down five of the Gimmer classics but the day of reckoning was near!

For some inexplicable reason, it seemed, everyone who was doing anything at the time was on Dow Crag next day. It was the day of the Heavies. The Big Men all seemed to be there and the lightest of them all, not only in physical weight but experience, was me. The distribution across the crag went something like this: Jim Birkett and party on Eliminate A, the Hargreaves-Cross combination on Eliminate B, Sid Thompson and Company on the Girdle Traverse. We, the rawest of recruits to the elite of new route makers, elected for Eliminate C. All went reasonably well until the traverse right, the third pitch, onto the arête. And, just as everything seemed to be over, confidence oozed from my finger tips and toes like oil off a glass plate. Jack Carswell, one of the (unsung) really fine climbers of his day was with us. He rapidly shinned up D Buttress, got above me and fished me off the corner. Jack has a blunt way of saying things. What he said to me at the top of C was said firmly, yet with kindness. As we sat there, the pair of us on our own, smarting, in my case, from injured pride, he said quietly 'You've come too fast and too far, too easily . . . Get into nailed boots and learn your craft . . .' I listened to him and my thoughts flashed back in time — to just over a year ago when I had done my first Severe and Speaker had said 'You climb too quickly.' I listened and thought hard about what they had both said . . . and started to climb in nailed boots a great deal more; I think I did learn my trade. There was, as it turned out, much substance to my lesson and the lectures. And so dreams of first ascents were set aside for the moment. We began to pick off the older established climbs. Confidence was returning . . .

A month or so after Eagle Front we returned to Eagle Crag, in Birkness Combe — again on the main face — this time just to the right of Central Chimney where the wall and ribs descended from our poor belay at the eastern end of the Terrace. The first one hundred and thirty feet or so are neither difficult nor attractive, but once on the wall above matters change more than somewhat. Again I was involved in long run-outs with no protection. A belay was found at ninety feet around a shaky looking pinnacle. Above this the wall continued steeply for another fifty feet and I had reached the poor belays at the eastern end of the Terrace. The climbing had been sustained, from poor holds to more poor holds, with no runners, for ninety feet. From poor belays the difficulty and steepness had continued. Fifth Avenue, as we named it, wasn't a climb giving the variety of moves and situations of Eagle Front but it was consistent. Now we'd had our fill — and in any case the weather broke! It was to be a long time before I returned to the main face of Eagle Crag.

Summer holidays were upon us. Bert and Frank had spent most of the week in Langdale. We were all to meet up for nine days in Wasdale.

The week began very well . . .

Then came Wednesday, August 7, 1940.

Just who dreamt up the plan to go to Pillar I now forget . . . probably me! It is a two hour walk from Wasdale but barely half an hour from Gillerthwaite, which was much nearer home. So why should we opt for a longer walk? . . . Yes! It must have been me! The plan was straightforward — we would warm-up on the South West, the beautiful rough slab climb overlooking West Jordan Gully at the right hand end of the superb western face of Pillar Rock, then descend around the north side of the Rock to the foot of Walker's Gully and ascend Grooved Wall, the much harder climb on the steep, grooved wall to the immediate right of the gully, this was to be climbed in nailed boots. The logic behind all this now eludes me but at the time it sounded a splendid expedition, even from Wasdale.

We were not alone at the Hut (I think, in fact, that it was a club meet) and one of those attending was a tall, well-built young fellow of about seventeen years of age who kept himself rather to himself, probably more through shyness than anything else. As we were about to take off for Pillar we noticed that the young fellow, whose name was David Horne, had presumably gone out for the day. And, of course, as one does, put the matter almost immediately out of our minds as we set off on the slow plod up Black Sail Pass to the High Level Route and the Rock.

As we neared the big north east face we could see clearly the impressive line of our route for later in the day — and then noticed that someone, a solitary climber, was winding his way up, and was fairly well established on the nearby classic North Climb. Even from our distance he was readily identified as young Horne.

Making our way up the eastern side of Shamrock we reached Pisgah, the point at which Pillar Rock, the promised land, is separated from the open fell side by Jordan Gap. Here we changed into rubbers and then descended to the foot of the South West Climb to sample the first item on the day's menu. As we had gone across the funnel shaped amphitheatre that debouches its scree into the top of Walker's Gully I recalled later that we had heard a strange flapping noise, like a flock of pigeons leaving a roof ridge and wondered briefly at the time why such birds should be so high up on Pillar. But this episode did not trigger off any other line of thought.

Our ascent of South West went easily and we arrived at the top of the Rock and eventually back to Pisgah where we changed into boots and I, as usual, tore off, before the others, to get down to the bottom of Grooved Wall to have a good look at the Big One for the day. It was there that I spotted young Horne's body some twenty or thirty yards below the base of the cliff.

Despite my several years in the mines I had been strangely sheltered from violent death or injury — this was my first experience. The shock was quite considerable. I called in a quavering voice to the other two who were coming down the scree behind me, about a body being down below. I think they realised immediately that things were not well, either with me or the body to which I referred. Some half hearted flippancy about dead sheep came back to me, but in seconds they were beside me and had taken over. The young man was quite dead and all that could be done was to get his body back to Wasdale. After a short discussion Frank said, 'Bill, you go back to Wasdale and get a rescue party. We'll stay here . . .' Glad to be able to do something positive, I set off for Wasdale Head.

In those days I prided myself in being able to get across the hills, and particularly down them, at a good rate, but I've no doubt that I broke any personal record I may have established as I hared back to Wasdale to assemble the Rescuers.

When I reached the Head all was very quiet. At last I found one of the locals and blurted out my story. 'I'll go down to Brackenclose,' I then said, 'and assemble the others,' and off I ran. At Brackenclose all was as quiet as it ought to have been on such a lovely day. So I left a message and took off once again for Wasdale Head. By now my new companion had got together a stretcher and one or two other necessary items — but no one else to carry any of them. The horrible truth was beginning to penetrate . . . 'Willie me lad,' I thought to myself, 'how would you like another trip to Pillar today, carrying that bloody great stretcher?' Consisting of two young trees wrapped round with canvas it was obviously highly suitable for carrying heavy loads, probably rocks, for short distances — by strong and multitudinous numbers of farm hands. It was not designed for carting back up the fell side to Pillar Rock, by two men only, one of whom for the last hour or so had been careering around the countryside as if all the Devils of Hell were after him. But that's the way it appeared to be . . . and that's the way it went! We got back to the Rock in the late afternoon without being able to pick up one addition to the party. We did pass one group going in the opposite direction, who evinced some slight interest, but doubtless feeling that the whole matter had nothing to do with them, kept on their way. At the Rock, Bert and Frank, who had now been joined by two fell-walking friends, were very glad to see us — thankful to have something to do at long last. They ran to us, took over the stretcher, loaded me up with all the unnecessary equipment and turned me round for home and said, kindly, 'On your Way', or words to that effect, with instructions to direct the additional help that would be coming (as, in fact it was) from Brackenclose to the High Level Route.

When I got back to Brackenclose, having passed all the help that was needed on the way down and given them details of what was happening, only one good Cumbrian word could describe my physical and mental state — knackered!

The reaction to this episode was quite marked. As Bert Beck said to me many years later, 'it slowed us all down a bit.'

For a long time after the event my own approach to a cliff face, and to some extent performance upon it, underwent traumatic moments. My eyes would scour the screes searching for bodies; a piece of bright coloured litter or lost equipment, or cached rucksack would bring a start to my eyes and a jolt to my heart. In the days of Eagle Crag we had climbed in a wonderful haze of confidence. Once every new thing we did, every new trick, added to that joyous feeling of invincibility. Others may fall off, but I? . . . Never! Now we had brushed against violent death. I knew that people near me could fall — so could I!

Eliminate C and the Pillar accident were a considerable steadying influence, but, nevertheless, the year's total of climbing began to show us, considering the fact that I had never led (or even followed) on a VS climb prior to mid-May, 1940, that something was happening — that experience, however harsh, was being gained; that one doesn't have to go under with the pressures. And it showed, personally, that climbing, for me, was the very stuff of life itself. When not climbing, I thought it, dreamt it, studied, read and breathed its every essence.

In the six months or so prior to winter we had managed to climb most of the Pillar Rock classics, including South West, North West,

Hadrian's Wall, Grooved Wall in pouring rain and boots, Scafell Girdle in similar weather and footwear. We had made several new climbs, which when compared in retrospect with some of those we had since climbed seemed to be standing up well in their own right.

Great Central Route on Dow paid for Eliminate C. Deer Bield Crack, Gimmer Crack, Asterisk (in boots), Botteril's, Overhanging Wall on Scafell East Buttress, most of the Kern Knotts problems — the Buttress, West Buttress, Sepulchre, Flake Climb, the Chain and the Buttonhook and many more, had given us their moments. We had had a good year.

It was around this time that the Workington and West Cumberland Mountaineering Club was born.

This 'great' and totally fictional club was invented to beguile away the time on the walk back from the crags. Under its banner songs and poems were invented — as were Kindred Clubs; the Herdwicks of the lonely wartime fells were the only audience to the spate of creativity that accompanied the long treks down to the valley.

We discussed solemnly the deeds of the redoubtable W. & W.C.M.C. members — both of them. The songs we spawned tended to be bawdy and the poems lewd (I recall faintly one that began 'Wynter is Icumen in' and which would hardly have been acceptable at the Vicarage Garden Party, having something of the flavour of the Ball of Kirriemuir). But it was with the Kindred Clubs that imagination took flight. The P. & B. New Routes Development Association accepted the credit for the planning of new climbs; the P. & B. Joint Mutual Admiration Society took upon its broad shoulders the challenge of explaining and justifying any set back the members of the parent club may have experienced. Failure — of any kind — became a virtue when the P. & B. J.M.A.S. had finished with it. Getting lost in the snow and mist on Grasmoor and Scafell, falling off a troublesome pitch, being unable to get up or making a hotch-potch of a move on this or that climb, falling foul of some other event or circumstance were all carefully, logically and soothingly explained away. But we had a special love for the Locusts Climbing Club (motto: 'We leave nothing behind — not even our thanks'). Despite the early war years the odd exotic tinned dish was not impossible to find. Bert and I tended to find them.

One winter weekend we were sharing Brackenclose with members of the Cambridge University Mountaineering Club. Our evening meal, served at the end of one of the tables consisted of soup, a boned chicken from a tin (an invention of our friends from across the Atlantic) and appropriate vegetables, a large steamed pudding (also from a tin) and a pint of Bert's custard made to a 'Creamy Consistency' — the high point of his culinary skill. One of the young C.U.M.C. lads stared for a while at the contents of our plates and then said 'Are you celebrating something?'

'No,' answered Bert, 'this is quite normal.' (Which wasn't, in fact, totally accurate.)

'Good Lord,' was the young C.U.M.C. reply after studying his own plate of uninteresting hash — a creation only equalled, I would say, in years to come by the less adventurous or esteemed of Motorway Caffs, 'and this is supposed to be our Annual Dinner!'

We didn't reply — what was there to say? The L.C.C. notched up another point.

At some time, early in 1941, one of us got the idea that the only thing missing from the W. & W.C.M.C. was a journal. In no time it was produced. It carried a title page with the inscription

Forsan et 'haec olim meminisse juvabit'.

and a complete list of office bearers and membership list which went something like this

President	S. B. Beck
Vice President	W. Peascod
Hon. Sec.	W. Peascod
Assistant Hon. Sec.	S. B. Beck
Editor	S. B. Beck
Assistant Editor	W. Peascod
Treasurer	W. Peascod
Committee	Messrs Peascod and Beck
Emeritus Members	S. B. Beck
	W. Peascod

(and so on).

It carried several articles (one on the Alpine Club); Editor's Comments; reports of the Kindred Clubs; a complete list of all the climbs we had done during the year — their standard and whether climbed in rubbers or nailed boots, and other items of mutual interest. Two copies were typed; one each. I kept mine for years but managed to lose it around 1970. Bert still had his a short time ago. It does, indeed 'delight us to remember this some day'.

We actually produced one more issue, later in the forties, then the W. & W.C.M.C. faded into the past. There is a time and a place for these things. Those first few years — their excitement and discovery and to some extent our naiveté — were the necessary catalysts that gave wings to our imagination.

The 1940/41 winter had been quite severe, but the sun arrived early. On March 16 Bert and I were again in Birkness Combe. Wilfrid Noyce once said 'Too much of Grey Crags after army diet is like champagne on indigestion.' But by March we were ready to uncork a magnum.

Up to this time most of the climbing on Grey Crags was on the arêtes or ridges of the various buttresses, and examination of the guidebook sketches by W. Heaton Cooper showed that there were good walls at the right of all the rock tiers which comprise this delightful climbing area.

The most blank of these is the one to the right of the Oxford and Cambridge Climb on the (top) tier Buttress of that name. It had cried out for a 'look' so here we were — to look! Dexter Wall, as we called it, is one of the very few new climbs I have done on a top-rope before leading. To provide a top-rope was so easy, and the wall, especially near the upper edge, seemed so bare we decided that, on this occasion, a little prudence could be profitable. It was, and we collected a nice little climb, which gets harder the higher one goes, a climb that turned out to be the hardest route on Grey Crags — an eminence it held for over thirty-five years!

But it was the right hand wall of the middle tier or Chockstone Buttress which yielded the highest dividend. We named it Grey Wall. It is about one hundred and fifty feet high and gives some pleasing situations on delightful rough rock. Of the three climbs we did there, Suaviter and Fortiter have turned out to be very popular and I believe justifiably so!

But if these two climbs sparkled like champagne, it was a slightly earlier expedition that could best be equated to army diet . . .

Warnscale is the short, wide based valley to the immediate south of Fleetwith Pike. It is ringed with crags. To the north is Striddle Crag (in 1940 it was quite unclimbed, but since then it has been given a good working over by Don Greenop and friends) with more broken crags to its right. Up the southern flank of Fleetwith Pike is a well marked track which winds up out of Warnscale to lead to the Dubs quarries and across to Brandreth and the Gables. To the right of the Dubs quarry path and straight ahead as one walks up Warnscale Bottom, is Green Crag (a crag which for many years was ignored until Odyssey was climbed in 1965 by Chris Eilbeck and Bill Young. The following year it became the 'in' place in Buttermere) and swinging to the right from Green Crag is the gash made by Black Beck as it pours down from the delightful plateau above and superb little tarn that bears its name. Still further to the right of Black Beck, facing across towards Fleetwith is the magnificently photogenic rampart of the Haystacks. This horseshoe of buttresses and gullies is one of the most attractive views in Lakeland. But in the middle of 1941 we weren't there for the view.

I always enjoyed gully climbing — maybe it's the 'head against the wall' syndrome; maybe it was the stirring tales of Jones, the Abrahams and Oppenheimer; maybe I just like playing in muck! And here, in the Haystacks were some of the most impressive gullies in Western Lakeland. There are three of them. From the right, there is firstly Stack Ghyll, already mentioned, a good climb, if you know what you're doing! In the centre, the second, is Warn Ghyll, climbed in 1907 by Fred Botteril, Oppenheimer and others, but hardly ever climbed nowadays. As long ago as 1926 A. R. Thompson, in his guidebook said, 'This place is *best avoided*. On the second ascent an accident took place owing to loose rock.' The third gully to the left is Y-Gully, so called from its shape. The rock on Stack Ghyll I had already sampled, that on Warn Ghyll I was prepared to believe was bad. When Thompson, in 1926 said of Y-Gully — 'its ascent was attempted long ago, but abandoned owing to bad rock,' I was fairly certain that any involvement with this part of the world would have very little to do with Grey Crags or champagne.

But whatever the reasons behind the decision to come near the place, the fact was that here we unquestionably were, on a warm summer's day, staring up into the dark upper reaches of a most impressive chimney and with serious intentions of trying to make the ascent of the same.

Bert's description *The Last of the Classics* (Fell and Rock Journal No. 36) written in 1941 soon after the event gives a clear enough picture:

'. . . The left arm of the Y offered little encouragement as it came to a premature end by merging into a smooth face, and the right and continuous arm was therefore our main concern. Its lower portion consisted of a wide, shallow trough, of mingled rock and turf, and set at an apparently easy angle, its lower lip ending fifty feet above us, and its upper end topped by a rock wall not more than twenty feet in height. Above the latter a short indefinite section led to the foot of the upper portion, and there our gazes quailed as they traced it upwards. One clear-cut, magnificent gash, black and forbidding, it seemed to curve forwards as it rose in a most intimidating manner. If the rock *there* was bad, no wonder its ascent was abandoned long ago! . . .'

A small chockstone at the foot of the chimney gave us a belay from which to commence operations — but technically sound though it may have been we could, for all practical purposes, have dispensed with it completely. A belay, at the *foot* of a climb, from which to safeguard the leader only becomes effective when he can arrange some satisfactory runner or runners as he makes headway. We very quickly found that good runners were *not* to be the norm on Y-Gully.

Above the chockstone I made my way upwards making for the shallow trough by way of a pleasant thirty foot slab with good holds. On entering the trough I found the cleanest rock was in the channel on the left where the waters had cut most deeply but scoured most smoothly; on the right the trough merged into steep insecure turf; and in the middle, on mingled rock and turf, the greatest care was necessary for the angle was much steeper than it looked! In a hundred feet I stopped. Not because the place was any better or worse than that above or below, but simply because I'd run out of rope. I had no runner on between where I'd reached and Bert at the bottom of the climb. There was little point in putting a sling round the odd loose flake that stuck out of the face. At my stopping place I found a spike that roughly suggested it might pass for an illusion of a belay. To find a stance to accompany the belay I excavated and finally dug out an earthy foothold big enough to accommodate one person. It was not a very promising situation — even less promise lay ahead! When we'd made the changeover on the stance and rickety belay I set off again, up the rotten rock and grass. The real fun began fifty feet higher — I had reached the wall against which the trough impinged! There was no possibility of a belay below it, nor any good standing ground, but only a smooth, shelving ledge — and it was even wetter, slimier and more rotten and hopeless looking at close quarters than it appeared from below. Added to this it overhung markedly. We were a very long way from the champagne of Grey Crags.

Across the base of this hopeless looking wall I scratched around without finding a line for any upward progress — certainly not any kind of progress that I cared to make, knowing the quality of the stance and belay occupied by the second. 'From a safe distance and the security of a belay,' wrote Bert showing once more that everything in climbing, as in life, is relative, 'I gave it as my opinion that the short buttress on the right looked more feasible than "this wicked wall, through whom I see no bliss". On examination, Bill seemed to regard the buttress with equal distaste, and declared the rock to be especially bad — of which statement he proceeded to give instant demonstration by plucking forth sundry lumps of it and hurling them from him. They were aimed for the channel on my left, but several ricocheted uncomfortably near and when one smallish one had zipped into the turf six inches from my nose, I was about to protest, but refrained on realising that the more he quarried the more determined he appeared to be . . .'

Very slowly and gingerly I worked my way up and across the buttress, onto the wall, trending back to the left as I gained height. The holds for the landing on the turf above the wall were particularly bad. I poised, some seventy feet above Bert, 'hesitating between advance and retreat,' searching for reliable holds and courage. Finally, both arrived in doubtful measure and the last steps were made. Thirty feet higher on what was now a firm ledge, below a very steep wall of apparently much better rock, I found a splendid spike belay — large, solid and secure! I lashed onto it as if I never intended to part therefrom. It was Bert's turn to drink his fill and again I leave him to savour the ascent.

'I had ample leisure to appreciate just what this pitch had involved . . . The wall itself offered no scope, even with a rope held from above, and after an extremely thin and airy movement to the right, I found the buttress to be much steeper than it had looked from below, the rocks to have an awkward tilt, the exposure to be troublesome and the technical difficulty considerable. After a

balance movement upwards on sloping holds it was necessary to
hang on two spikes, fortunately sound, swing the feet across to the
left, pull up, ease delicately upwards until the feet could be placed on
the spikes, step up and make that landing on vegetation . . .'

We had now ascended some two hundred feet, about half the
height of the climb, we weren't sure what lay ahead, but had a fair
idea, or so we thought!

A traverse led back to the left from the belay into the final
chimney. At first the going was easy, although hampered by bad
rock. In fifty feet I reached a chockstone, which although loose was
likely to offer shelter from anything that might fall from above — be
it rock, water, grass or leader! And better still I discovered behind
the chock a fine spike belay. I can well appreciate Bert's satisfaction
when he said, '. . . at least it was welcome as a shelter from any falling
stones. There were many, too, as Bill conducted further "quarrying"
operations above, but I could see them hurtle past me and hear
them rebound in the trough and then crash on the scree without
discomfort — or rather, to be exact, without physical discomfort!'

Up in the final chimney at the point where I had now reached,
things had not been going at all well. Smooth walls hemmed one in;
upward progress had ground to a halt, and finally feeling very much
in the need of some moral support and a friendly face, and having
wedged myself in the chimney, I asked Bert if he would like to come
up and have a chat.

Again I leave Bert to speak. 'I would, and emerged from
underneath, and passed above the chockstone on large sound
satisfying holds. (This and the thirty foot slab were the only sections
of the four hundred feet of Y-Gully where they were found!) I joined
Bill at an extremely uncomfortable position where everything sloped
the wrong way, nothing was secure, and there was neither definite
belay nor strong stance. Immediately above us was an awkward
bulge, and higher still the cleft became much more deeply cut and
narrow between smooth sheer walls. And the back of this chimney
bore out our worst fears by curving *forwards* so that it was necessary
to bridge and work upwards and *outwards*. And to crown all, the rock
was still bad. I do not think I have ever been in a more hopeless
looking place . . .'

We decided in this least congenial of places to hold a staff meeting!
We had been in the gully for some six or seven hours. There was still
plenty of light left but the toll on physical and nervous energy had
been quite considerable. I had given the final chimney a good
working over but it was proving in the depleted circumstances, to be
a tough nut to crack . . . Retreat, whilst some energy was still at
hand, was the prudent course.

Back we went to our splendid belay on the green ledge. The
options open to us were (a) to climb down the bulging wall, (b) to

abseil off the big belay, or (c) to traverse right or left out of the gully
and either ascend or descend one of the flanking walls.

There was no way in the world that option (a) was to be invoked,
(b) was little better; we only had a one hundred and twenty feet
hemp rope. Even if tied off to the spike it would land us barely half
way down the rotten rock and vegetation; we would then have to do
the remaining section unroped. To use a double rope would barely
have taken us down the wall and we knew there was no belay below.
There remained option (c). True we had never been on those
bounding buttresses before but they didn't appear to be insuperable
— rickety they may be, but there would be a greater variety of route
than in the depths of that black chimney. So (c) it was. The wall to
the right appeared to be the most amenable and 'not even the ascent
and crossing of a crazy ridge of badly-balanced flakes, and a long
sensational traverse above the depths of Warn Ghyll and the ascent
of the face of disintegrating rock and vertical vegetation beyond it
gave us any regrets as to our choice of route.'

In the late evening sun we reached the top of the Haystacks,
staggered down the fellside beside Black Beck, picked up our gear
from the foot of the gully and ran down what scree we could to
Warnscale Bottom. It had been an epic day! But obviously matters
couldn't rest there. A return journey had to be made.

The first return was a dismal failure. We tried to take a short-cut to
the top of the Haystack instead of the obvious roundabout route
following the path around Black Beck Tarn or up from Scarth Gap;
this involved us in more rotten rock and steep drops. Morale was as
shot through with holes as a good Emmental cheese, long before the
pair of us found the top of the gully and peered into the 'vast vacuity'
below. But we did, at least, see the finish and below we could see the
point we had reached on the last attempt — and the bit in between,
the unclimbed section, whilst not engendering in us thoughts of 'an
easy romp' did not determine us on total rejection.

On the second return we went back well-equipped. Bert assures
me we had three ropes for abseil purposes, three slings and actually
three karabiners — never had the pair of us approached a climb with
so much gear. This time we wasted no effort on niceties. We abseiled
off on two of the ropes over the breathtaking upper wall to the fine
belay we had reached from below.

We had been away from the place for a few weeks and in that time
we had done some good climbs elsewhere. 'The appropriate rites had
been performed,' wrote Bert. The time of trial was nigh.

'Were our spirits thus really purified or was it a purely fortuitous
combination of circumstances? Whatever the cause, in the event the
profundity seemed less profound, the walls of the temple less smooth
and unyielding, its roof protruding less inhospitably above our
heads. And, when the back was kept unwaveringly on the left wall

the feet of the faithful found support on the right — and those supports were occasionally secure! Slowly I watched my leader rise upwards and outwards in the prescribed manner, until he disappeared from my sight and signified in the usual way that I must follow . . .'

And that was it — all over! There was not the glow of Eagle Front nor the delectation one was to find on Suaviter and Fortiter, nor the same stabbing sharpness of Dexter Wall . . . but there was a deep satisfaction!

The Y-Gully is not likely to be on my Desert Island list, but I'm glad that we climbed it.

It was the last big new route Bert and I did in 1941. In July he was in the Royal Artillery. We had been climbing together for just over twelve months, we had been out on the rocks together on seventy-seven occasions; we had done over one hundred and fifty climbs together, the majority either Very Severe or Severe and of which ten were first ascents; we had climbed most of the classics — gullies as well as face climbs; including most of the hardest climbs in the then guidebooks. These are the bare statistical facts. What cannot be tied in to the numbers game is what it all meant; the way in which we worked as a team, the unspoken reliance, the joy of clean rock and air and good companionship . . . It had been a good start to a climbing career.

6

War-Time Wanderings

S. B. Beck and I never climbed together again for some four years. Whilst he was away 'fighting for King and Country' in the Royal Artillery, I stayed in Cumberland and filled coal for a living, getting onto the fells whenever I could. Soon after Bert went into the forces I met Elwyn Banner Mendus and Austin Barton. Elwyn had recently arrived in Workington from South Wales to join his brother in legal practice, whilst Austin managed the family Men's and Women's Outfitting firm.

Despite a recurring illness affecting the spine, Elwyn was quite competent on steep rock. When he died, after hospitalisation, early in 1952, he was only thirty-five years of age.

Both Elwyn and Austin brought with them a more general attitude to the mountains and valleys, and I found myself, on several occasions, doing things that the weather and the bug that gnawed at my 'vittles' would on other occasions have demanded I spent on a rock face or in a gully. I remember, for instance, spending days searching for the nesting site of the great crested grebe around Loweswater, where Austin, a very keen photographer, intended to make a film of its nesting habits — and days around St. Bee's Head, not for climbing, but to photograph the sea birds. The first time I ever put on skis was with Austin on Grey Knotts above Honister. During the hard winter we skated on Derwentwater and on West Cumbrian ponds. We still climbed — although transport began to be more of a problem. Our first new climb together was Resurrection on High Crag, which goes up the fine crack with the double-bunger overhangs in the corner to the left of the steep Eastern face of High Crag Buttress. It is true that the route is rather contrived but the climbing is varied and the crux, up the top part of the steep Eastern wall referred to, was alarming enough at the time — especially in nailed boots. We named the climb Resurrection because we felt at the time that we had infused a little life into this somnolent crag above Gatesgarth.

Later in the year we began to explore the cliffs at Honister and one or two crags attracted our attention and time was spent upon them. But the most significant non-climbing event of 1941 for me, was of an altogether different nature to any of these perambulations. In December I got married!

When we went to our virginal cot I was twenty-one and Margaret, my wife, had just turned twenty. As in many marriages, one is led to believe, a euphoric haze caresses the early vision — before evanescence reveals the path on which the feet and hearts are set. We had our share of ups and downs with, as time went by, more downs than ups! But self-delusion can overcome many a potential crisis, and life went on.

With my dedication to whatever I happened to be involved in at the moment, I must have presented a problem to the most liberal and understanding of thinkers. I never could, nor can I still, do things by halves. Of course, it has to bite me, but if I am in something then I have to give the new interest the care and attention it deserves. I couldn't give up climbing — not even when my small son was born eighteen months later. I possessed what every married climber must possess — the ability to cut loose from family ties the instant one's foot trod a mountain or hand touched a rock.

During the moments before leaving on a climbing trip the pull of conflicting wishes created unspoken resentment. If in those early years the causes of doubt and rancour had been 'another woman' there would have been some tangible opposition against which to raise the barricades, but when the rival for attention is a rope, a pair of climbing boots and a rock face, a situation develops, in time, which demands a greater maturity of thinking than I believe either of us were able to bring to the circumstance. Perhaps the aptitude to balance the pull of heart and mind in two directions is a function of mature years — a skill borne of suffering or need.

In 1942, on the domestic front, matters had taken a new turn. We had moved to a suburb even further away from the mine in which I worked. This now meant that I had to leave my bed at half past three in the morning, get into my pit clothes, eat breakfast, ride my bike into Workington where I caught the bus at twenty minutes past four in the morning. At the mine we just had sufficient time to be given our lamps, collect our explosive and sharp picks before the first cage went down at five o'clock.

On my journeys to and from Workington I passed a new colliery — Solway Colliery. I discovered later that it was intended to be one of the show pieces of the British Mining Industry — that it never really did become one, in terms of output, is someone else's story!

One morning during the long walk from the shaft bottom to our working face, I said to my father, 'I'm going to look for a job at Solway . . .' His reply was immediate, 'Aw reet!' The pair of us started work in the new mine the following week. The difference was the change from night to day — true, not a terribly bright, shiny kind of a day, but a day of hope nevertheless. Solway was the last mine at which my father worked. He was killed there eleven years later, a few days after my young sister's wedding.

I had enormous respect for my father. He, in his turn took a great pride (always under-stated to others and *never* stated at all to me) in my doings. He was one of the finest miners I ever knew. He could wield a pick or a shovel and swing a hammer with the care he would give a precision instrument. To him that's what they were; and that was the state in which they had to be kept. When I first became his apprentice he showed me how to make the coal 'work' — 'to talk' as he called it, by the process of 'liggen it in', that is, undercutting the seam, and keeping 't'fast and for'ard' (skills that may well have totally disappeared by now). He knew precisely where to hit a large stone with the seven or fourteen pound hammer to make it split into more easily handled pieces. If it was necessary to use a wedge then it was my job to hold the wedge in the bedding plane of the rock whilst he swung the hammer with all his strength. On the first occasion that this happened my hand shook slightly with nervous anticipation of what would happen if he missed. At the first noticeable quiver of the steel wedge in my hand he said, 'Keep t'bloody thing still or I'll knock thee hand off . . .' And from that instant my faith was established — and through all the hundreds, nay thousands of tons of rock or coal we handled together there was never a time when that faith was called into question. His death came very easily . . . whilst examining the seam after firing a round of explosives (he was then a Deputy Overman at the mine) a small piece of coal fell off the side and broke his neck. He was alone at the time. But this was years later, long after I'd left his guidance and protection.

In June 1943, my son was born. We decided to call him Alan Gordon, after the Connor twins, but whilst walking to the Registry Office in Workington to record the event, I suddenly decided to add William as well. As far back as I could determine the first born son of the first born had been called William — usually the only Christian name. This poor little fellow had three to carry!

Later in the year I was told I'd won a Miners' Welfare Scholarship. I had been attending evening classes for three evening a week for the last three years, now I was to be given time off work for one day per week to attend the Technical College. The difference that time off makes to one's ability to study is considerable. The only trifling problem about my particular circumstance was that at the time I won the Scholarship the Mining Department got a new Head. His policy was quite without frills or sentiment. If you can study three nights a week whilst being employed full-time, you ought to be able to study three nights a week if you've been given a day off was his simple dictum. So our new programme required us to attend one full day at the Tech plus three nights per week — I loved it! . . .

In 1944 and in contrast to my own decreasing pace of discovery, things had begun to hot-up on other climbing fronts. The most noticeable of these were the attentions that Jim Birkett was giving to Esk Buttress, in particular. In that year Birkett produced five new climbs on the magnificent crag — more were to follow in 1945.

It is difficult to over emphasize the impetus that Jim Birkett gave to climbing in the Lakes at this time. I never climbed with Jim, although we got near to it once or twice — yet for one reason or another never quite made the final contact. I watched him climb on occasions — the first time was on the Buttonhook on Kern Knotts. A superb climber — a combination of grace, delicacy and considerable physical strength — he was a man who believed profoundly in keeping himself in top physical condition.

There are many stories of Jim's agility. Charlie Wilson tells of how he and Jim were standing on the roadway near Seathwaite when Charlie happened to mention he'd seen someone in the gym do a back somersault. 'Do you mean like this?' said Jim and performed a perfect back flip — in heavy nailed climbing boots! Jim didn't mess about on a climb — his movements flowed. The traverse on the second pitch of Buttonhook he made look easy (he had not been there before — this was probably the second ascent!). It was only when one saw the difficulty experienced by the second that one realised that all was not what it seemed. Our ascent made a short time later confirmed the impression gained from the second man's performance. In many ways, one gathered, Jim Birkett was a shy man. He shunned publicity like he would smallpox, although occasionally the limelight was impossible to avoid. He was not a club man but he had his small band of loyal followers. Len Muscroft, Charlie Wilson, Chuck Hudson, Joe Williams, Tommy Hill, Vince Veevers, fine climbers all, who would have followed him to the very portals of heaven — or hell with complete faith in Jim's ability to take them there and get them back again. Jim loved to climb in nailed boots — thus were May Day on Scafell East Buttress and Central Buttress climbed with Charlie Wilson — the flake Crack being led clean without slings on the chockstone!

I used to meet Charlie Wilson quite frequently in the early days. He was the power behind the Carlisle Climbing Club. During the War Charlie was in the R.A.F. and stationed at Harrogate. Occasionally, to escape the monotony of Service life, he would take his bike and head for Almscliffe. One day whilst resting at the base of the cliff a young lad came up to him and said, 'Do you climb?' 'Aye,' said Charlie, 'I do a bit.' 'Would you like to climb with me?' the youngster queried. And off they went!

To see this young fellow ascend Frankland's Green Crack with handjams and friction was a revelation to Charlie.

Later he wrote to Len Muscroft . . . 'I've just met a young fellow who climbs nearly as well as Jim Birkett. When he starts moving in the Lakes you'll hear quite a lot about him, I bet! His name is Arthur Dolphin.'

Lakeland loyalty did not take long to reply, 'Nobody climbs as well as Jim Birkett!'

And of course we did hear a great deal about Arthur Dolphin. Like so many fine climbers, before and since, his initial introduction to climbing was on gritstone, and when the technique acquired there was translated into action of the most determined kind on Lakeland crags it was inevitable that the results of that action would leave a mark comparable to that of his slightly older contemporary.

I got to know Arthur and Bruce Gilchrist soon after they began to operate in the Lakes — but strangely enough it was not here but on Almscliffe that we first climbed together. The time was 1944 and I had gone to Leeds to take an examination. The day before the examination, being a Sunday, we decided to spend on Almscliffe. Transport out there was by bus . . . The mind just cannot recall all the routes we did that day. The boys took me round and pointed out all the party pieces, several of which we did, then we adjourned to the Quarry. Here, names like Josephine, Bonaparte, S Crack ring a bell. It was a long day and as long as the sun shone sweetly there was very little thought given to time. I recall that Arthur was wearing ordinary street shoes — but one got the distinct impression that it wouldn't have mattered terribly much if they had been scuba diving flippers; they would have presented little problem to Arthur. He was brilliant.

We had had a full day by the time we got back to Otley to catch the bus back to Leeds. 'What bus?' you may well ask; the last one had gone ages ago. Well! What does one do? It's war-time, there are very few Sunday drivers and even fewer who would pick up a group of scruffy climbers. So we did all that we could do — we walked back to Leeds. I thought it a long way. As I sneaked into my hotel in the early hours of the morning, with feet blistered from the miles of tarmac I felt distinctly that this was not the kind of pre-examination preparation that was guaranteed to give an A grade pass mark. I was right — I failed.

At this time, 1944, Jim Birkett was climbing at his peak. He had been down to Wales with Chuck Hudson and cleaned up most of the then known routes on Cloggy in the, for him, most appropriate footgear — nailed boots. In the Lakes, Esk Buttress, White Gill, Scafell East Buttress, Castle Rock of Triermain had become and were to become even more so, his most cherished stamping ground.

But so *complete* a climber was Jim that the same high quality of climbing that he was able to bring to familiar crags can also be seen in the one-off routes that he made on those cliffs which we tend, far less, to associate with him. Tophet Grooves is one that comes to mind . . .

Arthur Dolphin's earliest new climbs in the Lakes are on the same crag — Demon Wall and Tophet Girdle, which I'm fairly certain, came about after he and I had discussed the feasibility of such a traverse — but there were much greater things ahead for Arthur!

7

Buckstone How and Other Places

With the end of the War came the long period of adjustment to Peace.

Our friends, some of them, returned, but rationing didn't go away.

Things would never be the same as they were in 1939. Too much had happened; too much had been seen and felt. There was a longing on the part of many experienced mountaineers to return to the solace and certainty of the hills. They came back slowly. Strangely there was no rush of new blood to the crags as there had been in 1919 and 1920. The names of 1939 were still very much to the fore — joined by one or two others from the war years. It was these who still continued the exploration of the Lakes. But the hills slowly became alive again. Young men and women gradually found their way to the crags and several made one or two minor first ascents but it was to be another five or six years before the new generation was to make its first decisive impact — the generation of Drasdo, Ross, Greenwood, Brown and Whillans had still to find the Lakes.

In 1946 it seemed that Birkett, Muscroft, Dolphin and ourselves were the ones still undertaking the major share of exploration. A Barnard Castle schoolmaster, Bentley Beetham, it is true, produced some fifty new climbs during the war years, and went on to make another sixty odd afterwards, in Borrowdale alone. Amongst them were the climbs on Shepherd's Crag — some of which, like the Brown Slabs climbs and Little Chamonix, are amongst the most popular in the Lakes. It would not be an exaggeration to say that Little Chamonix is climbed by at least one party every day for most of the year. I have seen as many as five parties all jammed on the halfway ledge because some reluctant beginner was having difficulty with the crux. But it is also not an untruth to say that many of Beetham's climbs are now rarely done — if at all. The reason isn't difficult to find. The climbs looked backwards not forwards. They

Above left: The writer's father (also
W.Peascod) aged about 20 (May 1918). His
father (another William) had been dead for
a year or so and now, as the eldest son in a
family of eight children, was the major
breadwinner - working in the mines.

Above right: The writer's mother, Alice,
probably in her mid-twenties.

Right: Family group, 1920. Left to right,
great grandmother, father, grandmother
(she was known as Mother Peascod) and
the writer.

Above: Eagle Crag, Birkness Combe - scene of some of the writers most memorable climbs. Eagle Front (1940) is shown. Central Chimney (1948) is the long chimney line to its left. Fifth Avenue (1940) goes up the clean wall between the two and gave a 90ft. run-out with no 'protection' whatsoever to a rickety belay. Eagle Girdle (1940) traverses the steep wall in the centre of the picture to join Eagle Front at the belay 3. It followed Eagle Front for three pitches (to belay 6) then traversed left and round the corner into Central Chimney. From this climb Easter Buttress, the left hand skyline was reached by a traverse to the left and followed to the top of the crag.

S.B.Beck and right, Bill Peascod in the summer of 1940 at the time of the Eagle Crag (Birkness Combe) exploration. The photo was taken at the top of Honister Pass - en route to Gillercombe.
(Photo: S.B.Beck collection)

Dexter Wall, Grey Crags, Birkness Combe - the first ascent March 1941. The photo shows Bill Peascod ascending the steep thin crack at the top of the wall (the crux) with Bert Beck on the belay. (Photo: S.B.B. Collection)

Bill Peascod on Pedestal Wall, Pillar,
the day after his 20th birthday, and the first
climb he did with Bert Beck. This was when
he was working at the coal face. 10 stone in
weight and very fit.

Left: Resurrection Route, High Crag.
The first ascent - made in new nailed
boots. (Photo: Austin Barton)

Below: George Rushworth and Bill Peascod in camp at Seathwaite (around 1948). (Photo: Bert Beck)

Above: Stan Dirkin doing the traverse on Newlands Buttress (1949). Note the typical equipment of the period. Corduroy breeches, cut-away raincoat, nailed boots, a pair of rubbers and one 'sling'. By now nylon rope is beginning to replace manilla hemp.

Left: Bert Beck.

On Overhanging Wall, East Buttress
of Scafell, 1941. Bert Beck is just
starting on the difficult section. Bill
Peascod's head can be seen outlined
against the white slab half way up
the climb.
(Photo: S.B.B. Collection)

With Bert Beck on South West Climb, Pillar.

Below: Bill Peascod leads Suaviter, Grey Crags. On the ledge is Ronnie Wilkinson.

Bill Peascod 1951, about the time of the first ascent of Cleopatra, Buckstone How. (Photo: Brian Blake)

Left: Bill Peascod leading the first attempt on Cleopatra (Whit 1951). New rubbers were used next day! (Photo Brian Blake)

Above: At the same spot some thirty years later. (Photo: Chris Culshaw)

were aimed at the beginner — not at the potential tiger. They did nothing to advance the art of rock climbing. In his welter of easy climbs Beetham produced some classics — more than enough to go round. These are hugely popular: the rest are justifiably forgotten.

Our return to exploration began early in 1946. Bert Beck was by then back in Workington and again teaching at the local Grammar School.

During the years of Bert's absence I had noticed one or two crags scattered around the North Western valleys that were obviously crying out for at least a visit. And the first one to be given a climber's look was a crag I had noticed in Honister. There is a great deal of rock in Honister — on both sides of the valley. By far the majority of it is unsuitable for climbing because of its vegetated nature. But when examined with more than a cursory glance, and from certain angles and directions of light, it becomes apparent that there are some quite good crags camouflaged amongst the grooves and broken terrain of the main fellsides — it was through going up to repeat the old pre-World War I routes, Yew Crag Gully and Charter Chimney, that we noticed the continuous buttresses around the Gully and thought they would be useful for low-level winter climbing. They are! We noticed also a steep little buttress known as Yew Crag Knotts a few hundred yards to the east of Yew Crag Gully which I thought might lend itself to short, steep 'climbs of the Kern Knotts variety'. On New Year's Eve, 1941, we had climbed the chimney and ascended a route which I thought may have been done before, although we never found any record of such an ascent, and christened it the Garden Wall. The rest of the Garden Wall would, I thought, keep for another sunnier day. How long it *did* keep I could scarcely have imagined at the time! And I never would have guessed forty years!

But it was not these crags, nor even the mass of rock on Fleetwith Pike that excited my fancy — rather was it the bulk of rock nearer to, and seen as a sharp arête from the top of Honister, that seemed so full of promise. We named the crag Buckstone How.

The attack began in March, when we spent a useful day exploring the left hand end of the crag. But the first actual climb that we did there, a fortnight later, was Sinister Grooves — because it is located near the left hand side of the crag and not because of any villainous connotations. Prior to these explorations neither of us had actually climbed on the crag; so far as we knew, no-one had. We didn't know quite what to expect in the way of rock quality. Would we find another, bigger Grey Crag, or would we have a face version of Y-Gully on our hands? In the event, neither transpired. Buckstone How turned out to be like . . . well, Buckstone How! And apart from steepness, as far removed from Eagle Crag type climbing as one could get. There is a tendency for the rock to flute into vertical

curving ribs and grooves. Because of its slaty cleavage, sharp-cut
holds alternating with blank facets occur frequently. Fortunately
belays are generally readily available; rock spikes (some good and
others not so good) turn up when needed. It is a kind of rock which
lends itself admirably to present day protection techniques. In 1946
such techniques had not even been remotely considered — by us, at
any rate — but recent visits have borne out the truth of this
observation.

Sinister Grooves, like nearly all the new climbs done in those days,
was led without prior inspection on a rope — any knowledge of a cliff
being picked up from visual inspection from below or from an
adjacent climb. There were no adjacent climbs on Buckstone How
— here we were with a steep, brand new, completely untouched,
unexplored three hundred foot crag to play with! How many such
cliffs can be found today? The climb begins up a steep wall, via two
vertical cracks, then continues up a scoop of sorts to the bottom of a
deep V groove. The ascent of this groove proved to us to be the most
difficult part of the climb (it is interesting to note that later writers
found greater problems higher up). The sides of the groove are
smooth, but in twenty feet a good handhold turns up. I climbed it by
facing the left wall until the handhold was reached, then, after
turning on the handhold, finished up on the right wall. Easier
climbing followed and an upper crack was reached. This crack is one
of those irritating features to be found on many climbs — a pitch that
looks as if it ought to be easy but turns out to be frustratingly
awkward. Finally, the crack yielded and easier climbing led up to the
top. For our first real essay onto the cliff we had notched up quite a
good climb, we thought, and were thoroughly pleased with the climb
— and ourselves. But there was more to come, we assured each
other. In the meantime, silence would be maintained — lips sealed!

May found us back on the crag again — this time in its centre
where, we thought, the climbs would be the longest and Honister
Wall was the result, a long pleasant Hard Severe with considerable
variety and some good situations — with a finish, on good holds, up a
short steep wall that looks down over the full length of the climb —
an airy place, but so comfortable, it was a total joy to be there!

Two weeks after Honister Wall we were in Borrowdale, to a crag
that everybody who has been down the valley (unless he's always
travelled by night or with eyes closed) must have seen. That fine
blocky crag, another Eagle Crag, at the corner of Greenup Ghyll and
Langstrath.

The first route we did on the cliff was probably the best. Falconer's
Crack, according to Walt Unsworth in his *High Fells of Lakeland*, 'set
a new standard of difficulty for Borrowdale' and 'was regarded as the
hardest route in the district' for some time. (Nearly ten years later,
Paul Ross did the first Extremely Severe climb in the area. He named

it Post Mortem and set a much higher standard of climbing in Borrowdale.) Two other climbs yielded — one near Falconer's Crack called Great Stair and the other to the right hand end of the crag. Postern Gate, a deeply cut chimney, was snatched from a weekend of pouring rain. In something like two and a half months we had had a good look at two virtually unknown crags and there were still things to come . . .

The next year, 1947, was also an eventful year. A new lecturer in Mining had been appointed to the Tech. His name was George Rushworth. He and I became firm friends and it was not long before we were teaming up together — not only on our new climbs but the old classics as well. There is a delightful though totally fallacious story that George only ever did *new* climbs. For reasons that elude me now, I find, amongst my collection of guidebooks, one to Gable which I had originally given to George. It shows that in 1947 and on Gable alone George did twenty-six climbs, including most of the Kern Knotts classics; and this was an area he didn't visit as much as he did, say, Buttermere or Pillar. He climbed extensively in Langdale and Borrowdale in the same year and in the following year visited Glencoe and Wales.

George's first new climbs were with Bert Beck and me. And the place was again Buckstone How.

At the right hand end of the crag are two obvious grooves which run almost from ground level to the full height of the crag. They ask to be climbed. The first one from the right is about one hundred and forty feet long and the holds are somewhat worn because the debris from the quarrying operations that used to be carried out above has poured down this natural drainage channel. The climbing in Groove One was quite straightforward and untroublesome, which was more than could be said for its neighbour, Groove Two, some fifty feet to the left. This climb began easily enough but soon steepened into a water-worn groove or scoop which led to a belay, sixty feet higher and just below the lower lip of the main groove. It was the act of getting into the main groove that provided the excitement. Twenty feet above our belay the base of the main groove was undercut into a 'pronounced bulge'. Getting to this point offered no great difficulty but the next move looked like being a problem. Groove Two, like Groove One, had also been a debris chute at one time. But fortunately, being much the smoother of the two, very little rubbish had collected in the groove; there are no pronounced ledges where it could have accumulated, nor were there any large holds just where we needed them!

Upward progress was noticeable by its total cessation for a while. I picked at the fine pebbles jammed in the base of the groove, searching enthusiastically for a handhold and finally my determination was rewarded by the unearthing of a tiny fingerhold, above the bulge, just big enough to take the tips of two fingers. With a heave I pulled on the tiny hold and got a knee jammed into the bottom of the main groove proper; an awkward shuffle or two followed and then I was standing up at last in the groove. It stretched up above me for another unbroken, unprotected seventy feet. But even though it was steep and somewhat strenuous, the climbing was straightforward until I reached the very top of the groove — and there on the sloping ledge, at which the groove ended abruptly, was a mass of fine quarry debris. Give me grass or heather any time on which to debouch but may the Mountain Gods protect me from landing on masses of small stones — or thick mud. The landing was quite scary. Anything I sent down would be heading straight for Bert, yet I had to clean the place up a bit in order to effect my own arrival with safety. I tossed a mental coin. Would I try and 'make it' and risk skidding on all those fine slate chips or would Bert be about to receive a shower bath of the same material? Bert lost the toss and I arrived safely! George was out of all harm's way during these goings on — but his turn was to come, when the time arrived for Bert to join me at the top of the climb. With George safely alongside we cleaned the landing up a bit and hoped we'd made it rather safer for others to arrive there. There is much to be said for the modern technique of abseiling down a new climb and cleaning it up with a wire brush. This was, in fact, an ideal example of where the procedure would have paid off handsomely.

The move up and over the large bulge at the bottom of the main groove was the crux of the climb as we did it. It is a great pity, one feels, that subsequent guide writers have felt it necessary to divert the pitch up a subsidiary groove to the left of the bulge. This move is then followed by a traverse back into the main groove above the bulge — one can't help but think that the major difficulty on the climb has thus been avoided.

Early in 1946, when I was in my penultimate year at the Technical College, it was decided at the colliery where I worked to widen the mine rescue facilities and form an additional rescue team. The mine rescue scheme was quite straightforward and had served the area well for many years. Briefly it was this: each mine was responsible for providing one or more voluntary part-time rescue teams, the actual number supplied depending on the manpower employed at the colliery, or some other consideration. When a team was formed it was given an initial intensive training at the Mine Rescue Station, then at Brigham, under Superintendent John Charlton; it then trained on a regular, but less frequent basis, to keep itself familiar with equipment and techniques.

The training scheme was really interesting. Much of the training was carried out whilst wearing self contained breathing apparatus, the wearer of which was fed oxygen from an oxygen bottle strapped on the back of the suit, through a mouthpiece gripped between the teeth, and exhaled air was passed through a breathing bag containing an absorbent which removed the carbon dioxide; the air stream was then cooled and replenished with oxygen from the bottle as it passed once again to the wearer's lungs. The whole suit weighed just over thirty pounds and had a bottle life of two hours. Team members were taught how to strip down, clean, replenish, re-assemble and test the suit for leaks. They were also trained in mine rescue and firefighting practice and first aid. When the new team was to be formed I volunteered for membership and was accepted. It would be a thoroughly useful additional training to that which I had already received in the mine and at the Tech. And it *did*, indeed, prove to be a most useful practical training!

In the event of a disaster at either our own or nearby mines the rescue teams were to be called out on a roster system. The main functions of the rescue teams were to explore for and locate survivors and get them to safety. This done, to locate the deceased and render what help was necessary in the restoration of mine ventilation so that the recovery of the deceased could take place in a relatively safe atmosphere. All operations would be controlled from an underground 'Fresh Air Base' which would be established as near to the irrespirable atmosphere as the undamaged part of the ventilation system would permit. It may be mentioned that because of the violence and carbon monoxide, created by the ignition of methane and coal dust, the ventilation control system of doors, brick and canvas stoppings (walls) would be badly damaged and the residual air and admixed gases, known as afterdamp, would be poisonous in the explosion area. The explosion area may extend over a radius of hundreds of yards away from the point at which ignition occurred. In some circumstances the explosion wave could traverse every mine roadway and even extend to the surface of the mine.

I had been a member of the Solway B team for six months when the news arrived that an explosion had occurred at Lowca No. 10 Colliery. It was feared that all fifteen men in the district in which the explosion of methane gas had occurred, were missing. As the most recently formed and therefore least experienced team we were the last to be called out. There was, as it happened, very little to do (except to search for one missing man, a task that took nearly a week) but this did not lessen the initial twinge of fear as we went underground and into the explosion area.

One feels it the most in the inactive waiting period. What are underground conditions like? Will a second explosion occur whilst rescue operations are taking place? Is an unsuspected fire burning out of control? How will one stand up to the emotional impact of death and destruction? It is a time of tension and apprehension. As we walked into the explosion zone wearing our breathing apparatus none of us knew quite what to expect. We were shown in towards the Fresh Air Base by one of the employees of the mine where we knew our first job would be as stand-by, that is, we would sit for two hours at the Fresh Air Base while the team that had been there before us went exploring. By the time they returned from their two hour exploration stint, another team would have arrived at the Fresh Air Base and it would be our turn to explore, whilst the new team stood-by. Obviously the function of the stand-by team at the Fresh Air Base is to serve as a back-up safeguard to the rescuers out in the irrespirable zone.

Apprehension mounted in me during the walk in, until suddenly I saw the first sign of damage, walls blown down and a roof collapsed, and a quite miraculous event occurred — every vestige of fear or apprehension evaporated. It was almost with relief I heard us saying to each other 'we're here'. I knew we had all hidden the same fear.

The damage was colossal. I had never seen such huge roof falls, scores of them; conveyor lines were twisted in all directions, the conveyor drive ripped out of its foundations. Water ran from the roof in thick streams, the whole place was still and dark and covered in slime. Over it all hung the dank horrible silence of violent death. Drama followed fairly quickly with one small occurrence, when we'd moved only a few yards from the Fresh Air Base through canvas screens and into carbon monoxide. A team member, Tom Graham, a fellow student, collapsed! In seconds we had him dragged back to safety and later found his apparatus' breathing tubes were perished, allowing carbon monoxide to enter his breathing circuit through pin-hole fractures in the air tubes. Thankfully his exposure to the poisonous gas was only of short duration and we were able to administer oxygen to him from the resuscitation apparatus at the Fresh Air Base almost immediately. Apart from this small flutter, the ensuing operations were fairly routine, and indeed, as time went by, somewhat boring. But it was our first blooding — and we were grateful, to have passed through the ordeal without serious difficulty . . .

It was August 9, 1947, a Friday, and there was a knock on my front door. One of the men from the mine stood there. 'William Pit has gone up,' he said, 'and you have to stay on the alert until your team is called out.'

'When will that be?' I asked.

'I don't know.'

'Is there much loss of life?'

'I don't know, but not many men have got out.'

'Are there any fires?'

'I don't know.'

There was not much point in pursuing the questioning. The messenger either didn't know or he had been told to say nothing about the disaster. It didn't really matter whether he'd told us anything more or not; it wouldn't have done us much good!

But gradually, when more details became known, I was struck almost dumb with horror. An explosion had occurred on the afternoon shift, it wasn't known where or how; there were one hundred and nineteen men underground at the time — of whom twelve, who worked near the bottom of the shafts, had escaped to safety. One hundred and seven were missing — (that old euphemism!). It was devastating!

The disaster was of such magnitude that every mine rescue team in West Cumberland was called in, ours included — and as the days went by, other teams from far away were brought in to help. As the hours ticked away hope for survivors of the disaster dwindled. More and more obvious did it become, from the searches of the rescue teams, that the whole of the principal workings of the mine had been affected. There were huge rock-falls on the main haulage roadways, the ventilation had been disrupted at a most critical point and had left all the far sections of the mine without air-flow — a vast gasometer of afterdamp. Access to some of the faces was almost totally cut off. Falls of stone blocked the belt-roads.

We had just been instructed to couple-up into our rescue suits to carry out the next phase of systematic exploration of the explosion area, by an approach through the return airway, when the miracle occurred. A gang of workmen repairing a fallen area in the main roadway, in fresh air, which the rescue teams had managed to re-establish, saw advancing towards them out of the murk of the explosion area three faint headlights. Three men, survivors of the disaster, had somehow managed to get through all the falls, through an almost lethal atmosphere, to safety. The story they had to tell was that, whilst trying to reach safety a few minutes after the explosion occurred, they had noticed their workmates, walking in front of them, beginning to collapse. One of them called to the others 'Where is there any water?' Two listened to him and said, 'In Skelly's End,' a dead end roadway! 'Well let's go there.' And they had turned and run back into the distant workings of the mine — there, in Skelly's End, they had huddled, conserving their lights and dipping their scarves in water before wrapping them round their faces. After a long wait — nearly a day, in fact — they noticed from the light of their oil-burning flame safety lamp that methane was beginning to migrate into their haven of safety. 'The rescue teams won't be long,' they'd been saying. But the area that the teams had had to search through was considerable and they hadn't got to Skelly's End when the three survivors began to notice the burning blue 'cap' on top of the flame — a sign that methane is present. So they decided to try and get out by themselves — and they did! There was just sufficient oxygen (and a reduced quantity of carbon monoxide) in the partially restored ventilation system to enable them to crawl through to safety . . .

Three men had survived because they had gone into a dead end . . . but they went in for the wrong reason — to find water — and they left their place of refuge for another wrong reason — because they had found five per cent of methane in the atmosphere. I wonder what they would have done if they had known that scarves soaked in water have no effect whatsoever on carbon monoxide, which is the killer, or that methane, although suffocating, is not poisonous and that men have lived in an atmosphere containing *ten* times the amount of methane that they had found in theirs. But this was all academic speculation for a later date. At the moment three men had walked out alive — hope sprang in every heart, teams began exploring in all directions, and we were switched on to a six hours on, six hours off roster. But that first bitter search after the miracle of survival will live, and has lived, throughout my life. Our instructions were simple — retrace the steps of the survivors and see if anyone else is huddled in a similar dead end.

In relative silence, because trying to talk is inviting carbon monoxide to sneak around the mouthpiece, with only the 'click-clack' of air valves and the occasional hiss of air escaping to the atmosphere, or the sound of our signalling horns strapped to the front of our suits — we walked and climbed over debris and along a belt-road. The first body we found was that of a big man. We could see that he was covering something with his open jacket. Pulling it aside we saw the something — a small boy locked in the older man's embrace for protection on the edge of and into death. The bodies became gradually more frequent, collapsed as in sleep. One was sitting on the belt, arms on thighs, head on chest. All were covered with dust. We came to the end of the line of victims. A lot more were still missing. 'Try and get onto the top of the overcast from the old left hand workings,' we had been told (the overcast being a brick and concrete structure which allows two air streams travelling in the opposite directions to pass one another), 'you'll get to it by going through a hole in the wall. It'll be covered by a canvas sheet.' We found the hole, lifted the sheet and passed through. There we located twenty-five missing men, a vast tangle of humanity locked together in death and carpeted in grey dust.

We completed our task and retraced our steps to the Fresh Air Base, to report . . . When I got home at the end of that first exploration I bathed and went straight to bed. The taxi would be back for us in a few hours' time; I must get some sleep . . . Before crawling between the blankets I sat for a moment on the edge of the bed. Suddenly the whole shattering experience welled to the surface and I did that which I had never done before . . . I wept for my fellow men.

By Tuesday all the teams were given twenty-four hours' break. It had been only work and sleep since Saturday. Back into operation on Wednesday, the mine had now been thoroughly scoured. All except two miners had been located. In one section of the mine the violence had been extremely intense. Humanity, in death, lost recognisable form . . . but by now we were too stunned with shock to register fear or pity. We just got on with the job. Small things probably saved us — the hot tea and sandwiches that poured into the Fresh Air Base and the humour that always emerges in desperate situations such as these, but my recollection is of one man, who stayed above ground, a lay preacher, and a man who never swore (and God help you if you did in his hearing — a straight left to the nose was guaranteed); an ambulance man, he had elected to do the most difficult job at the mine — to wash and identify the dead, to put together shattered frames and to help the next of kin who came to claim their own. The courage and sense of duty of such men surpasses my understanding.

By the following Saturday it was all over, so far as we were concerned. There was still a prodigious cleaning-up job to do, but that was someone else's task!

A few days later the letter I had been waiting for arrived: 'We are pleased to inform you that you were successful at the recent examinations for the First Class Certificate of Competency . . .' I now held the necessary paper qualifications to be a Colliery Manager — I had been studying since September 1940 — seven long years.

'Where do I go from here?' was the question I would be asking myself for some time.

8

The Start of the Good Years

At the end of February 1948 we struck beautiful weather. Sour Milk Ghyll which normally pours down below Red Pike into the lower end of Buttermere seemed cased in ice from top to bottom. Higher up the valley the streams and the water in Yew Crag Gully were also frozen. But we passed all these by, for once again our eyes were on Buckstone How.

As we approached up the long scree slopes from the foot of the first steep section of Honister the air was still, the rock was dry and the sun shone warmly. Our objective was the Girdle Traverse of the crag. This, we knew, started easily enough up Groove One then, after sixty feet it would go past an exposed pinnacle and, eventually, in ninety feet, across a steep wall to the ledge below the undercut second pitch of Groove Two. From a point sixty feet up this hard pitch of Groove Two we would then set off on what was, to both of us, totally unexplored ground until we got onto the familiar sections of Honister Wall. Some of the finest climbing in the valley would lie on this stretch, we were to discover.

On the wall to the left of Groove Two I had found a small ledge, about sixty feet up. Here there were rather poor flake belays. This point was reached without serious difficulty and morale, confidence and excitement were running high. After Bert joined me I set off into terra incognita across a bottomless slab to the left to a narrow crack. Awkward flake handholds led upwards and in forty-five feet I had reached a ledge and belays. The situation was superb but the belays were not of the first order of perfection, so when Bert's turn came to cross the slab I got him to work below me to the left, around a steep nose. Still good belays did not turn up, but eventually, taking over the lead and passing Bert, I climbed a splendidly airy rib and found a good sound little block belay. From here there were two options open to us, either down a bottomless groove or an ascent of one or another of two grooves away to the left. After exploring the former and reflecting that, if we managed to get down the groove onto unfamiliar ground and failed to make any further progress leftward, we could be in trouble, I turned my attention to the second alternative. The first groove I entered proved to be somewhat obtuse and as it was leftwards I had to go anyway. I passed quickly to the next groove, beyond it. This was strenuous but short and I was soon up and working across the face to a stance and belays. We had now reached, roughly, the halfway mark. The climbing across these walls, grooves and ribs had been superb. The airiness had been exhilarating.

Another fifty feet of climbing then continued leftwards and to my joy I found myself overlooking the Black Wall pitch of Honister Wall. Things were working out splendidly. From here on the journey would be more familiar if not necessarily easier.

Black Wall, with its poor holds, led downwards. We had been on the cliff for some considerable time working out this move and that and weariness was beginning to be noticeable, particularly in Bert who had found the paucity of holds on Black Wall to be more tiring than difficult. On the good ledge and from the comfort of a splendid belay we basked in the sun, assuaged the inner man and recuperated generally. But despite the comparative luxury the worm of exploration began to gnaw and I was off again, finally settling on the horizontal traverse (not too easy at first) into the main groove of Sinister Grooves, as the best line of progress. We were now back into the fine groove system of which we had made the first ascent barely two years before. To continue up this to the summit seemed the most logical finish. The main groove of Sinister Grooves looked very impressive when approached from this direction. 'How holdless it looked,' Bert wrote a little later. 'Twenty feet or so down appeared a good foothold, and after that only the smooth vertical walls! We shuddered deliciously and passed on . . .'

After crossing the top of the groove forty feet of easier rock took us up to the final one hundred feet of cracks and chimney of the finish. The top was in sight. Normally one would stop half way up the chimney for a stance and belay. But I, too, was beginning to wilt and I ploughed straight to the top. Bert joined me after a rest at midway 'feeling' as he said 'as though another ten feet would prove impossible.' We had been climbing more or less continuously on quite steep rock for four hours or so. The route we had done was just six hundred feet long. Perhaps it wasn't such a bad time in the circumstances.

Two weeks after the Buckstone Girdle epic the three of us were again at Buttermere, by courtesy of the Workington Ramblers' Club bus. Bert was on duty leading a group of non-climbers to Pillar for an ascent of the Rock. George and I went to Birkness Combe. Again the weather was excellent. We started off the day by making the first ascent of an amiable little climb on Border Buttress, which we named Tailgate — a term any miner would know; it is the name given to the end roadway at the extremity of a longwall face (hence it seemed appropriate enough!). The climb went without any problems and we returned to the base of the crag to pick up our gear. 'What now?' we said. Eagle Crag lay just away to our right. I looked at George and he at me. We were both thinking exactly the same thing and in a few minutes the pair of us were roping-up at the foot of Eagle Front. Beck and I had made the first ascent in June 1940. Here it was, the fourteenth of March 1948, nearly eight years later and the second ascent had never been made.

I took the lead and, as I wrote later, 'again lived each pitch, nor did I find them less difficult or exposed. The long run out on the second pitch still felt like ninety feet, and the small gangway and slab at its upper end was still as awkward. The bulge above these was ascended with the most tongue-sucking delicacy, and relief to be handling the magnificent flake handholds below the great black overhang was just as marked. The next pitch, the bulge and scoop, went with a little more difficulty than on the first ascent, and the grass terrace was reached in high spirits. After the long traverse to the left we decided we must have decent belays instead of the loose block S. B. Beck and I had used in 1940 (after tying on to this block, Beck had sat on it to keep it in position while I negotiated the overhang above). Our efforts were rewarded by a thread behind a doubtful flake, and a rounded knob which would remain adequate only so long as it wasn't used.' A thread, of course, meant a small stone jammed in a crack behind which a sling could be threaded — these were a primitive form of 'stopper', not to be compared either in ease of insertion or efficiency in operation with the thin wired 'stoppers' or elaborately evolved alloy 'chocks' and 'friends' much in use today. By this time, 1948, I had three pitons — metal climbing pegs which I'd had made by the colliery blacksmith, but I had no faith whatsoever in their application and seldom used them for belaying purposes. I did, in fact, reach the quite erroneous conclusion that Lakeland rock was totally unsuitable for pitons. My pitons had blades some five or six inches long and were quite thick and broad — on reflection I imagine that they would have offered substantial resistance to a runaway carthorse — but my dependency on such safety devices had been substantially coloured by earlier writers of the old British school who derided such aids and I had little, if any, faith in the pitons and certainly of their ability to restrain a run-away *me*! But back to our climb . . .

Above the thread belay is the wall and the bulge that leads to a sloping stance and another poor belay. (We had used a six inch nail here to try and supplement the poor natural belay — but, with very little belief in its effectiveness.)

Nowadays there are three satisfactory piton belays with the remains of several others at this point (and, on the ledge below, near our loose block a good crack is available for nuts). This 'is probably the finest situation on the climb . . . The view of the Combe below is interrupted by neither rock nor grass. The walls above and to the left may be written off; only to the right does the way seem feasible, and on this ascent the traverse, across a water-worn slab on rounded holds, became increasingly interesting when a film of water made its presence felt on rubber soled footgear. When one gets into such a position — the second none too happily placed, the ground a long way below, and progress in any direction only possible by movements which are attended by natural hazards — I think a climber must cease to regard himself as a member of a party, welded together by three strong strands of rope, and climb with the intensity and concentration of a man going solo on similar rocks . . .'

This was written in 1950. Since then attitude of mind, equipment and standards have changed markedly — the one obviously conditioned by the others. I am told technique has changed too, but this I find less easy to accept — 'back-and-foot' is still 'back-and-foot', bridging, wedging, hand jamming, mantelshelfing are still the same. Today, however, they are pushed to a higher standard of difficulty — I hesitate to say in more exposed situations; there can be few situations in Lakeland climbing which are *more* airy than, say, the top of Overhanging Bastion on Castle Rock — and Jim Birkett led that in 1939! Yet there is no doubt that the standard has increased remarkably and doubtless will continue to do so — that climbs which, in 1940, we thought were getting near to the limit are now often considered to be little more than pleasant outings. Will the same thing happen to the Blockbusters of today? I doubt if I'll see it — others might!

Above the traverse lay the splendid final crack. We romped up it and sat quietly on the summit. Rethinking the moves . . .

Still the dry weather held — and barely a fortnight after our ascent of Eagle Front, with Easter upon us, George, Bert and I were at Wasdale Head. Transport was again by train, which should have left Workington at 8.10 a.m., but was over an hour late. From Seascale we took a taxi and it was after eleven o'clock before we reached our base for the weekend — Brackenclose, the mountain hut at the head of Wastwater. The day was cold and windy but fine. We were in good form, the sun shone, the world was ours. Despite the lateness of the hour the objective was Scafell East Buttress. This magnificent crag had an impressive reputation. C. F. Holland, in his historical review of climbing on Scafell for the Fell and Rock Guidebook to the area said 'the wetness and ubiquitously vertical character of this region may well give it the right to challenge the present supremacy of Clogwyn du'r Arddu as the wettest, most dangerous and altogether most formidable crag in the British Isles . . .'

At the time the hardest climbs on the crag were considered to be Great Eastern Route, Overhanging Wall and May Day Climb, the first ascent of which had been led by Jim Birkett ten years before. May Day, it was thought, took the honours for difficulty. We had climbed the first two, it was now the time for the third. We could have picked a better, warmer day, but our enthusiasm and confidence were running at peak flood point, so, despite the cold March wind and the shadow, we went in to the attack. The first thing to catch one's eye on the lower sixty feet was the presence of three pitons. Whatever reservations I may have had about pitons I wasn't going to ignore them — rusty though they certainly were. As it turned out, not only were they not ignored, they were well and truly used — rust and all!

The fun began at a sloping three inch ledge some fifteen feet up. I led up to the ledge and hung a karabiner on the second piton then descended again. Bert, with his rope through the karabiner I'd put on, then went up, tied himself to two of the pitons and took his stance on the three inch ledge; then I climbed back to him. 'A short leader' Dolphin's guidebook was to say later, 'may need his second on the three inch ledge to give a shoulder on the difficult part of the slab.' At five feet six inches in height I considered I qualified for such assistance! From the perch of Bert's shoulder I could reach the top piton and then was able to work round the corner to the right to a piton belay. The next pitch, a 'ferocious looking scoop', overhangs slightly at its base, and having very little faith in the rusty old piton to which eventually Bert and I were tied, decided I would feel happier with another one in as a back-stop. This, as always, took time. But eventually a somewhat shaky second anchor point was established and I then addressed myself to the scoop. The cold was beginning to tell on both of us and the small finger holds which save the day felt more rudimentary than they probably are. But after repeated attacks and retreats, getting higher each time, I finally attained the delicate slab which follows and traversed it to a thread belay. The stance was euphemistically referred to as a 'friction stance' which means there wasn't much there at all to stand on. But it had to serve.

It was now George's turn. We had been a long time on the first two pitches. We were cold; George was frozen. He got as far as the three inch ledge and then elected to retreat. This left Bert and I on our own and so, anxious as we were to leave the climb as we had found it, I lowered him my piton hammer (a cut-down bricklayer's hammer) for removal of my extra piton — an act which presented no difficulty whatsoever. Bert was so relieved to get away from the stance below that he rejoined me in good time with, as it happened, a not very high opinion of the difficulty of the pitch — thinking, as he wrote later, that it was not as hard as the hard pitch on Sinister

Grooves or the bulge on Groove Two. At the belay I made a tactical error. I had place two thread belays; these were two short lengths of rope threaded round stones jammed behind a flake and tied round the rope. Thinking, for some reason, doubtless concerned with the optimistic nature of our stance, that it would save time and increase safety if I *pulled* the rope through the rope loops onto which I was belayed rather than untie, I got Bert to hang on to the belay loops whilst I commenced this operation. As one might have guessed the rope became kinked and difficult to get through the threads. We finished up in a remarkable tangle and utter insecurity. In the end the only solution was to untie and sort the whole thing out, which meant Bert untying and hanging onto the belay with no stance for either of us, while I, equally unprotected, got the ropes free, running properly and finally, the pair of us latched back on again with some degree of safety. It had been another of those glorious balls-ups that occur periodically in the kind of awkward situation where the last thing in the world one needs is the capriciousness of a reluctant rope and nothing much to hang on to. But, in time, all was well and I set off.

Round an overhanging corner, first high, then low, then back up high again and, on sloping footholds and wrinkles for the finger tips, the traverse left led me to a slab and a grassy corner. A further twenty-five feet up and we were no more than a hundred feet from the top. The angle and the severity had lessened so I took the remainder in one run-out. It had been a good climb in the lower sections, but, like Overhanging Wall, tended to deteriorate in the upper reaches. Nevertheless for the conditions it had been a trying enough expedition.

Next day, Easter Saturday, we had optimistically decided on the Central Buttress of Scafell. Colder, even, than the day before, we got up to the Oval, the large ledge at the bottom of the notorious Flake Crack. Bert climbed up to the lower chockstone and tied on. I went up past him and headed for the large jammed crux chockstone near the top. The holds got smaller, fingers more frozen and the rigours of the day before kept recurring more frequently the higher I got — it took no persuasion whatsoever to reach a mutual conclusion to retreat to something easier, which, as it happened, was to cross onto Moss Ghyll Grooves and descend that climb to the path below.

Later the weather turned really wet and windy and little more was done that weekend . . .

Early in April George went to North Wales and Bert and I, having got a lift with the ubiquitous Ramblers' bus, to Borrowdale, wandered up the Old Quarries track to find ourselves at the col between High Spy and High Scawdel. Below and ahead of us the valley dropped into the long furrow of Newlands and to our right the crags, which we knew were there, stretched in a broken line of buttresses along the western face of Eel Crags. Here, subsequently, George and I identified four distinct areas of rock. The most northerly, a steep little buttress of beautifully rough light grey rock we christened Grey Buttress, next to it a crag of quite different character and reddish colour is to be found — this, too, succumbed to the colour scheme nomenclature. Red Crag, is in two tiers, the walls being separated by a large heather shelf. The biggest crag is next in line, and because it lies directly above the waterfall in Newlands Beck, was christened Waterfall Buttress. The best of the four is the most southerly and offers three separate climbing areas — a lower crag facing west, then, higher up the fellside to the south, a series of slabs overhung by ribs and grooves and highest of all, above what was later to be called the Quartz Rake, a wall of grooves and pronounced overhangs which eventually became known as Terrace Wall. This southern crag we called Miners' Crag. And the whole range kept several of us occupied for much of the year.

Newlands Gully, the gully bounding the northern edge of the west face of Miners' Crag, had been climbed as long ago as 1913. The crag was not revisited until Whit 1923, when Chorley and Harland did a climb on the west face which has since defeated all attempts by climbers to find its location. After Chorley and Harland's visit in 1923 the whole valley fell back once more into sleep and was neglected by rock climbers. It was to try and find Chorley's climb, Newland's Corner, that Bert and I made the first successful visit there in twenty-five years — the beginning of a rapid exploration. The first new climb, some two hundred and fifty feet in length and named Newlands Buttress, is now a fairly popular climb of Severe standard. On the same day we did Double Slab on the south wall. This route enabled us to have a look at the steep grooves in the locality and three weeks later George Rushworth and Walt Dennison put up Corkscrew, a pleasant climb that works its way through one of the best areas of Miners' Crag. George and I repeated it a short time later. Weekend after weekend one or other of us was working on Miners' Crag.

But we had not forgotten Eagle Crag. It was a good early summer — and it was obvious that Eagle Crag would have dried out nicely. Central Chimney is the most obvious 'line' on Eagle Crag. Descending in one great fracture down the near centre of the face it is somewhat grassy and green in its lower reaches but in the upper section, just after it cuts through the obvious escape ledge near the mid point, its character changes completely, giving two hundred feet of fine, deeply cut, typically classical chimney.

Recorded information on Central Chimney had been hard to come by. It was said that Binns and Raeburn, two fine climbers of the old Gully Epoch, had tried it in 1918. All we knew about their efforts was that they were 'said to have traversed out of the chimney half way up', but there is no record so far as I'm aware of their return or ascent of the upper pitches. We determined to put the ascent beyond question. Two early attempts were already to our credit — or otherwise. Lyna Kellett (later Lyna Pickering) and I had walked from Brackenclose in Wasdale Head to Birkness Combe one summer's day in 1943 and, as I said in an article written in the 1950 Fell and Rock Climbing Club Journal, had 'ascended the cleft to the first major problem in the upper section. Only extreme tiredness, and the knowledge that the return to Brackenclose had still to be undertaken, made us give up at seven o'clock in the evening. I remember how, dirty and dishevelled, we flopped down in the smoke room of the hotel at Wasdale Head, and Pollitt said: "What have you been up to?" "Buttermere," I answered evasively. "What have you climbed, then?" countered Laurance, getting to the point. "We tried Central Chimney, but we didn't get up," was my reply. "Better luck next time," condoled Laurance, and we drank his beer and accepted his good wishes . . .'

But the next visit didn't fare much better. Bert Beck and I had arranged to meet some beginners in Birkness Combe and take them for a day on Grey Crags. As we were in the Combe fairly early and our friends were nowhere in sight when we neared Eagle Crag I conceived the idea that we should have another quick look at the Chimney. All went well until we reached the base of the impressive upper chimneys — the same point as Lyna and I had reached earlier. It was then that we noticed our friends climbing into the Combe. We had the perfect excuse for traversing out of the Chimney as we had done before, and, probably, as other explorers had done in the past, telling ourselves that we had only come to have a look anyway and that we weren't really serious about 'pushing' it and so on . . . the Simple fact was that had the rest of the climb looked less impressive we would have pushed on regardless — and rationalized by saying it was just as straightforward to head for the top as it was to traverse out and descend . . .

The third, and as it happened, final visit waited until May of 1948, five years almost to the day after our first reconnaissance. Our plans had been carefully laid (apart from one small problem — I was on night shift and would have to go straight to Buttermere after working all night!).

Bert and George, who had recently got back from ten days in Glencoe, were the advance party. They would set up camp at the head of the lake in the Buttermere valley and would get off as early as possible up into Birkness Combe to clean out the lower pitches of the chimney. I would cycle out to Buttermere and join them on the crag for the big push through the upper unclimbed sections. As it happened they were rather behind schedule, and I was in front, and was already up in the Combe before they had made much progress in the Chimney. When I reached them they had changed to rubbers. I stuck to my nailed boots — and we roped up. George was sporting a new nylon rope; Bert, his manilla hemp cable. I took the lead, Bert came second and George was tail-gunner.

It was a perfect day. We had plenty of time; we were all fairly fit.

Later I wrote: 'Without incident we reached the major problem (or so we thought). This is a steep chimney, with the left wall overhanging badly and the right wall cut away about half its height into a small sloping ledge. The top of the chimney also leans out, and at that time a large cannon of rock stuck out at the top of the cleft, barring progress. After ascending on to the ledge on the right I managed to work into the groove formed by the left wall and the back of the chimney, and with difficulty and considerable thought to those below I worked over the cannon which was dangerously loose. After climbing above it I sent it hurtling down to the scree below, to join the rest of its companions. Above this the chimney was still steep, but in ninety feet it eased off, and a comforting belay was reached. We were now in a large overhung cleft, with a narrow exit between the overhang and the right wall. The exit, guarded as it was by an intimidating bulge, proved to me to be the most awkward section of the climb. This pitch is also an anxious one for the leader because of the tricky landing, and ascent of rounded slabs to a corner. The pitch is eighty feet long and the belay is reached thankfully. Once there, however, all is over . . .'

It was after nine o'clock at night when the last of us crawled up the final slabs. It was ten o'clock and dark before we got back to the tents. The fire was lit and cooking began and we ate in Bert's tent by candle-light. The night sky was clear with a brilliant moon bathing the surrounding fells in a silvery glow. Bert's final words on the day had about them, as it turned out, a prophetic ring . . .

'It must have been nearly one when we finally turned in' he wrote, 'but no one cared. I did not care whether I did more climbing or not, I had already had a good weekend.' One wonders now what conscious or sub-conscious yearnings gave rise to that remark. After that weekend Bert and I only climbed together on one more occasion — on Dow Crag of all places, when we indulged in a quite ferocious ascent of the old classic, Hopkinson's Crack, in the foulest of conditions imaginable — howling wind, rain, thick mist and water pouring down the climb. For twelve months more or so, Bert, now in his forties, enjoyed taking beginners or introducing newcomers to the gentler climbs of Lakeland. In August, 1949, he and Tom Price spent a holiday in Chamonix. Thereafter, he mainly walked . . . It was almost as if he had seen Central Chimney as the climax of his climbing career — as if, on its completion, total fulfilment had been experienced.

Many years later (thirty-three to be precise) I wrote to him about some photos and to clear up a point about his earlier climbs. He wrote back to me:

'Dear Bill,

. . . You asked about what I had done before we met. It seems I was leading "severes" — this quite surprises me! — such as "Rib and Slab" and "Nook and Wall" on Pillar, "Arête, Chimney and Crack" and "Southern Slabs" on Dow Crag. "Pisgah Buttress" and "Jones Direct from Lord's Rake" on Scafell and "A" and "B" on Gimmer.

'I think my trouble was that I fell in with a very fine natural climber whom I soon realised I could never hope to rival and so accepted a second man's position quite resignedly — and lost my zest for leading, since I couldn't hope to do the climbs we did otherwise.

'No complaints! We got in some very remarkable — and plentiful — routes! When I look at the list I am amazed — and impressed.

Best wishes, Bert.'

When I received this note in Bert's long-familiar hand, showing little of its seventy-five years, I felt deeply moved. Bert Beck died some two years later in June 1984 in the West Cumbria Hospital at Whitehaven, his heart gave out a week or so after an operation for appendicitis. He was only two days away from his seventy-seventh birthday. Vale! Bert.

For my part, 1948 was the beginning of a very satisfactory period of climbing, a period which lasted pretty well up until my departure for Australia in August 1952. It was (I realised years later), the time when I did my best climbing, when confidence was backed up by experience and good physical condition, when anything might have happened . . .

9

Out of the Depths

Soon after the William Pit disaster of the previous year (1947), the Manager of the mine at which I worked called together all front line supervisors — deputy overmen, of which there were about twelve, including my father and myself, overmen and other officials at our mine and made an announcement.

'I propose to appoint a Colliery Ventilation Officer,' he said, 'this is the first such job of its kind in the area . . .' He then went on to expound on the duties and responsibilities of the new official and finished by saying 'And I've selected young Bill Peascod for the job.' I could hardly believe the news! It was a job completely after my own heart, offering not only a practical challenge, but an opportunity to apply and develop whatever theoretical knowledge I had acquired in my College years. It meant that I was very much a free agent, responsible only to the manager and undermanager, with virtually unlimited freedom of movement in the mine. The terms of reference I had been given were indelibly etched into my thinking — 'make sure we don't have the same kind of thing that happened at Whitehaven.'

It was a splendid job. I learned a great deal about the problems of airflow in a coal mine. Very little precedent to the job existed — no one to turn to, to ask 'What do I do next?', because no one in my immediate vicinity had had such a job before — or knew of anyone who had. But gradually, the work expanded — a perfect example of Parkinson's Law — and filled the void created by the hours of my employment. Yet, out of all the expansion and note taking, and graph drawing began to emerge some intensely interesting and useful patterns on gas emissions and air quality and the care and use of explosives.

From mine ventilation I then moved into mine management — a decision forced upon me by the need for a still wider mining experience.

I went to be the undermanager at William Pit in Whitehaven which had been the location of the frightening explosion of 1947. From here I was next transferred to a much larger mine — Risehow Colliery, near Maryport — and I seemed set for the long lonely road to Mine Management. Then two things occurred — both of which had considerable influence on my journey through life.

In 1948 our climbing group was joined by Stan Dirkin. Stan lived only for climbing, fast motor bikes — and weightlifting. In 1948 the pair of us launched out onto a 'three-times-a-week' weight training schedule — a programme that we rarely broke for four years or so and its effect on our mental, as well as physical well-being was remarkable.

Then in 1950 a vacancy occurred on the lecturing staff of the Cumberland Technical College at Workington, my old *alma mater*, where I had been a part-time lecturer almost from the time I had qualified. I was appointed to fill the vacancy. After fifteen years, some good, some achingly depressing, some happy, some sad, I said my farewells to the depths of the mine. It was a move I have never regretted.

George Rushworth had joined the college three years earlier and so he and I were now on the staff together. George had a delightful sense of humour. On certain matters he formulated 'laws'. A couple of these, which I christened Rushworth's First and Second Laws, were evolved in respect of the department's curriculum. 'Change is inevitable' was R.L. One and the other . . . 'And when it does come it'll be for the worst!' Thank goodness Rushworth's Second Law didn't apply to changing jobs! Some of George's other pronouncements used to cause not a little fuss — delivered always in a serious voice (but, I think, more often designed to jolt the complacent than to espouse a deeply held belief) — for instance, 'There is no such thing as rape! It's difficult enough when you're both trying,' and another, which also tended to rouse feminine ire, 'When all the chips are finally down a man owes it to himself to survive.' The one in which he believed most deeply stated that: 'When, for any reason, a friendship is heading for extinction it is better to cut it clean, whilst the best of it is still in the memory, than to let it grind to a slow death.'

I have rich memories of the years George and I climbed together. The guidebooks would suggest that most of it was in Newlands in 1948 — in that year the pair of us, either together or with others, did twenty new climbs in the valley.

George's infectious humour stood by us on many an occasion. And there is no doubt in my mind that this was one of the characteristics that endeared him to his few close friends. George's friendship, when he gave it to any man or woman, was real and very precious. Friendship, to him, was an experience to be treasured. 'The most noble of human relationships,' he called it.

I recall once, that my climbing boots were falling apart — and beyond repair. Rationing was still with us, but all my clothing coupons had gone. George insisted on me taking his — 'It's more important,' he pondered, 'that you get new climbing boots than that I get a suit!'

There was one winter's night when we had imbibed long and rather pleasantly at the 'Scafell' in Borrowdale before setting off across Sty Head Pass for Wasdale Head and Brackenclose. It was throwing out time before we left the warmth of the pub and by the time we reached Seathwaite we were both feeling very hungry. In my rucksack there happened to be a self-heating tin of soup. This ingenious product had a tube running through the centre, a kind of heating device which, when ignited, made the soup quite hot — in fact the lip of the tin became *too* hot to put into one's mouth. Since we had no drinking cups available there were obviously serious technical difficulties in respect of this particular can of soup, but the truth of the matter was that we were far, and happily, 'gone'.

We were sitting on top of a heap of coals in the Edmondson's coal house at Seathwaite Farm, where we had adjourned to escape the wind. The soup experiment was being conducted in stage whispers and slow moving actions worthy of Laurel and Hardy, that had the dogs joining in all around the farm. Suddenly I had one of my rarer ideas. In my rucksack I had a pair of new plimsolls and giving one to George and retaining one for myself I carefully divided the hot soup into each plimsoll. Even our prior alcohol intake did not blind us to the foul relationship of hot soup and new rubber! After we'd dined we set off for Wasdale — still to the accompaniment of the farm dogs.

At the gate near Stockley Bridge two huge horses stood outlined against the moon. It would be difficult to say which of us were the more startled, but at least the great horses could run — and they did, their shoes flashing sparks off the beck stones as they crashed into the night like avenging demons. Even this failed to sober us.

It was a hard winter that year and the Wasdale side of the Sty Head track was sheeted in ice. I had never seen it quite like that before. To be perfectly honest, I didn't even see it when we went over it that winter's night, for our knowledge of its state was picked up next day when, with some little difficulty, quite sober and in broad daylight we retraced our steps! There is, it is said, a special Spirit that takes care of small children and the inebriated. I feel that on that occasion we gave him a hard night's work!

I draw a veil over our arrival at the Brackenclose hut, when we were greeted by an extremely large black dog, which, inadvertently, I let into the men's dormitory. Here it went round every attainable bunk licking and sniffing until with considerable delight, it found its beloved master . . . By which time everyone in the men's dorm was awake and I produced, politely, brightly and with feeling I thought, one of my lesser appreciated remarks, 'I hope we're not disturbing you! . . .' I felt, somehow, that we were.

10

In Gullies

The early guidebook writers had a fine turn of phrase . . . Thus it is, that when climbers find themselves 'in perfect physical condition' on 'a warm, dry, windless day' with feet encased in 'glove fitting rubbers' on the quiet of Scafell Pinnacle or in the evening sun on the West Face of Pillar wandering wherever inclination takes the party, feeling at peace with mankind, tuned in to that sense of ease and fulfilment that good form, confidence, perfect conditions and ideal companionship can engender, that the apogee of the rock climbing experience is attained.

And yet . . .! The moments that are so often recalled are not those of idyllic traverses on warm slabs in a summer dusk but the thrashing and scraping and hauling over chockstones, or in waterfalls, or through powder snow, or up icefalls — in other words . . . in gullies!

These days gullies do not receive the favour or offer the same attractions that they once did — not unless, that is, they are encased in ice, sufficient in depth to allow secure purchase for front-point crampons and short axes.

Even in the forties the gullies did not have the same appeal as they had had for the pioneers of forty years earlier — at the turn of the century. Yet on reflection, it seems to me that though the School of the Forties is mid-way in time between the High Peak of the Gully Epoch and the Modern Movement, its exponents leant much more towards the tastes of Haskett-Smith and the other pioneers when it came to gullies.

I learned my trade in a school that favoured gully climbing. If gullies contained sufficient firm snow to make an ice axe necessary, then so much the better. If they didn't, then we still went up them, anyway! In gullies boots were proper — and by that I mean nailed boots. Ice axes, which were common enough when conditions demanded, tended to be of greater length than today's models. My first one was some forty-two inches long in the shaft, with a very small step-cutting edge and a rather long spiked end. Seen in profile it appeared to be distinctly out of balance — a diagnosis that was shown to be accurate when the thing was put into use.

Ice axes were used for cutting steps in snow, for hacking ice off handholds and for belaying. Crampons were not used. In fifteen years of climbing in Britain between 1938 and 1952 — when I never missed a winter climbing season — I saw no one climb in crampons.

Bentley Beetham wielded an ice axe better than anyone else I ever knew. On a perfect day on Great End in the mid forties Beetham, who was some forty years my senior, was leading. Although there were several other parties either above us in the gullies or on the lower snow slope beneath them, Beetham declined to make use of any steps the others had made and cut his own. His skill held me spellbound. Two steps required three strokes — two for the left foot (we were on a rising traverse to the left) and one for the right foot. These were made with a clockwork rhythm and at such speed that I, who was following on behind, could barely keep up.

Nowadays, of course, the slope would be walked up in crampons!

January of 1941 gave quite remarkable conditions — not only in the gullies but on the snow and ice-caked open fellsides also. Bert and I had decided on Wasdale for the weekend — and so, on the Saturday morning, with snow chains fitted long before we got anywhere near to the valleys, we wended our way to Brackenclose.

Dumping our surplus gear in the hut we made for Brown Tongue, the long, dreary trod up to Hollowstones, between Scafell and Lingmell. We had expected new snow but hardly the quantity we met below Lord's Rake. Any old snow that there was lay deep below this mass of fresh powder. Half way up the Rake we roped up. Deep Ghyll was totally unsafe. The mass of soft new snow sitting on the steep hard old snow in the Ghyll was poised ready to defend itself against any intruder. The Pinnacle Face lay encased in a fantastic shroud of wind-feathered ice. A fierce wind drove powder snow across the Red Ghyll cols — but that, in preference to the insubstantial nature of the snow in Deep Ghyll, was where we had decided to go. Bert led up to the first col to be met by howling wind and fine snow. Sheltering as best he could he belayed me on the second leg. Where the old snow had been cleared of powder by the gale it was possible to cut steps but higher we took to the rocks, iced as they were, in preference to the powder. The wind screamed up the Ghyll; suddenly it would change its mood and scream down again — driving with it powder flurries in both directions. Near the top we were forced back again into the deep snow and waded, waist deep in parts, through the loose mass of powder.

Emerging onto the summit plateau we headed for where we thought the summit was. It couldn't have been more than one hundred feet away from us but we never found it. The wind raged, driving the snow which stung us like a million midges. Visibility was down to a few yards. Heading away from the rocks we aimed for the direction of Burnmoor, thinking quite rightly that that way back would take us longer but would be safer ... But so much for guesswork. Eventually we found ourselves descending steeper slopes with the visibility improving as we gained some shelter from the wind. Below us we saw not Burnmoor but Brown Tongue, which we had ascended that morning, and behind it a white Lingmell. We had gone round in a large semi-circle, fortuitously avoiding the rocks of Black Crag. Out of the wind we compared notes. Across my chest, where a thick woollen scarf that I used (almost as a pullover) had poked through between the lapels of my climbing jacket (a cut-down gaberdine raincoat) lay a thick slab of ice; frozen condensed breath on my balaclava helmet had case-hardened this too; eye lashes had frozen together. Yet this hill, Scafell, by all those other standards is just a little hill — not really the roof of anybody's world.

In the Hut that night we were short of kerosene and had run out of water. All night the gale roared outside. On Sunday we hardly ventured beyond the door, until it was time to pack and return to Workington. In the afternoon the sun shone; the gales had practically swept the roads clear — enough for us to get through! We left while fortune smiled.

Birkness Chimney is precisely what the modern guidebook says it is — 'an exacting and strenuous chimney, particularly when wet ...' When I wrote the Buttermere guidebook in 1948 I described it as 'extremely strenuous under bad conditions ...' It seems that despite the lapse of years the various guide writers are consistent in their respect for this rather splendid cleft.

The first of the several times I have climbed the Chimney was in April 1941. Wintry weather was still around but we had not taken ice axes with us to Gatesgarth.

Morale was fairly low as we wandered up into Birkness Combe and there was little appreciation of the scenery as the grind took us up amongst the old moraine heaps. Birkness Gully, we thought, might clear away our depressions — but one sight of the huge ice-mass on the top pitch left us even more disconsolate.

Then we had a bright idea. The chimney, we rationalized, even though classified as harder than the gully (in fact, in its day, rated as the hardest climb in Buttermere) might, because it is less of a main drainage line than the gully, be freer from ice. Because it's steeper, too, we assured each other, there's less likely to be as much ice around and so on and so on ...

We should have been warned off before we even started on the climb proper. The scramble up over snow and ice-covered rocks and vegetation might have been no problem with crampons and an ice axe, or in summer sun. We had none of these — and the 'easy' slope was far from being such.

The guidebook was very succinct.

'A wet chimney,' it says of the first pitch! There wasn't a sign of wetness anywhere — it was all ice!! Up the narrow chimney we squirmed and soon arrived at a big snow terrace below the continuation.

Here we had expected trouble but somehow nothing of great seriousness presented itself and so, after putting a sling on at the top of the pitch through which to run my rope, I ploughed on up the next short crack to get a look, as soon as possible, at the real difficulty, the crux, the guidebook said, which lay ahead.

Below the crux pitch I ascended a small snow slope with protruding rocks up to a stance below the main difficulty and here I belayed — to an icicle.

When Bert joined me he nearly had a fit. I hadn't been terribly kind to him in the last hundred feet or so. I had no ice axe but I had boots — and if there is one thing one *can* do better in nailed boots than in Vibrams it is kick more effectively. During my upward progress I had used them energetically — slabs of snow, ice spicules, frozen vegetation and at one point a large sized rock had fallen about him. These had done nothing for his morale.

I had asked Bert to bring up with him a suitable stone for hacking purposes and when he saw my belay he went back down the snow slope to find a larger one. Just above me was a small chockstone completely iced into the parent rock. With our primitive tools I attacked the ice, hoping to break a hole through behind the chock to form a thread belay. Hacking at ice, frozen pebbles and clay is painful work, particularly without gloves. Soon the gore from cut fingers mingled with the ice and clay to form an unpleasant melange. Exhausted from standing in a cramped position and fingers raw and cold I finally handed over the mining operation to Bert.

'My smaller, thinner fingers were an advantage for getting out small pieces of stone,' he wrote afterwards. 'In fact, jammed into the chimney with my face against a wall of ice, standing on a snow ledge with one hand paining me as it recovered circulation and the other scraping and picking at filthy cold stones I realised that I was just beginning to enjoy myself ! . . .'

We alternated again, turn and turn about, working on that line of weakness and finally we got a hole through — just big enough to take a karabiner line. Cold, chopped, bleeding fingers dragged the line through the hole and at long last we had a firm belay.

This was the turning point in the whole expedition. With warm hands (however temporary the sensation) and with the thrill of success in the hunt for security still glowing inside us we knew that the problems ahead would have to be fairly considerable before there was any question of defeat. In imitation of those stalwarts of long dead years 'the cry rang out to the echoing crags — Vorwarts!' Whymper or Carrel themselves couldn't have yelled it better!!

I let Bert tie himself on to his own satisfaction — for, as he said, he 'knew what was to come!'

Progress is barred by a great bulge on the left wall, which narrows the back of the chimney to a thin crack. The right wall is smooth — not at all given to large holds. And in this instance the whole issue was wreathed in a liberal coating of black ice. 'A shoulder,' says all guidebooks, 'is permitted' and I intended to take one — and more if they were available.

Bert's stance in the chimney was as high as the anchorage would allow. With one boot on the snow and the other on a foothold on the left wall Bert braced himself while I prepared to use him as a human ladder. With nailed boots mangling into his collarbone I tried to find sufficient purchase to get me moving in the crack. Time and again I tried to force the ice laden crack but my hands got colder and colder and more and more painful. Finally I had to retreat down my human ladder and I crouched on the snow doubled up in agony, hands under armpits — searching for warmth and life. In the meantime Bert rearranged his position. With back braced against the right wall he was more able to use his hands to assist and so finally, circulation returning, I went for it again. I knew that it had to be this time . . .

I hand the story to Bert . . .

'Bill got onto my shoulder and then on to my head — luckily I had on a balaclava. He left it and a fierce struggle followed as he jammed between the wall and the chockstone. Footholds were practically non-existent, fingerholds small and poor and the wall of the crack was iced! But still he struggled up, and reached the bottom of the upper chockstone . . .'

At the chockstone I was able to arrange our other sling (one each was our normal complement in those days). With now some degree of security I heaved up over the top chockstone and found a good stance and belay. Ice showered down onto Bert, but he, like me, was past the stage of caring about such trivialities — victory was within sight.

He wasted no time in following me. He had no shoulder to stand on but he had a rope from above and we had plenty of slack rope to spare. In it I made a couple of loop handholds and hung it from the belay, then, with me taking his weight on his waist loop the pair of us hauled like mad things and within minutes he was up beside me — all rope and two slings recovered and all that remained, according to the guidebook, were 'a chimney with good holds' and 'an easy grassy chimney'.

Unnoticed by us lower down a strong wind had sprung up and some of the ice chips that were kicked down the chimney met the gale blowing over the crux chockstone and were actually being blown back up again past us and away out of sight. But nothing now could stop us — not even gravity-defying ice . . . and as it happened there really wasn't any great difficulty from here on. Within a few minutes the pair of us were at the top of the climb. It had taken us three hours; we had been on ice most of the way. With proper equipment it would have been much easier — but it would not have been half so satisfying!

Not all gullies were fights against the elements. Y-Gully which followed Birkness Chimney some few weeks later was climbed in warm sunshine and rubbers — the only time I can recall, or my records indicate, that I climbed a gully in something other than nailed boots.

We occasionally got into strange places, just to see what things were like — Walla Crag Gully, Spiral Gully on Grasmoor, Penrith Gully on Dollywaggon Pike, Yew Crag Gully and Charter Chimney as well as the great classics like Intermediate on Dow ('One of the finest gully climbs in the district'), Hopkinson's Crack on the same crag, Moss Ghyll, Stack Ghyll, Sergeant Crag, the Gable Crag Gullies and Chimneys and of course, the Screes Gullies and many others — some of which were visited on several occasions and in different moods. Like Great Gully on the Screes, for instance!

Early in 1944 I received a letter, dated January the Twenty-fourth, from Elwyn Banner Mendus. It said:

'Dear Bill,

'I have been studying my Guide and Ordnance Survey maps and I am keen on the idea of doing one of the Screes Gullies. It appears to be no more than seven miles from Drigg — we could start climbing at eleven!

'What about it for Sunday week, if you think we could make the climb "go" given reasonable weather? (Reasonable for the time of year, I mean — of course if it turned out to be a balmy day with larks singing and so on and you insisted on "H.C.B." or "T.T." [*High Crag Buttress and Tophet Traverse had not been climbed at this time.*] I wouldn't complain!) Shall we make a date — the cycle ride is so short the weather doesn't matter as long as it permits us to get up the gully?

Yours hopefully, Elwyn'

February the Sixth, a week or so later, found us riding in the train to Drigg and pedalling our bikes from that well-known watering spot up to Nether Wasdale. The larks were not singing!

Despite the non-appearance of song birds the weather, for so early in the year, was relatively mild — or so we thought, from the shelter of the farmyard. The clouds hung low in dense skeins, blanketing any view we may have had of our objective, and we decided to leave our ice axe with the pushbikes — the thaw had set in, we were assured by the kindly farmer when we met in his yard; his next shots were somewhat more personal. Had we been there, on the Screes, before? 'Well, no,' we had to admit. 'They warn't like t'crags at Wasdale Heed,' we were advised — there were 'greet big hangowers' — (reserved for and enjoyed, it was suggested, only by experts and we, it was vaguely hinted, didn't quite fit into his vision as such exalted personages!).

'Aye! It's a bad day,' was the final shot. 'Rain after frost . . .''

We set out across the fields. Almost unnoticed the wind had got up and was driving the fine rain before it. On the open fellside we hid beneath the intake wall to try and identify our position relative to the crags ahead. Our tactics were rewarded by a sudden rift in the cloud. Through it we spotted a gully, 'white with ice from top to bottom'. I retreated for the ice axe.

On my return I found Elwyn almost paralysed with cold and so action of one kind or another — push on or back off — was imperative. We pushed on!

The first snag was to identify our Gully. We could see two lines which may or may not have been the famous pair of gullies knows as Great and C. Elwyn voted for C and Great, in that order of approach; I was more inclined to the belief that the first vague break in the mist didn't indicate anything and that the next one was C. At least we agreed that the second one was *something*, whether Great or C, and so we went for it! As it turned out we finally identified it as Great — but by that time this information was of little more than academic interest!

'We made our way up to its foot,' wrote Elwyn later 'and decided that the "long approach over boulders" agreed with the Guide and that this must be Great Gully. The pitches receded between tall black walls hung with fringes of enormous icicles, and there was the roar of much falling water. Seen through the driving rain it looked overpowering and the ascent seemed hopeless, but I remembered that the first duty of a second man is to nurture the leader's morale (a plant of tender growth according to Mummery) and when Bill asked "Do you think we'll get up?" I tried to combine honesty with encouragement by promptly replying "No, but we can try," and in that slightly irresponsible mood we started to climb.'

The guidebook gave the climb as six hundred and seventy feet in length, comprising seventeen pitches. It was not very long before the guidebook description possessed little, if any, relevancy.

By the time we had got up the first hundred feet we were soaked through to the skin — too wet to care! But we were going well and provided we could keep out of the main water channel there was a chance that reasonable speed would maintain adequate warmth.

Soon we reached the rib that divides the gully. Up to now we had been climbing over rocks caked with black, crusty ice but here the right hand branch of the gully, which we had to cross to get onto the rib, was free of ice. The wall to its right, across which we had to traverse, was difficult enough in the conditions but its most alarming feature was the presence of some gigantic icicles suspended like an array of Damocletian Swords high above our heads. One shake of the great wall, we imagined, would send these huge darts spearing downwards to impale the pair of us, like butterflies in a display case, against the black rock beneath our feet. The belays on the wall were not good but I didn't waste time looking for more. As soon as Elwyn reached me I was away with all the speed I could muster, up and across the rib and a very unstable grass traverse into the bed of the main channel — technically the most difficult climbing up to this point but, encouraged not a little by those suspended javelins above my head, its difficulties melted away. Elwyn was as clearly aware of the icicles as I and in a very short time he had joined me. The gully now closed in. Rotten ice caked every hold except where the main water spout crashed down. After a scramble up the gully where the relative shelter of some large boulders had been reached we decided that a short halt to reappraise the situation would be useful — in any case, Elwyn demanded a smoke.

We had now, officially, climbed six pitches. There were eleven more to go — the next four of which didn't appear to be too bad, if one ignored the presence of the ice on the slabby water slides. Beyond the water slides, about one hundred and fifty feet of them, was an eighty foot Easy pitch, according to the book. By the time we got there, we reasoned, we would have the bulk of the climb behind us. In any case neither of us was particularly keen to descend the icicle rib . . . It was push on, then, with all speed and get to the top and down to tea as soon as we could.

Barely giving Elwyn time to savour his Craven A I made off up the water slides. One had the option of climbing on easy-angled iced rocks or in the water. In either case one got cold.

'It is difficult to tell at what stage we ceased to look upon the climb as a lark and recognised it as a serious struggle with the issue no foregone conclusion,' Elwyn recalled. 'We had no watches but by the time we reached the Amphitheatre we seemed to have been climbing for hours up endless ice walls. The lake framed between the retaining walls, seemed a very long way down, but we knew that we still had a long way to go. We were tired, soaked through and through and half frozen. We tried to wring some of the water out of our clothes and laughed at the squelching sound in our boots as we walked.'

The only phrase to describe the Amphitheatre, as we found it, is again Elwyn's — 'darkly magnificent; a place for calling up spirits.'

As long as we had only one or two optional lines of progress, route finding hadn't been such a problem but now, in this gloomy cirque, we hadn't the slightest idea where the main line of the gully went.

'The wind was strong and cold' Elwyn continued, 'and mist raced across the crags in the folds of the grey curtains of rain. I remembered Mummery again — "grim and hopeless as the cliffs may sometimes look when ebbing twilight is chased by shrieking wind and snow" — and shivered. I wondered if his "but brave companions and a constant spirit will cut the gathering web of peril" also applied, and vaguely felt the humour of so presumptuous a comparison.'

Working first right and then back left we found the gully bed. It was choked with ice and we went up back and foot between ice walls having to hack ice away from a chockstone in the face of yet more water.

We were tiring visibly. Pitch twelve is described in the guidebook as containing an awkward traverse — but for some reason it presented no problems whatsoever. We were heading for the simple bed of the gully — pitches thirteen and fourteen — and these because of the ice turned out to be the most difficult we met on the climb!

Our safe stance was in a pool of water — over the boot tops! 'We stood in the pool and howled like dervishes while we tried to beat some life back into our hands. The howling had a more warming effect than the beating. From our stance the gully bed rose steeply in a narrow corkscrew to a big bulge of black ice which apparently hid a chockstone somewhere inside it. The water was pouring over the bulge and shooting down the corkscrew. There were no degrees of wetness for us then; but there were still degrees of coldness, and we were reluctant to face more falling water compared with which the water filling our clothes was relatively warm . . .'

I tried, first, the right wall, to get up and away from the water — but the rock was hopelessly rotten and I had to descend again, dropping down the last few feet to join Elwyn in his pool. There was nothing else for it, I thought, it has to be the water corkscrew.

The speed with which I went up the water corkscrew was described by Elwyn as 'remarkable', as apparently, were my gurgled comments when I reached a ledge below a thickly iced bulge where I was able to traverse out of the water to the right for a momentary respite.

From the ledge I attacked the ice on the bulge and cleared away several holds, while Elwyn, below, dodged masses of flying ice. The way ahead eventually became clear enough. On the bulge itself I had de-iced a small foothold, but to reach it I had to go right through the path of the falling water. There was a chance I would get washed off.

Several times I tried to get up the wall to the right of the bulge but this, though drier, proved quite abortive.

I invited Elwyn to join me on my ledge, small though it was and with no belay that I could find, though doubtless one existed somewhere under the ice.

Glad to get away from his goldfish bowl Elwyn ascended the water corkscrew and joined me on my ledge. Now with moral support and encouragement close beside me I attacked the ice on the bulge — half in the water, half out! Slowly more holds were revealed, then finally, resorting to combined tactics on the ledge and, be it admitted, a little desperation I got onto and up the bulge, and to security, where Elwyn with all the aid we could muster, cast compunction to the winds and rapidly joined me.

There were now, we estimated, some one hundred feet of official climbing between us and the finish, and we scrambled up the easy bed of the gully to where the next item of delectation was awaiting us. We expected to find a crack on the left of the large chockstone spanning the cave. What we saw appalled us!

The large chockstone existed all right and so did the crack, the chimney and the cave — but the whole complex was buried under a vast accretion of ice — a vertical wall of hard ice down which poured a daunting spout of water. There was no way in the world that we, with our primitive gear (although we didn't think of it as such in those days), in the physical condition in which we found ourselves and with the remaining light we had at our disposal, were going to be able to get up that iced waterfall. The walls immediately adjacent to the icefall were very steep and clearly rotten. One chance of escape was possible. At the top of the last pitch we had noticed that the gully wall to the left had looked feasible and to this we back-tracked. 'We took,' as Elwyn summed it up later, 'a shameless delight in the prospect of getting out of the gully.'

'The wall was steep,' he goes on, 'and thickly covered with heather and grass, and Bill soon discovered that the rock underneath was as rotten as the vegetation. He progressed slowly, mostly by driving in the pick of the axe and hoisting himself on it. Just how he managed the status quo while he drove the axe in higher up, is, for me, another of those unsolved mysteries. Every other tuft of heather he stood on gave way beneath him, and it was a very long time before, with most of the hundred feet of rope out, he reached the top of the wall.'

The 'easy ground' I had got to was as rotten as the wall I had just left. My belays were poor and I drove the axe into the ground and used that as an extra anchorage — then, with words of warning to Elwyn that belays and stance could be better, invited him to join me.

I leave him to tell of his own experiences on the wall . . .

'After warnings that his belay was poor and that he could not help me, I started. The axe was being used as an extra belay and I had to rely on hands alone to get a grip on the vegetation. The rope ran diagonally at first and was little help in a disintegrating world. It was a case of digging frozen fingers into the earth and pulling until either a foot was gained or something gave way, and one slid back again. There were places where a mouthful of heather was thankfully used as an additional support. It was not climbing, and it was not magnificent, but it was terribly exhausting after all that had gone before . . .'

But we were up! There wasn't much of any consequence left to do — although what there was took on another dimension because of our physical condition — a state near to complete exhaustion. The 'walk up grass on to the pleasant summit plateau' (*vide* Guidebook) was a scramble up snow and ice, where even step cutting was necessary, in the teeth of driving rain and strong wind and in thick mist . . .

Sometime later, having gone to considerable pains to avoid striking downwards onto the dangerous rocks that skirt the Screes Gullies, we finally, in the gathering gloom, retrieved our bicycles and pedalled back to catch the train from Drigg — very weary and very wet we may have been, but, in that most inexplicable of ways, not dissatisfied with our day's endeavours . . .

11

'Group C'

Apart from the usual kind of Poly-tech students such as those who were studying Mining Engineering in the hope that one day they would reach the top echelon of mine management, or those specialising in mine surveying or mine ventilation, George and I had to teach the Mining Entrants. In our locality the Entrants were an innovation that did not receive universal approval.

After the nationalisation of the mining industry someone, in his wisdom, had decreed that all new entrants into the mines under the age of eighteen had to have some academic as well as practical training in the fundamentals of mining. The academic strand would be conducted by the Technical College and the practical sessions would be undertaken in a specially constructed Training Gallery, under the supervision of a qualified Training Officer at some selected colliery.

On paper it sounded rather fine and was certainly a far cry from, and distinct advancement on, the initial 'training' I had been given when I first went to work underground. In my case, I recall, on my first day below ground, someone had said I was to be sent to work for a week with 'Daft' Harry. At the end of the week my 'training' would be reviewed. So, on the first day I went as instructed with Daft Harry — in an isolated locality far away from anyone, with tubs, empties and fulls, coming into a tiny underground marshalling yard from three different directions. Our job was to allocate and distribute the empties and attach them to ropes to be dragged away into the darkness — into I knew not where. The entire operation was carried out by the faint light of a four-volt hand-lamp hanging from one's belt. In theory fulls were lowered down inclined roadways to the marshalling yard where I worked, under the control of a haulage engineman who operated a fixed electric haulage engine which turned the rope drum to which the haulage rope was attached. There

is a rigid code of signals which has to be learned and the signal to
'lower', 'stop', or 'pull away', and so on, is transmitted to the haulage
engine driver by rubbing together two copper signalling wires which
extend the full length of the roadway or incline along which the tubs
have to travel. When the fulls arrived safely I would stop them at the
correct place by signalling the driver, then unclip them and attach a
new set of empties onto the rope to be taken away into the workings of
the mine. When these had gone the recently arrived fulls had to be
disposed of on another rope and replaced by new empties. Thus was
the dark mysterious maw pacified. In theory, the engine driver
would not allow his fulls to run straight down onto my marshalling
yard without my signal because I might be doing something with
another set of tubs or on another rope. But the theory didn't always
work. Sometimes, soneone in the far distant places of the mine might
have forgotten to couple together some of the tubs, or they may have
become unclipped from the rope, or the rope may have broken or a
shackle may have pulled, in which case one or more or even all the
full tubs that, in theory, were being lowered down towards me under
strict control would arrive with unseemly haste. If one knew the
sound of runaway tubs, the rapid 'clicketty-clack' of loose couplings
hitting steel floor rollers and the rumble of the runaways at high
speed — then one rapidly assessed from which direction they were
coming and got out of the way as quickly as one could. Refuge holes
four feet square at the base were cut into the sides of the narrow roads
or the marshalling yards at frequent intervals and we would dive into
these as fast as our legs could propel us, whilst the runaways either
raced past us or piled up nearby in a tangled mass of broken tubs and
coal — the air dense with coal dust.

Day One passed without untoward incident, the newness of it all
still rather frightening. Day Two arrived — but no Daft Harry!
Harry didn't turn up any more that week. I have always assumed,
since, that having got someone to take over from him he was
luxuriating in a self-imposed holiday — or maybe it was just
professional jealousy. At any rate, from and including Day Two I
was doing Daft Harry's job. So ended my period of introductory
training!

The training schedule that had been introduced on
Nationalisation was much more elaborate than the one that I had
experienced. The new entrants were all assembled in the first
instance at the colliery training gallery and by some process of
assessment were finally re-classified into three groups A, B and C on
some vague academic basis. Group A were those lads who showed an
inclination towards or aptitude for some higher kind of training —
possibly an apprenticeship or even higher; Group B did not shine
with the same lustre; Group C — well, it would be kinder to draw
a veil over the academic potential of Group C! George and I got

Group C.

One Group C still lingers in my memory. There were twelve in the class most of whom came from Whitehaven. They ranged in stature and presence from the tiny, little Jonty to the hulking Fred. Jonty possessed a squeaky voice and his elder brothers' half worn-out clothes, sleeves doubled up to free the hands and an even bigger roll of ragged trouser cuff framing his feet. Utterly incapable of pronouncing my name (Mitta Peatod was the nearest he got to it and that was delivered at thirty second intervals throughout the day) he was the tiniest and noisiest student I ever met. Fred by contrast was big, slow and enormously strong for a seventeen-year-old. In fairness to Group C any shortcomings that they may have exhibited could not entirely be laid at their door. For years they had been at school, fighting their own paths to any scrap of sunshine that dared to intrude into the hardness of their lives; longing only for the day when they could get into the mine; to have money rattling in their pockets; to be able to demand as their right a fag, a pint and a girl. The last thing they wanted was more schooling. They were prepared to work like hell in the mine for what they wanted. But dry theoretical clap-trap got them nowhere — and got nowhere with them.

At that time the campus was shared between the Technical College and the Grammar School. There were unmarked boundary lines beyond which the two authorities did not transgress. The nearest approach to a community spirit was in the College refectory, where the Grammar School students were not permitted but where their teachers sometimes joined us in morning tea.

To be a Grammar School student in those days was quite a laudable achievement, and it was often to be noted that it was not entirely the fault of the student that he became aware of the fact that he was a cut above ordinary mortals. There were those staff and students, from both sides of the campus, who felt that somehow the tone of the place had not been improved by the presence of Group C.

Group C came to us on Wednesday afternoons, Thursdays and Fridays.

On the second Wednesday Jonty spoke up. 'Mitta Peatod, can I go to toilet?' So off he went. A little while afterwards, another of the boys was taken short and, within seconds, yet a third. Whatever they had had for lunch had certainly affected the entire group because a fourth one disappeared soon afterwards. When more revealed an urgent need of adjournment, I knew that the toilets by now would be completely occupied and suggested that they try to contain themselves until a vacancy occurred. Eventually the first victims of whatever complaint they had contracted returned — and one or two others took their places.

The following Wednesday, to my considerable surprise the

affliction recurred. Jonty was again the first out rapidly followed by three more. I gave them time to settle down, then went to explore.

I found them all, on forbidden ground, arms round each others' shoulders — an ardent and admiring cheer squad for the splendidly built sixth-form Grammar school girls in their very short blue shorts and far too tight white blouses playing netball under the guardianship of a comely young gym mistress. It was difficult to determine whom the boys admired the greater — the girls or their mistress. Group C had disovered 'P.E.' day.

I dragged my crew back into their classroom and the balloon went up next day. Fraternization was OUT; there was to be no intrusion onto sacred ground; no ogling from corridor windows. But restrictions and deprivations were the daily bread of Group C. The boys quickly found out which girls went by bus in the same directions as they did — and joined them; to the mutual satisfaction of both parties. There was nothing the fulminators could do about it. Ranting at the girls had as little effect as stingless threats to the boys. My scruffy heart-warming crew, completely lacking in any vestige of couth, table manners or working knowledge of King's English, were winning all along the line! I was secretly near the point of wetting myself with delight.

A few days later Group C was 'in the gun' again. Away across the street was a high wall and beyond that an orchard. Somebody had climbed the wall during a lunch break and given the apples a fair working over. The message came back 'chastise those miners! . . .' It couldn't have been the Grammar School boys, for two good reasons. One was that no Grammar School boy would do such a thing, and the second was that, just in case temptation *should* raise its head, they had been told they must not leave the grounds of the Grammar School during lunch breaks except with permission . . . And the Grammar School boys always did as they were told . . . (I had worked in the Survey department in the mine, for a while, alongside some ex-Grammar School boys and they didn't strike me at all as being people who had been poured into *that* kind of mould!) But my instructions were to reprimand Group C.

'Which of you lot have been pinching apples from Mr. Whatsits' orchard?' I thundered. No answer. I ranted on again, putting on a performance the like of which would have warmed the heart of Orson Welles. No answer; the ranks closed against me. I raved on for a long time, trying to penetrate their armour of loyalty and principle. Finally it was Jonty who broke silence — not because of fear for himself but more likely out of a sense of pity towards me.

'It warn't any of us, Mitta Peatod.' 'Well, who was it?' Silence. 'Come on, I want to know.' More silence . . . faltering at first but later with a rush: 'It was them Grammar School lot. They knew we would git t'blame and nae body would believe us if we sed we didn't dyuh it.' It wasn't self pity; Jonty was merely stating a fact. And I knew he was telling the truth!

Next day I went in to bat for them. I said my piece where it mattered and left no doubt in any one's mind that I thought my boys were victims of plain malice, bigotry and snobbery. The following day was Friday. I had the boys on Friday afternoon. Nothing was said by me, nothing by them. Came the end of the day and they all began to troop off home 'Tarah, Mitta Peatod' as I cleaned the blackboard — and then, they'd all gone . . .

As I turned round to pick up my books and chalk I noticed it sitting on the edge of my desk — a beautiful big, shining apple as fresh as the day it was picked!

Group C possessed an infectious and irrepressible source of energy. They were tough boys — they could give it; they could take it. The world to them was a living vital place. They were at their happiest when involved in any form of hard physical contact. George and I recognised this and had long talks about how to get our messages across — to explore *their* values and to let them question *ours*. Sometimes we had to take them for 'P.E.'; this was the session they really enjoyed.

I don't know how we got involved with the next phase. In one of the laboratories was a large circular steel crushing disc with a hole through the centre and rounded edges. It weighed eighty pounds. 'Can you lift that, Mitta Peatod?' demanded Jonty. Apart from needing to be fairly strong one had to have a big hand to span from the centre of the disc to the edge and strong fingers into the bargain. Fortunately, with weight training for so long I was able to lift it first to my shoulder and then above my head. 'I bet Fred can do it, Mitta Peatod.' I had been sucked in as neatly as a goldfish taking an ant's egg. Fred, with all the grace and finesse of a rather large bull in a very small pot shop, lumbered it above his head with ease. During these activities there was absolute silence from the rest of the boys and then loud cheers all round for Fred.

It was now the last session of the day which for them was 'P.E.' time and someone suggested a wrestling contest. I could see the danger sticking out like the teat on a lemon. After the preliminaries had been gone through . . . 'Mitta Peatod, I bet you can't wrestle Fred.' It had arrived! I had pondered the possibility of wrestling Fred. Fred was little more than half my age but he was bigger and possessed a raw natural strength. Any that I possessed had been acquired with a bar bell, hot-house grown compared to Fred's birthright. But I felt that I might have the edge on him in agility. So I accepted the challenge. Group C was agog with excitement. The gym floor was cleared; the other staff had gone home. It was 'on' between Group C and me.

The style of wrestling had, of course, to be 'Cumberland and

Westmorland'. We knew the rules but neither of us possessed any technique to speak of. It was to be largely a contest of brute strength and ignorance.

Coats, shirts and shoes came off and we bent down, heads resting on opponent's shoulder and hands gripped across opponent's spine; a pause whilst we sized each other up. I could feel the big lumbar muscles flexing and thought, 'If this boy gets hold of me properly he'll break my back!' Then suddenly the tussle was on — bodies straightened and crashed together, arms strained. I dropped my hand quickly a couple of inches, then got him up in the air. With a thud he was on the floor and I was victorious. The cheers had barely started when the yell went up 'Best out of three!'. I knew that that one would come, too! We had a short rest and then dropped into the preliminary posture again. Fred had learnt rapidly in the last couple of minutes. I tried to swing round and hook him behind one leg but he had me up in the air and then flat on my back in seconds. With a big broad grin he helped me to my feet again. One each, now! I've *got* to win this next one, I thought, otherwise I'll never have control of this class. (I wonder how true that would have been?)

At the third round both Fred and I tore into each other, but I got the better hold first and we both crashed together, Fred hitting the floor first. I was declared the winner . . . and it was time to go home. Those Friday afternoon wrestling contests went on for two or three more weeks before that particular Group C's session finished. They certainly weren't in any formal curriculum but I think, somewhere along the way, a message was communicated, something to do with mutual respect.

The end arrived for Group C. One more wrestling contest for old times' sake and then we said our farewells — a dozen of the world's roughest diamonds; I had quite an affection for them as they trooped away — with a squeaky voice fading last of all calling 'Tarah, Mitta Peatod.'

There were more 'Group C's', before and after the Whitehaven crew. None had quite its composition, thank goodness, but there were others that linger in the haze of distance, like the young lad of Irish extraction who exhibited a total aversion to any form of restriction placed upon him. On one memorable occasion he none-too-politely told a teacher where to go and was reported. George and I could see that any disciplinary action was going to lead to a fairly dramatic occurrence. It did. The young fellow went on the rampage and a Head of Department, imagining himself to be a black belt judo exponent, but whose only contact with the sport had been the book he'd read about it, was demanding 'let me at him — I'll put a Half Nelson on him!' The Irish lad obliged by leaping on *his* back and the pair of them were to be seen running round the Common room as if in preparation for some human 'horseback' race. We never did discover who was quite putting a Half Nelson on whom. Eventually the protagonists were separated and, in time, the decision was made to send the Irish lad 'down'. But down to where? Was there any place more 'downer' than Group C?

Came another day and another Group C and George said to me, 'Have you seen Aaron?' I admitted the pleasure had not yet been mine. 'Well he can't read.' Two thousand school days had failed completely to arouse in Aaron the least desire to render or recognise the written word. His mathematical skills, we were to discover, were of similar standing. There was not much we were likely to achieve, we thought, in the twenty-four days at our disposal — but we'll try something. George started off by putting Aaron at the back of the class with a book. He said to Aaron, 'Now Aaron, I want you to try and read this story. If there is any word you don't understand put your hand up.' Aaron nodded his head and bent over his open book in ardent concentration. Aaron read away for nearly the whole of the class time; George was delighted; maybe we were underestimating the lad. He went to investigate . . . Chapter I began 'The pirates . . .' and George thought, well that's a good start! 'What does *that* word say?' said George, pointing to the second word in the book. Aaron pondered a while then looked up at George and said 'I don't know, Sir, I haven't got that far yet.' It was back to the drawing board for George and me.

Then George had a splendid idea. He said to me. 'Look, we've got to get him to recognise something; supposing there's a danger sign placed somewhere underground and he doesn't understand it — he could walk into an accident or even get killed!' 'True,' I agreed, 'so what are we going to do?' George had given this a good deal of thought.

'Well, what are the most important signs he should recognise? First, there's the word "Danger" and there's "Keep Out" and just so that he won't walk past a sign where Shotfiring is going on we should teach him to recognise that word as well. We'll teach him,' said George, 'how to read and write four words — "Danger, Shotfiring, Keep Out" and we'll do it by giving him a sheet of paper with a slit cut in the paper. We'll then write the four words at the top of another page and if we make the mask only big enough to expose two lines he'll be able to copy the line above until, in time, he can write the four words without resorting to copying.' From such small beginnings are Ph.D's evolved!

So Aaron was put to the back of the room and all day long whilst the others were studying formal English or any matter which involved taking down notes, Aaron slowly shaped the words 'Danger, Shotfiring, Keep Out'. At first they were badly formed — an agonised script — but gradually they began to take on recognisable imagery. We began to feel rather proud of the solution and achievement. Aaron spent many, many hours on those four words. He worked hard; he did not waste time; he took it all seriously and in his kind good nature — his slowly formed smile gradually lighting up his face whenever either of us addressed him.

And finally it was the end of the course. For reasons far too abstruse to explain someone required the various Groups to be given 'tests'. George and I set formal exams which were marked with due seriousness. Then we came to Aaron. He sat at the back of the class and painfully and silently through all the examination sessions wrote those four words. At the end of the session everyone was trooping home but I called to Aaron as he was making for the door. 'A moment please, Aaron.' He stopped, silently, dutifully, beside my desk. When the room was empty, except for ourselves, I said to him, 'Well, Aaron, we can't let you go without giving you an examination, can we? Here,' giving him a stick of chalk, 'write on the board Danger, Shotfiring, Keep Out!'

He walked up to the board; he looked at the chalk in his hand, he stared at the board, he turned his head and stared at me — then his face broke into his long slow open smile 'I can't, sir!'

The following week we were assembling the marks for all the examinations. Aaron, not unexpectedly was the bottom of every list — until we came to 'metalwork'. Not only was Aaron top but he was away out in front, we went to talk to the Metalwork teacher. 'The boy's brilliant,' he said, 'all I have to tell Aaron is what we are going to make today and whilst I am explaining to the rest of the class what to do and how to do it, Aaron is away working at his bench and has the job finished to perfection before most of the others have got started. He's a born blacksmith.' Whether it happened through us or whether someone had worked it out for himself I do not know, but we heard a short time afterwards that Aaron had been put to work in the blacksmith's shop at the mine, where he was doing very well . . .

A few weeks later I was walking through the town's main shopping street when I saw a small group of young lads coming towards me intent, quite obviously, on a pleasant night on the town. Amongst them was Aaron. As he drew level with me he gave me that long slow grin . . . which I returned with a 'Hello. Aaron!' 'Poor old Aaron,' I thought to myself.

I had walked about twenty paces when the truth began to penetrate. Poor? Aaron? He's survived ten years of schooling untroubled by, and untroubling to, anyone who'd tried to teach him; not the least concerned by the pressures of the academic Joneses; with friends; doing a job that he likes and that he can do extraordinarily well; possessor of a happy gentle nature; a man who clearly would be incapable of harming his fellows and who would probably make an understanding parent . . .

I caught my reflection in a shop window. Could I say the same thing? Maybe Aaron's riches were far greater than mine could ever be!

12

A Final Fling

I had taken up the full-time position of lecturer in Mining at Workington in March 1950. For many months prior to that I had worked underground on the night shift. Because I had to be at the mine six shifts per week it had meant that every day was affected by my work hours. If I wanted to go climbing on a Saturday it had to be straight after coming off night shift, without any sleep. If I went on a Sunday then, when most people would be expecting to have a meal and go to bed to recover from the day's exertions, I had to get changed and go to the pit.

There is little doubt that this was a considerable factor in my desire to 'humanise' my existence.

Thus when I went teaching, with a five day week and a nine a.m. start to the day, I felt almost a sense of guilt in my new situation — and coupled to my very civilized work load were the long holidays which added still further (though honesty compels me to state, only temporarily) to the feeling. I recall, even now, how eagerly I looked forward to the long summer vacation. I reflected on how Bert and George had been able, almost, to squander their holiday — a week here and a week there if they felt like it, or a few days' loafing, if the urge so took them. And this was now to be my privilege.

Stan Dirkin, Rushworth and I had spent quite a lot of time together. Both Stan and George owned motorbikes. Transport was now less of a problem.

The old classics were repeated time and again — routes such as Tophet Wall, Moss Ghyll Grooves, the climbs on the Pinnacle Face and the West Face of Pillar. We poked about in unfrequented valleys and wandered onto, then, unrecorded crags. We found time to take out beginners. I acquired the Guide's Certificate of the recently formed British Mountaineering Council (I recall that George Spencely was the assessor for the B.M.C. and, because we knew each other quite well, the matter of 'assessment' was little more than a formality, but I insisted on taking him up Zigzag on Castle Rock, a climb I'd done several times before, but which had acquired a reflected glory from its association with Overhanging Bastion, the magnificent direct route up the main face of Castle Rock).

The previous year I had made my first trip to Scotland. This was in the company of Graham Macphee. Macphee's name is something of a legend in mountaineering circles. Whenever one starts delving into the history of mountaineering in Britain one, inevitably, turns up his name. He had been with Kirkus on the early exploration of Clogwyn du'r Arddu; had made with A. T. Hargreaves the first ascent of one of the hardest climbs in Lakeland in its day (and still highly respected a good long time afterwards) — Deer Bield Crack. It was, perhaps, inevitable that a man whose name comprised the initials G.G.M. should make the first descent of 'Moss Ghyll Grooves'. He had been associated with Scottish climbing, the Scottish Mountaineering Club and the Guidebook to Ben Nevis for many years.

I first climbed with Macphee in 1945, at Buttermere, when we produced three new routes on Grey Crags. The next occasion, for which there are records, was in Newlands some three years later. Amongst several climbs we did were two more first ascents — Waterfall Buttress Direct and, probably the best route in the valley at the time, Miners' Grooves.

The first pitch of Waterfall Buttress Direct is quite long — some one hundred and ten feet, and as I negotiated the slabs and ribs Rushworth and Macphee whiled away the time in conversation on the heather shelf at the foot of the crag. The weather had been good, the rocks were dry — so was the heather. And George felt like a smoke! He lit up, flicked the match away; there was a yell; I looked quickly down and saw, to my dismay, Macphee surrounded by flame and smoke. At this point I was left entirely to my own devices whilst the pair of them attacked the burning bushes intent, as was right and proper and a first priority, to save a distinguished mountaineer from incineration. The fire extinguished, and order restored, the climb settled down once more to a gentle amble.

On the first trip to Scotland with Macphee, who picked me up on his way north from Liverpool, our initial objective was Clachaig Gully. We would climb this, then head up to Fort William and the Charles Inglis Clark Hut beneath the North East face of Ben Nevis. The time given for the ascent of Clachaig Gully was seven and a half hours. We, Macphee assured me, would try to reduce that time. I concurred, mainly because I couldn't think of anything else to say. This was my first visit to Glencoe; I had never even heard of Clachaig Gully before! Somewhere halfway up or thereabouts was a wall called Jericho Wall. This, Macphee told me, would present the most difficulty. I thought it a pleasantly Biblical name for a wall and wondered about the religious background of its first ascenders.

The Gully, when we reached it, did not look particularly impressive — a vast gashed hillside; it is only when one gets into it that the atmosphere closes in. I remember very little about the lower pitches, except that we were making good time. I kept wondering where Jericho Wall was, had we passed it? Then we reached it — a dark, slimy, shattered wall barring all progress. It looked to me as if it were built up of black bricks without the benefit of mortar to hold them together. But our eyes were also on the clock and there didn't seem to be much point in standing around to frighten oneself. So with little hesitation, but more than a little concern for the brickwork, I went up the seventy feet wall. It yielded a lot more easily than it looked as if it might, and our path continued upwards without any further noticeable event. To the top we went, and then, after seventeen hundred feet of climbing, we reached the open hillside and hurried down to the base of the gully — we had knocked three hours off the recommended time . . .

The weather on Nevis, when we reached it, held very well — which was all to the good considering the programme Macphee had in mind.

To someone, like myself, who had been used to guidebooks which give almost a hold by hold description, the guidebook to Ben Nevis came as somewhat of a shock. More accurately, I suppose, it would be nearer the truth to say that *Nevis* was the shock and that the guidebook doesn't do much to lessen it!

My introduction to the Ben included A. T. Hargreaves' Rubicon Wall and the Long Climb. The former had the reputation of being the hardest climb on the cliff in the 1936 guidebook and the latter the longest. Macphee needed to do them both for the new one. Rubicon Wall was followed without much difficulty and proved to be, as its description suggests, an airy climb, some five hundred feet long and decidedly delicate.

The Long Climb, as its name implies, was given as being some fourteen hundred feet in length — and thought then to be the longest face climb on the Scottish Mainland. The principal difficulty so far as we were concerned was route finding. The climb lies on the magnificent North-Western wall of the North East Buttress facing across to Observatory Ridge. A huge spur or flying buttress projects from the face and into the large amphitheatre between the North East and Observatory Ridges. This is where the climb starts and it works more or less straight upwards to the highest point on the North East Ridge, at least that was where we finished!

Macphee possessed two hundred feet of very lightweight (about 7 mm diameter) abseil line. We decided to use this and climb on it doubled. As events transpired it was a fortuitous decision. Up the flying buttress and onto the main face all went fairly well. Above lay a vast area of slabs and ribs steepening higher up into quite pronounced walls. Run-out after run-out, hour after hour we pushed our way upwards, with the difficulties not excessive but with a decided shortage of protection points. About three-quarters of the way up the face this feature became most noticeable. I was now up onto quite a steep bare wall when Macphee let me know that the rope had almost run out. Search as I might I couldn't find any anchor point, and so I took the best option left open to us. Hanging onto the face with whatever handhold I could find, poised on footholds that could never be described as large, I managed to untie the doubled line and retie onto one end. With Macphee then tied onto the other end and back onto his belay we had, at least, mobility — if not necessarily any extra security. High above me on the wall I could see a niche, about the size of (and about as inviting as) a two-man coffin. We had only a couple of slings and these had been used on exiguous spikes below me — only to promptly fall off as I had moved above them.

I headed for the coffin and got there with just enough rope to spare. It was a v-niche with a flat triangular ledge for its base — and attached to the wall above head level was a perfect little spike of rock.

I looked at the spike; I tapped it; a crack existed all around its contact with the wall; it looked exactly as if it had been stuck on with epoxy resin. I was doubtful about its efficacy in the event of a fall and yelled down to Macphee to that effect. 'Don't fall off, the belay's not much good.' So I gingerly tied on to the fragile spike, took a firm stance and surveyed the world around me, the vast wall below my feet and Observatory Ridge across the amphitheatre, as Macphee climbed up to join me. It was a most exciting situation.

The nook was just big enough for the pair of us. 'Where's the poor belay?' said Macphee in his polished Scottish accent. 'There,' I indicated. He then did something which even to this day, when I reflect upon it, causes butterflies in my loins. He grabbed my rope which was tied on to the tiny spike, gave it a heave, then hung on it with his full weight and announced 'That's all right.' There was no point in saying 'But what if it hadn't been?' He had just proved that it would take the weight of one man hanging from it — and I hadn't the slightest intention of taking the demonstration any further. After getting him tied on to the spike I got up the remaining section of the face, to real security, as if all the bats in hell were after me.

We didn't stop to readjust the abseil line and I led out as much of the two hundred feet as circumstances allowed, on each run out. When the pair of us reached the top we had been on the climb for nine hours . . .

Back in the Lakes again, the climbs, for sometime afterwards, seemed fairly predictable.

In July 1950 Stan Dirkin and I were in Langdale, staying at Raw Head. A young chap was the other occupant of the hut and we introduced ourselves. His name was Brian Dodson.

He was a lad of twenty-two — medium height, open faced, strongly built and, I was to find out, possessed of a remarkable repertoire of songs of the kind that are more frequently enjoyed in the showers at the Rugby Club. (I became an eager and, with modesty, an apt student of this particular art form — and sang them on more than one occasion on Lakeland fells, Queensland mountains, in the art gallery circuits of Sydney and the sake bars of down-town Kyoto.) He was extremely fit and, I discovered, climbing very well.

Brian had begun climbing the previous year, he told us, and now, having been released from National Service early in the year, was preparing to take examinations that would finally, he hoped, get him into medical school. In the meantime he had spent the summer climbing.

Next day the three of us did Stoat's Crack, a good climb on Pavey Ark, which strangely enough none of us had climbed before.

I told him of our intention to stay at Gatesgarth during August and invited him to join us. Despite the rain this was a plan that eventually was adopted. It was my first long holiday. Like George and Bert I had now time to play with. For much of the week we were there it rained. In the dry spells between the showers we got up into Birkness Combe and on to Buckstone How.

Almost the first climb we did together was Dexter Wall. It had waited for nine years for this second ascent. His lead of it was a masterpiece of concentration, delicacy and fine climbing. My turn came next, a lead of Fortiter — much easier than Dexter Wall, nevertheless this, too, had not had a second ascent. A few days later 'Ginger' Cain and Brian climbed Fortiter in nailed boots, just to show how really easy it was!

By now the rain had set in and our activities were fairly restricted but despite this, we made the second ascent of Cumbrian's Climb — a route on Buckstone How — the first ascent of which my fellow Cumbrian Ronnie Wilkinson, a reporter on the local paper, and I had made just a year before; it is a climb which, I feel, doesn't get the credit it deserves. It is no more artificial than many hundreds of others to be found in Britain and possesses a very good first pitch of seventy-five feet which is not without its moments for the middle grade sort of climber. Brian led this in the pouring rain in socks. (It has a modern grading of '5a'.)

The rain kept us barn-bound for much of the remaining time and we began to discuss the effects of the rope, particularly the waist loop, on a freely falling leader. Throwing a rope over one of the trusses in the barn roof we tried dangling in a waist loop, above the ground. We also experimented by jumping off the stacked hay, to try and get some clear idea of the effect of a free fall. We tried to lift each other (the 'patient' being in a state of 'unconsciousness') to see how easy it would be to haul a fallen leader out of a crevasse or up an overhang. We made some alarming discoveries; that it is virtually impossible to hang freely and in a conscious state for any length of time without the additional support of the arms; that one can't lift a freely hanging body (unless, of course, one is equipped with phenomenal strength). Coupled to all this there is the great danger of rupture to internal organs caused by the constriction of the waist line. Which all appeared to add up to the fact that if a leader fell off into a free situation the best the second could do would be to hold him whilst the most the leader could hope to do would be to relieve the strain on his waist by hanging by his arms on the rope above him — and he wouldn't be able to do this for very long. What was needed, we decided, was some kind of harness or sling that would take the weight of a freely fallen leader but not subject him to the agonies of the kind of suspension that the waist-line technique induces, and one that would reduce the injury on the internal organs in the event of such a fall.

The result of this elementary research was the Gatesgarth Sling. Thus, in 1950, was (so far as we were ever aware) the first British climbing harness designed, built and used. It was made out of one continuous piece of three-quarter weight nylon rope. It comprised a waist loop and braces which crossed at the back between the shoulder blades; the braces then passed over the shoulders and were attached to the waist loop through 'eyes' spliced into the rope ends. The assembly was held together at the front by a screw lock karabiner and the leader's rope was attached to a second karabiner (which clipped over the braces where they crossed) by means of a Tarbuck Knot — a sliding knot which permitted some give or elongation in the rope, in the event of a fall. (This is achieved, these days, by using ropes of greater elasticity.) The difference between hanging from a waistloop and the Gatesgarth Sling was tremendous. We both made the Slings. I climbed in mine for years afterwards.

When, twenty years later, I saw my companion in Japan (Takada San, one of the top Japanese climbers) donning a Whillans sit-harness, the first I had ever seen, my interest was considerable.

Another visit to Scotland had been planned with Macphee. So Brian and I decided to hitch and spend a couple of days on Buachaille Etive Mor before joining Macphee in the C.I.C. Hut on Nevis.

We didn't make much progress on the first day and had to spend the night in our sleeping bags just off someone's private driveway on the Bonnie Bonnie Banks. It was mid-afternoon, the next day, when we reached the S.M.C. Hut beneath the Buachaille — and my first taste of those ferocious little midges. A dutiful ascent of Crowberry

Ridge and we were away again, this time sitting on the top of a cartload of bricks, heading for Fort William.

It was dark when we reached the C.I.C. Hut on Nevis — and we were exhausted. The haul up from Fort William to the Hut, a climb of two and a half thousand feet, had not been as easy for me as it might have been. I tended to take my hill walking at a steady plod; Dodson at a restrained gallop! We still do!

When we arrived at the Hut Macphee greeted us with the working rules and procedures we were to adopt for the week. We should spend as much time on the crags as we could — good! There would be a minimum of washing up — splendid! We kept our own plates and knives and forks and spoons and each meal will be finished with half a slice of bread. With this bread our plates, knives, forks, spoons would be cleaned to individual satisfaction . . . it was all well organised — and suited us fine . . .

We had a good few days and the weather was very kind. On the first day, descending down No. 3 Gully after completing one of the standard routes on Tower Ridge, I noticed a pleasant-looking buttress to the Tower Ridge side of the Gully — No. 3 Gully Buttress, and we picked off an interesting and not very difficult new route which we christened Gargoyle Wall, because of certain protuberances on the face.

But it was the great Western face of the North East Ridge, that was claiming our keenest interest. The principal gullies on the North East face of Ben Nevis had all been numbered off to the right from Observatory (or No. 1) Gully as Nos. 2, 3, 4 and 5 Gullies. When later-comers began to discern other gullies, or at least fracture lines to the left of No. 1 Gully, the numeral system of nomenclature was continued and the names 'Point Five', 'Zero', 'Minus One', 'Minus Two' and 'Minus Three' followed with little hesitancy. Zero Gully separates the massive Western flank of the North East Buttress from Observatory Ridge, and it is on this flank that Minus One, Two and Three Gullies are to be found. On the day of our visit Minus Two had not been climbed; a state, we decided, that should be rectified.

Accordingly the three of us roped up at the foot of the gully — myself in the lead, Brian second and Macphee third.

The gully in its lower sections is really a succession of chimneys and grooves which run eventually into a black overhang. At this point it was clear that we would have some open face climbing for a while before the rock reverted once more into a chimney/gully system.

The first one hundred feet were fairly easy and I took this section as one run-out. Bringing Brian up I then pushed on for another eighty feet or so into a cave. We were now all nicely strung out on the climb with me placed some two hundred feet or so above Macphee. It was whilst I was taking in the slack rope between Brian and myself that the rope tweaked a small stone off the face below me. It wasn't very large, but it did have quite a distance to fall. It leapt past Brian, bounding gaily off the rock in impressive leaps — straight for Macphee. We all saw it; there was little any of us could do about it. It glanced off the rock in its final bound and hit Macphee square on the side of the head. In those days we never wore helmets; Macphee on that day didn't wear headgear of any sort.

We watched him collapse against the rock and, even from my distance, saw the blood pouring down the side of his head. 'My God,' I thought, 'Poor old Macphee, first we try to set fire to him and now we try to bash his brains in!' I was horror struck . . . He lay there for a few moments whilst Brian and I began the operation of getting off the climb to try to assess the extent of the damage. Slowly, to our indescribable relief, Macphee got to his feet, examined himself, put a handkerchief to his head to staunch the flow and announced that (a) he was all right; superficial cuts only, (b) that he would return to the Hut, (c) that we were to go on.

It was with no small sense of relief that this information was received and, as he seemed to be quite capable of movement and in command of his faculties we pushed on somewhat reluctantly, with the climb, whilst Macphee collected the second rope we had thrown down and made a determined, if somewhat shaky, journey back to the Hut, watched by either Brian or myself from our respective perches on the climb.

With the party down to two climbers we were able to move much more quickly and to alternate the leads — nevertheless, with all the antics we had been up to and the grease and moisture we found on the most awkward parts of the climb (including a black undercut slab, where the chimneys merged into an overhang to temporarily bar our progress), we were on the route for seven hours.

But finally, somewhat tired and still a bit concerned about Macphee, we crawled out of the top of the gully onto the ridge of the North East Buttress and scurried down the latter and the scree and broken ground below it to reach the Hut.

Macphee was in excellent spirits and had caught up on needed rest. It had been a good holiday — injuries apart — and we returned to the Lakes not displeased with the climbing we had been able to achieve.

Around this time the Scafell Hotel in Borrowdale was owned by Sandy Badrock and he and I had become quite good friends. Sandy never aspired to the harder climbs of the valley but he got an enormous kick out of ascending some of the more amiable frolics amongst the mass of climbs that Bentley Beethan had produced and was continuing to produce in the area. One of these was called Sybarite; it is now, for some reason, called Woden's Face. The climb was almost hidden by a large tree. Sandy managed to persuade the

National Trust to have the tree removed. Its removal certainly has improved the climb and doesn't appear to have done too much harm to the environment.

Sandy's influence on me had little to do with climbing, however. His secret passion was painting . . . and so, after a lapse of fifteen years or so, I began to paint again. Sandy loved his valley and the South West of Scotland — Dumfriesshire and Galloway — and again I found myself, on occasions, going to the mountains for other reasons than to climb them — to paint, or just to look. It was with Sandy Badrock, walking up Combe Ghyll early on a beautiful summer's morning, that I first saw the sparkle of jewels on the grass — refracted sunlight on the droplets of morning dew; colours that changed through the full spectrum range as one gently shifted one's position on the fellside. I began to discover that the mist forms or rain skeins that hung or shroud a mountain's shoulder are not necessarily things to be cursed — that they may be things of grace and mystery — even promise! That a mountain's outline can possess drama or tenderness; that vertical edges, indicative of cliff faces, need not necessarily be an absolute essential in the criteria of mountain beauty. It was Sandy who first talked to me about Turner and Constable and who gave me my first original paintings — two delightful small watercolours by an old man who lived a shy and secret life in Rosthwaite. (His name was David Baxter.) I still have the paintings . . . they are just as fresh and lovely every time I look at them. They've gained with time rather than lost; isn't this what painting is about?

When 1951 arrived, I, still in 'my thirtieth year to heaven', did not question that I would still stand on that same hill in 'a year's turning' — but it was a question I *should* have asked myself, because it was to be my last full year in England . . .

It was in the late forties that I had met 'the other Brian', Brian Blake.

Brian had graduated from Cambridge, where he had read Geography, around this time and had moved into Maryport as the Warden of its Educational 'Settlement', a kind of Workers Education Institution which brought interest and cultural values into the lives of many young people in the area who would otherwise have had little opportunity to satisfy needs beyond the football field, dog track and pub. We were introduced through Bert Beck.

I met Brian for the first time on Grey Crags in Birkness Combe. A number of us sat in the sun below the start of Harrow Buttress and we watched Brian toiling up the scree towards us. Shirtless, I could see that he was of muscular build (he had swum for his College) and was slightly taller than me. He was possessed of a very dry humour and an engaging frankness. I could see that we were going to get along very well together.

In the next couple of years or so Brian Blake and I had paired up on a number of climbs. Most of the time it had been in Buttermere or Borrowdale, largely because his caravan had been permanently sited at Thornythwaite which, with our tent pitched alongside, gave us all the facilities we needed for a comfortable joint family outing. In 1951 my son, Alan, was eight and had already proven himself on the gentler Shepherd Crag classics.

At Whitsuntide, 1951, we were in camp at Thornythwaite, both of us pretty fit, and, given the right weather, we had decided, we would have a look at that imposing face between Groove Two and Honister Wall on Buckstone How — a face that we had crossed on the Girdle Traverse but not yet ascended. And the weather *was* right . . .

We went in to the attack early in the week. As we roped up at the bottom of the crag it was apparent that the first problem was going to be the line of overhangs some fifty or sixty feet above our head. Higher up there were more — but there were also grooves and ribs and flat faces cutting through them and with luck there, too, we would go!

The first pitch went easily enough and I got up to the overhangs. The difficulties began at this point. To get through the first line of overhangs was the initial problem. A short steep groove off to the left between a block and a vertical leaf solved this and led up in twenty more feet to a flake on the left of a steep flattish wall.

Upwards progress seemed out of the question — but to my right, across the flat wall, a line of footholds hypnotised me. If there were suitable handholds the traverse across the face could be superb.

About four or five feet to my right, at just the proper height I spotted a tiny hole in the wall; just adequate, I thought, for one finger. The trouble seemed to be that it would be necessary to change hands at the tiny pocket — but having done this more and better incut holds seemed to lead right across the face.

It was a wonderful situation. The traverse worked out beautifully and I arrived on a good ledge, with belays, at the far side of the wall, at the foot of a steep groove. Here Brian joined me some minutes later.

The groove was a tempting line to follow but the real challenge lay out on the main face which swept upwards *above* the overhangs and wall I had just crossed.

My next moves were up onto the wall on the left. I was now above the second line of overhangs and some sixty feet above these were the third set, up yet another steep wall. The first few moves up onto the upper wall were not easy, but once established it was easy enough to move back to the left to a small bracket. The situation was breathtaking. Above me lay difficulty and unknown territory, below my heels, fresh air. High up above the bracket I could see a hold, it looked suspect but it could be good. If it was a good one it would solve the problem of progress . . .

Two days later we were back. I'd gone round to the top of the cliff and climbed down until I could see the hold. It *seemed* to be adequate. We retraced our steps to the bottom of the crag and climbed up again onto the bracket half way up the upper wall where there was a rudimentary belay, low down. The straight-up ascent from the bracket proved to be very hard. I just couldn't reach the hold. Suddenly, I thought of 'combined tactics'. With Brian standing on the bracket and a now utterly useless belay underneath us I climbed on to his shoulders, made a couple of airy moves, then got the hold. It stayed secure. With a whoop of delight I was up the difficulty and I hung on to decent holds whilst Brian climbed down off the top of the bracket to get himself belayed again. Then I moved on.

Up the wall the third overhangs were reached easily and I traversed under them to the left to a good belay. The stance to accompany the belay was rudimentary but adequate — and I called for Brian to join me. When he reached me I moved out up the wall to the left then, in about twenty feet, moved back once more to the right, via a delightful, though short traverse, into the shattered groove immediately above the third line of overhangs. The left hand wall of this groove led straight to the top of the crag — it was all air and light and joy.

We called the climb 'Cleopatra'. The date was May 18, 1951. It was one of the best new climbs I ever did . . . What is it that Shakespeare said about 'Age cannot wither her nor custom stale Her infinite variety' . . .?

That night, a Friday, we went to the Scafell in Rosthwaite. On one of the upper shelves spanning the width of the front bar, was a magnificent collection of liqueurs — all lined up in splendid array for the delectation of any who cared to dip into their seductive ranks. It was hereabouts we decided that Cleopatra should be saluted. But it was to be no gentle dipping; it was to be a straightforward, whole-hearted traverse — starting at the first bottle on the left and going straight across the shelf — in liqueurs!

I remember starting the traverse; it was a blue liqueur, with a Drambuie next to it . . . But I do not remember reaching the end of the shelf. I am assured that we did. My notes do not say. In fact there are no notes for the following day, which suggests that maybe we were successful in our salutations.

Cleopatra launched a spate of names of notorious ladies for new routes — Delilah, Jezebel, Eve. There were others that we never used — Salome was one. We reserved these names for climbs that we felt had special qualities . . .

Whatever the guidebook's List of First Ascents may say to the contrary the 'four ladies' were all ascended in 1951. Cleopatra, on Buckstone How, May 18, 1951; Jezebel, on Miners' Crag, July 29,

1951; Delilah, on High Crag Buttress, August 10, 1951. Eve, on Shepherd's Crag, August 11, 1951 — with a free drink at the Scafell that night; the barmaid's name was Eve!

Jezebel came about in a rather special way. Stan Dirkin and I had been to Newlands and Honister on many occasions, where he'd led some of the better climbs in both valleys, and we realised eventually that Miners' Crag in Newlands was a cliff that lent itself to a Girdle Traverse — as much as any cliff of similar size. Yet none had been done.

As I said in an earlier chapter, the cliff presents a flat west face towards the valley and then a rising cliff line which ascends the scree to the south to finally connect with the wall, rich in overhangs, which overlooks the Southern face — Terrace Wall. A girdle traverse starting at the left hand side of the West Face and working round onto the rising Southern Face to finish up Terrace Wall would be quite long and would, if the best parts of the existing climbs could be worked into it, be of some quality.

We did the climb on the same day that we ascended Jezebel; in fact the latter was the last three pitches of the climb.

Newlands is a strangely lonely valley for such an otherwise busy area of Lakeland and many times, even at Easter time, when hordes are to be found crawling over the popular routes in Borrowdale, one usually finds in Newlands the same sense of solitude that we discovered in the forties.

Jezebel is a pleasant little climb, quite under rated, I feel — as is the valley — with some lovely moves in an airy position.

I climbed it again with David Craig in 1982 and again, later, with Chris Bonington. They both liked it; one wonders why no one else seems to have been there! One never hears it mentioned in climbing talk.

Our explorations in Buttermere were still unfinished. For years, off and on, we had been looking, from a greater or lesser distance, at the face of High Crag Buttress. I'd already been up the right hand edge of it — Delilah goes there! And so, later in the year, Stan Dirkin, Brian Dodson and I found ourselves roping up once more. In the forties (and 1950/51) the chimney line which splits the main mass of High Crag, the front face of the Buttress, was loaded with a massive, continuous growth of hyacinth grass and old nests — the greatest collection of useless and unstable material I have ever found on any climb. Back in the late forties Bert Beck and I had had one session trying to get some of it out, with little success. It hung out of the 'caves' in huge tussocks; the loose sticks of nesting debris were many feet higher. It was painfully clear that any successful attempt on High Crag Buttress would require us to move this continuous line of junk from the main chimney system. I preferred to attack from below rather than on a rope from above and so, with Brian and Stan on the ledges at the foot of the cliff, I set off upwards and eventually into the 'hanging gardens'.

Brian Dodson maintained afterwards that he actually stood at the foot of the climb belaying me for four hours. I think that is probably an exaggeration — although I was a long time; but be that as it may, I did work my way right up the chimney caves — sending literally tons of material, dirt, mud, rocks, grasses of many kinds, sticks, all pouring down onto the ledges below — and their occupants — and finally, to my joy working my way right out to the top of the chimney out onto what is now the fourth pitch. The way ahead looked straight-forward enough — stepping first to the right and then up; this looked 'thin' but feasible and after moving out to a rib on the right, I tentatively fingered the wall above. I found it *was* delicate; not only that but I was covered in mud and dirt. My rubbers were encased in slime, my arms, hands, clothing were equally greasy, and the past few hours of toil had left me fairly drained of energy. Discretion taking contol I called for a rope from above and Stan, only too anxious to be doing something besides dodging falling vegetation, dirt and rocks, soloed up nearby Gatesgarth Chimney and threw me down the end of his nylon. I tied on and stepped up to the right after having cleaned off as much of the mud as I could. At the critical point, I recall, footholds almost disappeared. A knob of moss offered itself and was accepted. In two or three feet more the difficulties disappeared. And we went back down Gatesgarth Chimney far too tired in my case (and far too late at night!) to make any further assault on the climb but content in mind that with all the filth now removed and after good rain to wash it clean the route would go. The top move from the rib would be hard but I'd done it on a rope. There was a thread belay nearby . . . Next time, we told ourselves, next time . . . (In the cleaning up operations I had actually led the first three and a half pitches of the climb in one run-out. It never crossed my mind, at the time, that I could have also done the crux — for six feet of which I took a rope from above — by putting in a piton and climbing on that. Apparently this was how the first ascent was made eleven years later.)

But there was to be no next time . . . I never went back again.

Two months later I applied for a job in Australia. Before we could get into the new climbing season I had been offered the job. From then, almost until the time of departure my thinking and actions were directed towards this new adventure . . .

In the June of 1952 I went to Buttermere once more to lead a Fell and Rock meet. But the weather was not good and 'nothing very much was done.' I said my farewells to Buttermere — leaving it by the same track from which I had first seen it; stopping at the top of Fangs Brow to take in one final time the scent and sounds of Loweswater. Would I stand here again?

For me it was the passing of a lifestyle. I had been climbing for fourteen years. Was this the end? And what of all the others? Bert had virtually stopped climbing three years before. George left the Lake District soon after getting married and, true to his belief, cut off all communication with all of us. Stan went to Hong Kong (where he still is) almost at the same time as I left for Australia. Ronnie Wilkinson, with whom I made the first ascent of Cumbrians Climb in 1949, left for Africa. Brian Blake rarely climbed again. Brian Dodson simply said to himself, 'I can't study medicine and find the time to climb as well as I would want to. One of them has to go!' He stopped climbing immediately I left.

A. T. Hargreaves died in an avalanche in 1952. Jim Birkett did his last new climb two years later. Macphee fell in the mountains of the Canary Islands and died in 1963.

And Arthur Dolphin . . . We climbed together for the last time just a year before I left, he leading one group and I the other up Overhanging Bastion. We laughed and joked all the way up the climb. After doing the 'gangway' and stepping around and up the flaky overhang Arthur had his team wedged in behind the yew tree awaiting my arrival. All was lightheartedness and laughter. As I went up the final overhang and having to do some fancy footwork on the loose flakes that were around, because I could not reach the holds that long-legged Arthur had attained, I cried out in mock horror for them to pass me down a handhold. I made some crack about Arthur's length and he said with a grin, 'It's being so short that keeps you down in our class.' It was said in fun, in a situation where, at that time in Lakeland, not many of us ever found ourselves — leading a climb of Overhanging Bastion's calibre. It may have been corny and said in jest, but I knew that in his gentle way Arthur Dolphin was paying me a compliment and I took it as such and have cherished it — and never forgotten!

He died, descending the easy way on the Aiguille du Géant the year I left . . .

Thus, rare friends and precious moments passed into memory. How would I fill the void of their departure?

13

Australian Interlude

We arrived in Australia on September 5, 1952, to begin a long and rich experience in a country which, with its people, was very good to me. The entire Australian story is far too long to be treated here in other than a cursory way. For present needs this Interlude must suffice. Australia was my home for twenty-eight years — almost as long as my life spent in West Cumberland and the Lake District.

Those years spanned a multitude of changes and events. They saw, as I had sensed they might, a run-down of my climbing activities. Life amongst Lakeland hills had no equivalent for me in Australia. The intimacy with the mountains and crags that I'd known in Britain disappeared. I doubt that I ever really found it again in Australia.

I discovered that one can't climb in a vacuum. One needed to talk about and to share an experience. I had to come to terms with a whole new spectrum of criteria.

The mountains were different and the crags, certainly where I lived, just south of Sydney, stood apart from my needs. There were miles of sandstone escarpment all around me but they did not beckon. The rocks stood aloof. They were difficult to get to. Water and, to a lesser extent wild life, could be problems. Access was not easy — bashing through dense scrub often left one exhausted before one started to climb. Almost every time I went to a crag in those early years the climb we did would be a first ascent — frequently of the crag. Above all no one really cared whether I (or we) got up or not. There was no one to say 'Good climb!' or 'Which way did it go?' or 'How do you rate it?' or 'You should have gone left at the top of the chimney' or 'You can't claim that one, Stupid Nit, it's been done twenty times already . . .'

Almost every time I went climbing it was with friends who'd never climbed before and who'd been pressured into having a 'go' at this rather ridiculous climbing thing.

The passing of the Lakes left an enormous void in my life. For years I dreamt of 'Home' and of being with old friends. But it was all delusion. Slowly, I began to decay and to grab at every passing straw.

True, we did some climbs that have lasted — the first ascents of the Breadknife and N.E. Ridge of Crater Bluff in the Warrumbungle mountains in central New South Wales. And something of the camaraderie of the Lakeland scene evolved when I met the Brisbane Bushwalkers — but they were five hundred miles away and I could only visit them twice a year (which I did, incidentally, every year between 1954 and 1961, when I went to Southern Queensland to write articles for a mining journal). There were rich moments with the Bushwalkers. With Neil Lamb and Julie Henry, the spearheads of the climbing wing within the club and others, I spent many days (and, frequently enough, nights, too — often unpremeditated) on the mountains in Southern Queensland when we climbed on Tibrogargan, Beerwah, Crookneck, Barney, the Steamers and Mt. Maroon, making first ascents on most of them or checking up on earlier ones that they had made.

As the climbing wound down I felt a desperate need to fill the void. I began to study painting at the College where I was teaching. I attended the courses in the National Art School up to 1959 — but always as a student; painting had not yet become the driving ambition within me that it was to become. This happened in 1960 — almost coincidentally with the time my climbing wound down to its lowest point.

In those early years in Australia I was easily impressed by other people's paper qualifications. I could never forget that I had left school at fourteen; that, until I went to Workington Tech., I had never seen an experiment in chemistry or physical sciences conducted (if we exclude that one which demonstrates barometric pressure using a jam jar full of water and a sheet of paper!). I liked mathematics — but trying to teach myself the elementary concepts of differential and integral calculus had presented considerable difficulty. When I settled in Australia I decided that I would rectify this position.

One of my good friends at the College (which then incorporated the local division of the N.S.W. University of Technology) was the mathematics lecturer, Austin Keane. Austin was a brilliant mathematician — First Class Honours, University Medallist, M.A. whilst still in his early twenties, Ph.D. a few years later. I have never met any man who loved his subject more. He persuaded me to study maths at the University College — this I did for three years until 1956. Austin and I had talked at great length about ventilation problems in mines. We did a series of joint papers — a mathematical analysis of air flow in a leaky duct system. These were published in Britain. I was invited by the parent University (of New South Wales) to lecture on Mine Ventilation, to its final year students, as a result. This I did for several years. Then Austin said 'Why don't you apply to the University as a person with special knowledge of his subject, to be admitted as a candidate for a Masters degree? There's provision for such things in the statute.' I applied; my request was refused.

In the meantime I was told by the N.S.W. Department of Technical Education, for whom I worked as a Teacher of Mining, that if I wished to progress beyond my present position it would be necessary for me to achieve a higher academic standard. This didn't come as a surprise to me. I was given a very extensive programme of work, which included topics like Maths and Geology to University exam level, Surveying Computations, Electrical Engineering, Technical Drawing to appropriate Diploma level and, interestingly enough, all the subjects in the Final Year of the Department's Coal Mining Certificate Course. I replied that I would be pleased to do this but pointed out that there was a slight difficulty — namely that I was the person who actually *set* the examinations referred to in the Coal Mining Course. 'Oh,' someone thought 'not to worry — we'll get someone else to set special ones for you.' And they did. The mining lecturing staff at the University of N.S.W., where I was part-time teaching was given the job . . .

Ultimately I completed all the programme to everyone's satisfaction and was accredited with the entitlement to progress to higher things. I was made Head Teacher.

By now I was biting hard on the academic bullet. I had decided that, having done all this work, I would get myself into an appropriate degree or diploma course so that my star, too, could glitter. I began to apply to various institutions for permission to be admitted to their external degree or diploma courses. The replies I received were varied and sometimes bewildering.

'Yes, you can do it, but it finishes this year.'

'No, we used to let *mining engineers* in but not now — you have to be a *civil* engineer.'

'No!' 'No!' 'No!'

And the most astounding one of all:

'We thank you for your application for the post of Professor of Geology but advise you that the vacancy has now been filled . . .'

I came nearer to home and applied to my own people for admission to the Engineering Diploma Course. I was told I couldn't do it because I wasn't, properly, an engineer.

I scraped the sides of every academic barrel that I considered remotely appropriate. The results were always the same, 'No!'

Finally in some desperation, I applied to my own Department. I thought, at least, I'll get a certificate out of it all; it's not very much —

a long way from a degree, I thought — but it's at least a piece of paper. A few weeks later I received the reply:

'No — because you haven't attended enough lectures . . .' I couldn't be bothered to reply that the reason why I hadn't sat in on lectures was because I was delivering them!

Suddenly the absurdity of the whole situation hit me like a bomb. 'You stupid bloody fool, what the hell are you wasting your time for — chasing bits of paper which could be of very doubtful benefit — just to say "look, aren't I clever"?' The doors in my brain slammed together with a resounding bang. 'Forget it, mate, get stuck into that which you *know* you can do. Get on with your bloody painting.'

At that instant my entire attitude towards painting changed — almost miraculously, I have reflected many times since.

In 1960 I threw myself into it. I painted at every available moment — weekends, evenings, holiday times. Almost overnight I switched from being a smug weekend hobby painter into an ill-equipped, desperately anxious and fairly unsuccessful professional painter. If hard work can change this position, I reasoned, I'll work like hell. And I did. I kept the pressure on myself and those around me for years.

In 1960 I held my first one man show in the local W.E.A. rooms in Wollongong, N.S.W. The opening was performed by the late Tony Tuckson, then the Deputy Director of the Art Gallery of N.S.W. There were many local artists, friends and well-wishers present; it was a heady occasion. A show in Sydney had to follow; the critics were guarded — but, importantly for me, they didn't blast. Other shows followed in Brisbane and Melbourne. I was not saying anything terribly new in them — I was, in fact, leaning very heavily on my contemporaries, particularly one of the most successful of the artists of those years, my friend Thomas Gleghorn, arguably Sydney's most exciting artist at that time. I didn't sell very much. That was not the point of the exercise. I felt I had to show, show, show; I set myself standards; I desperately needed experience.

Gleghorn opened the doors of the Sydney Art scene for me. It was a wild time. Like the lead climbers of the forties everyone who was painting anything significant or regularly was known to the other performers. We met at weekly 'openings', galleries and pubs. A marvellous 'in-thing' developed.

Despite my age, in my early forties, I was seen (by myself at any rate) to be very much the lad around the place. Then in 1963 came, for me, the big breakthrough!

In Sydney, in those years, abstract art, for want of a more accurate term, carried the day. Nearly every newcomer leant towards non figuration, as opposed to Melbourne's concern with the figure and mythmaking. Yet, in the best of Sydney painting at the time, the abstraction was landscape based. One detected, amongst the gestures and noise, the colours and forms of the outback, the harbour side, the structures of the emerging city skyline. We struggled hard to acquire individuality. My own efforts were rewarded almost by accident. At the time I used oils. One day, after many fruitless attempts to make a painting 'work' I decided I would strip back the board on which I'd been labouring and start all over again. I poured some paraffin over the painting and set fire to it. The oil burnt merrily. Flames and smoke leapt into the air then gradually subsided. The results of this happening left me spellbound. Certainly the composition was no great wonder, but magical things had happened to the paint itself. Where harshness of colour and crudity of brushwork had previously existed there was now a great subtlety. Colours had fused delicately and become softened under a charcoal haze. The surface had become blistered and careworn — I felt, exultantly that from the ashes of this fearsome holocaust a delicate, almost poignant, phoenix had arisen. I was completely entranced. Obviously, much work had to be done. I had to find ways and means of greater control — but for me there was a message and a direction. In one ferocious shrug I managed to cast off the influence of my contemporaries.

My show of the 'burnt paintings' went on in the Blaxland Gallery in Sydney in May 1963.

Wallace Thornton of the Sydney Morning Herald said '. . . In this show he reveals qualities not even hinted at before. Here are resources of mind and heart, that show in completely new order, a new perceptive quality.

'A poetry of nuance, an inflection of forms that dissolve into strange mists, or shapes into disciplined lines that suggest subtle changing planes, touches on real beauty in these paintings. It is a beauty of a world evoked, of a man's strength and tenderness fused into an expression of echoes and half realisations. The mystery is established . . .'

James Gleeson of the Sun went on along similar lines 'By far the most powerful and impressive paintings he has shown us in his brief exhibiting career. The total impact is unnerving . . . This is post Hiroshima. Peascod has painted a world surrounded by devastating heat . . .' and so it went on. I wasn't sure what it all meant, but it sounded terrific. That year I won three art awards including the Maude Vizard Wholohan, in Adelaide (which at the time was the biggest art prize in South Australia). The painting was acquired by the South Australian National Gallery and went into its collection.

The next year I was invited to exhibit in 'The Rubinstein'. Entry to this competition was probably the most coveted prize in the Australian art scene in the late fifties and early sixties. Helena Rubinstein, of cosmetic fame, had set aside a large sum of money to allow one artist each year to travel overseas and study. The sum, with the odd additional grant that could be prised out of various Foundations was sufficient to keep an artist in reasonable comfort for the Grand Art Tour of Europe. Each year from the whole of Australia eleven painters were selected. Each had to submit five major paintings to be hung, in the first instance, in the Art Gallery of N.S.W. Here they were subjected to the scrutiny of a selection panel who then decided who would be the lucky recipient of the Rubinstein Prize. Just to be there, amongst the eleven, was an adrenalin charge that comes only on hard rock climbs. I didn't win; the winner was a young friend of mine, Colin Lanceley, who deserved the award. But the experience was a tremendous boost to me. For a short time I felt infallible.

I represented the country internationally in the U.S.A. and South Africa on several occasions; my work was acquired by many of the leading National Collectors — the N.S.W. Art Gallery, the Victorian National Gallery as well as the South Australian National Gallery, Newcastle, Wollongong, various Universities, Institutes of Education, Banks and Municipal Galleries and so on. I won numerous awards and prizes. I was accepted amongst the avant garde. It was a short-lived glitter.

By the mid sixties this particular avant garde had been swamped by a younger, more vociferous one which waved hard-edged blockbusters at our now sterile abstraction. These 'colour field' specialists had an even shorter reign. Before the sixties had run their span 'colour field' was being swamped by 'new figuration', then 'conceptual art', which seemed to be little more than a fleeting gesture. The whole gamut of new '-isms' rushed to the shore like artistic lemmings and were seen no more.

In 1967, after fifteen years in Australia we returned to Britain for the first time. I was overjoyed at the thought of meeting old friends, of getting on the fells, possibly, even, of climbing. When we reached the Lakes in December the foot-and-mouth ban on access to the fells was still in existence. I attended a meet of the Fell and Rock Climbing Club at the Old Dungeon Ghyll. Apart from Sid and Jammy Cross I didn't, for a long while, recognise anyone. Even worse, no one recognised me! It was, for me, a sad homecoming. Maybe I'd expected too much.

Had it not been for the interest of one short and bearded young man I feel I could have returned to Australia in a very dispirited state. He was someone I'd never met before and didn't know of, or what he did. We got into conversation. He knew the current scene intimately. We talked well into the night. He told me he ran a climbing shop in Ambleside — and if I would like to go along next morning about eleven he said he'd meet me there and show me what the current gear situation was all about. His name was Frank Davies, now one of the best known personalities in the equipment scene.

He never knew, nor did anyone else at the time, how much his conversation meant to me. He made me a present of several different items of modern climbing technology and showed me how to tie a tape knot. He told me of the new climbing areas and who was doing what. It was a breath of fresh air to me.

But, my visit to Europe in 1967/8 was more than a return to old stamping grounds. For years I had devoured the glossy Modern Art magazines. I had a knowledge (even if only superficial) of every American and European painter who had managed to make the glossies on a regular basis. These I came back to Europe to see. Oh, I knew of the Old Masters, all right. Yes, I'd heard of Giotto, Piero della Francesco, Masaccio, Rembrandt and so on — but they didn't interest me one little bit. Turner and Constable, I was prepared to admit, would be worth going to see — although I think this may have been out of some loyalty to Sandy Badrock, more than any turn-on I could expect from them.

We 'did' Rome rather quickly but not before we had seen Michelangelo's Pieta in St. Peters and the ceiling and end wall of the Sistine Chapel and the Raphaels in the Vatican Museum. I found them all rather disturbing.

But walking down the Viz Nazionale and seeing a sign inviting me to visit the Rome Biennale of Modern Painting I felt happier. I said to myself 'This is what I've really come to see.' There were several floors of their creations — although in fairness, I should say that they didn't include the familiar names I'd found in the coffee-table mags. I started my tour on the top floor and worked downwards. All the paintings were done in imitation of the recent (and sometimes not so recent) styles of the American International Abstract School. From room to room I wandered. I seemed to pass through acres of similar canvasses — all fairly uninspiring and (it slowly began to dawn upon me) all increasingly boring and pointless. On the next floor down the offerings were of the same order — and all about as memorable.

I began to wish the exhibition would terminate. Yet one more floor down and I felt the artistic vomit rising in my gullet. I had to get out of it all. On a landing I spotted an open door which led out onto the busy street and bolted for it — feeling very much as if in another minute I would be physically sick. Outside I breathed deeply of the Roman air — car fumes and all — and felt an enormous sense of relief. From that moment I ceased to be enchanted by the latest offerings of the international glossy art magazines.

From Rome we moved to Florence, to Botticelli, Masaccio, Giotto and Piero. London and Caravaggio, Leonardo and Van Eyck. The Impressionists in Paris and Goya in the Prado — those fearsome Black Paintings and the lyrical Majas — with side trips to Cuenca to see the wonderful Casas Colgadas (the Hanging Houses) Gallery

First ascents in the Warrumbungle Mountains, Central New South Wales.

Left: Crater Bluff. The first climb anywhere on this face went up the rib near the right hand side of the face (outlined against the shadow). It then went into the deep alcove, in the shadow and finished up a series of ribs (just seen in the sun). The first ascent was made by Bill Peascod and Russell Kippax (alternate leads) in August 1954. (Photo: Neil Lamb)

Below right: The Breadknife, South Ridge. The first ascent of this remarkable pinnacle in the Warrumbungles was also made by Kippax and Peascod in August 1954.

Below left: Bill Peascod leading up from the gap on the first ascent of the Breadknife. The route then moves slightly left of Peascod and goes straight up the wall. This pitch was led by Kippax and although not hard was very exposed.

Painting 'Snow Country'

Above: In Australia at the time of the Burnt Paintings - 1963.

Below: At the opening of the writer's studio - 1964 - Near Wollongong.

Above: Etsu and Emma (aged 4) at the Drum House above Honister, New Year 1979.

Left: Etsu at Ardshiyama, near Kyoto in 1974.

Left: Tom Gleghorn

Below left: Bill Birkett

Below Right: Scottie Dwyer

Bill Peascod at the top of the Great Flake, Central Buttress, Scafell. (Photo: Bill Birkett)

Right: Brian Dodson on Suaviter, 1981.

Below: Bill Peascod at Melbecks Studio.

Plotters - Tony Greenbank, Don Whillans and Bill Peascod, Buxton 1984.
(Photo: Bill Birkett)

At the top of Eagle Front. Chris Bonington and Bill Peascod.
(Photo: Border Television)

with its faith restoring exhibition of modern Spanish Masters — and
to Vienna and the exquisite Brueghels all followed. But it was in
Amsterdam, firstly with Van Gogh (seen by me for the first time in
depth) and, in the Rijks Museum (where I really encountered
Rembrandt) that I finally capitulated to the non-moderns. In front
of *Night Watch*, a vision for which I was totally unprepared and which
came after the wonders of *The Syndics* and *The Jewish Bride*, I stood in
total aesthetic disarray. The tears literally coursed down my cheeks.
My artistic values had taken a terrible hammering. I was completely
and totally overwhelmed — not just by the Rembrandts — these
were merely the final swipe of the sledgehammer — but by the total
cultural shock of those old painters whom I'd heard of but in my
naivety had written off without seeing.

I returned to Australia in a turmoil. I recollected many times the
comment of my old friend, Tom Gleghorn, who had undergone a
similar experience a number of years earlier, 'Who do we think we
are?' he had said, 'Compared with them, mate, we're chicken shit!'
For a year I couldn't paint. When I started again the results were
very introspective. In the great big Sydney Art World the Hard
Edged Boys had moved in. The New Boys and their admirers let us
Oldies know in no uncertain terms that we weren't much 'chop' —
but they needn't have tried so hard; Rembrandt had managed that
much more convincingly and he'd never said a word!

*   *   *

In the mid sixties I had managed to do a little climbing just two or
three times a year — more, I have no doubt, as a reminder of what
I'd lost than as a desire to hit new form. I had found the cliffs of Mt.
Keira (the 1500 ft. peak that overlooks the town in which I lived)
away back in 1954 and at the same time had discovered a disused
basalt quarry just a few miles to the south on the sea-coast. Over the
years with several friends I had made half a dozen or so climbs in
Bombo quarry as it is called. One of these, a beautiful expanding
crack which splits a seventy foot high prism of basalt off the main face
(which I climbed in the sixties with Bryden Allen) is the best of them.

My son, Alan had left High School in 1962 and, after a year of
trying to find out what he wanted to do, elected to study Ceramics in
the National Art School in Sydney. Eventually after much hard work
and intense study he was to become one of the most respected of
Australian potters with an international reputation in lustre glazes
— but that was to be much later.

On a more personal front it sadly has to be said that things had not
gone so well between my wife Margaret and myself. No one can point
to a spot and say 'this is where it happened; this is what went wrong.'
There was just a slow erosion of our relationship over the years and a
great deal of unhappiness on both sides.

The pressures and chains I'd felt in the old days of climbing were still there. I was nearing fifty. I no longer climbed with any success. My painting didn't feed my needs as it used to do. There was nothing about the future that looked particularly bright. Simple conversations between us changed rapidly to argument. And as the years went by these became more brittle and meaningless. I felt very strongly that life was phoney; that I was a phoney.

By 1970 I had held over thirty one-man exhibitions throughout Australia, then I was invited to have a one-man show in Japan! This was organised by the well known Japanese calligraphist Shotei Ibata. The challenge was what I desperately needed. I rose to it and in May took the exhibition to Japan and stayed there, with the Ibatas, for four weeks.

It was an unbelieveable experience. For the first time in years I felt the pressures lift. I felt an enormous sense of freedom. I found myself laughing at nothing terribly much and somehow I felt clean and honest. I was enthralled by the landscape, my friends and the Japanese aesthetic.

The experience in Japan gave me strength. But I wasn't sure whether what I'd seen and felt was real or wishful thinking. I returned to Japan later that year and stayed until the end of January 1971. I thought I saw the sun of hope through the depression. By now I was determined that, come what may, I must return to Japan to live for a while.

In February 1971 I won a large art prize and this provided the funds. I made plans to return to Japan in December to study at the Kyoto Seika College of Art. The intervening months before December 1971 was a period of intense unspoken aggression. But I left for Japan in December, again I stayed with the Ibatas until I could find my own accommodation. During this time my wife came through Japan on a world trip. Her visit was not a success. I felt the return of all the aggression and hopelessness.

After she left Japan I moved into an International Hostel in Kyoto and settled in to work in the College. I had few contacts there and none (apart from one or two of the teaching staff) who spoke English well. In the large studio shared by the Post Graduate Year I was allocated working space and the eight or nine of us worked slowly and with increasing confidence to establish communication. It was not easy for either side but we managed somehow, with their halting English and my rudimentary Japanese, to share ideas. The College was very well equipped. As well as the Painting School and a large English Department it operated an excellent Design School, a Sculpture Department, Textile Design and Printing Schools.

It was in the Design School that I became friendly with two of the final year students. Peko, a small, neatly-built intelligent girl with twinkling eyes and a great love of rich pastries. Her friend Thuto was tall by Japanese male standards. A kind of Japanese Marcel Marceau, his mime and humorous attitudes were a source of constant amusement — particularly in busy streets where his tall lean frame and long limbs, bedecked in a knitted woollen poncho of ancient vintage, would leap into wild gesticulations to the obvious dismay of the highly conservative passers-by. Peko took it all in dry silence her face straight and eyes laughing, with a resignation beyond words — 'Here he goes again' they would be saying. We were good friends despite our difference in years, culture and language.

After some three weeks Peko said to me in her slow studied English 'I would like to bring a friend. Her name is Etsuko. She speaks good English.' She joined us the following day. Etsuko Michihata was in the same year as Peko. She was a tall, slender, very attractive girl who did, in fact, speak good English. Not only that but she was, I later discovered, intelligent and possessed a lovely sense of humour. Her manners were impeccable; her sense of standards in behaviour and dress could not be faulted. Coupled to all of that she demonstrated a considerable ability to absorb information and was the owner of a remarkably strong will power. We soon became friends. She rapidly picked up the nuances of English which I had found so difficult to convey to most other people I met in Japan. We found we had a common interest in art and ceramics. We visited galleries and, with Peko and Thuto, travelled all over Kyushu and Honshu, the main island, tracing the locations of the Seven Ancient Kilns. We explored the less popular, smaller (but still exquisitely lovely) temples that she knew of and I was welcomed by her family, whom I liked immediately. Some weeks after I met Etsuko I realised that the time had come when I had to make a very positive decision about life — whether to join my life with hers or return to the phony front I had built up.

Those who have made such a decision will know it is not easy. I returned to Australia in the middle of April 1972 to face whatever music was being played and to sort out whatever moves had to be made. This unhappy business was spread over several weeks. The pressure and strain were intense.

Etsu came to Australia on the twenty-fifth of May 1972. Within ten minutes of her arrival at the place where I was living I collapsed with a massive coronary. This was one event I hadn't bargained on!

We were married in December 1973. (Margaret, incidentally, was herself married a few months later.) Life for Etsu and I took on a wonderful new glow. We had very little money but somehow managed to build a house and then, three years exactly to the day of Etsu's arrival in Australia, twenty-fifth of May, 1975, a lovely sweet little lady came into my life. We called her Emma Satsuki Peascod.

Our happiness was complete. The only problem that might arise was my health. I knew another kind of fear for the first time. 'Shall I climb again?' I asked the physician. 'No,' he said, 'But why do you want to? There's not much point in it is there?' I couldn't answer this, but I made a secret promise to myself — I will climb again, I said, I'll find the mountains! And I did. First through cross-country skiing in the Snowy Mountains, which I took up after years of inducement from a G.P. friend of mine, David Oliver. Etsu started, too, and as I might have expected, became completely efficient in no time. We skied every season in the mid and late seventies — and David kept a very professional eye on me all the time (I found this out after one superb ski tour of the Mt. Hotham ranges). The skiing experience was very valuable as a guide to my recovery. I found, and this was supported later by extensive medical checks, that I still had a high exercise tolerance. I could stand up to heavy physical going — it was obviously emotional stress that knocked me cock-eyed.

Soon after the first skiing holiday I prevailed upon another close friend, Les Zietara, who was in the same practice as David, to accompany me climbing. Two trips to the Blue Lake cliffs in the Snowy Mountains and several visits to the sandstone cliffs of Mt. Keira confirmed that I *could* climb again. True, they weren't very hard, or long climbs, and they may never ever be written up as classics — but they were rock-climbs, and it was steep rock, and above all, I *was* climbing.

Gradually all these new experiences — happiness, the mountains, the Japanese aesthetic began to fuse together and my paintings came to life with new meaning. I didn't, as I'd done twenty years before, run away from the image. The mountains came through in all their love, hope, gentleness, strength. I felt at long last that something very positive was happening.

In 1974, 1976 and 1979 we returned again to Britain and Japan.

The first time Etsu drove with me alongside Crummock water and up the Buttermere Valley the clouds hung low over Grasmoor and the Haystacks. The mood of the mountains was threatening and mysterious. Occasionally the clouds lifted and a touch of light sharpened a fell side and crag, promising new things. 'This is what you've been painting all these years,' she reflected. I realised quite forcibly that she was right.

In 1979/80 we spent the winter in a cottage in Lorton to see if we could live in the Lakes. We were certain we could and we began the business of trying to find a permanent home. We found Melbecks, and we returned to Australia in April to wind up our affairs and say farewell to Alan and friends.

Our departure for England coincided with a final art happening in July 1980.

For many years I had been in contact with the art scene in Australia and particularly in the City of Wollongong where I had lived. For the last few years of my sojourn there I had also been the part-time lecturer in Art History at the University of Wollongong. These two latter, the City Council and the University, with the help of the local T.V. station gave me a retrospective exhibition called simply 'Bill Peascod 1950-1980'. The show was held in the splendid new City Art Gallery and was organised by the then director of the Gallery, Tony Bond. Some seventy works were on display, spanning thirty years of my painting life. They included most of the largest and best paintings I had ever done, borrowed for the occasion from various national, educational and private collections throughout Australia. It was the widest ranging artistic statement I had ever made. For the first time in thirty years I could see what I, as an artist, had been trying to say — tracing the thread that touched on all the work.

I had been talking about life, my life — about the ageless hills and the promise that lay with them, about the marks of man on the landscape and the scars that it could inflict on man. At times I'd whispered of love and hope; on other occasions I had savagely attacked my themes — almost to the point of destruction — to find, as in life, that something of tender beauty may emerge from the stirred ashes.

It was, for me, a very moving experience.

A couple of days before the final departure I was given a farewell dinner in the Gallery surrounded by this enormous array of paintings. As the guest of honour I was asked to give a farewell address — and for the first time I, who had made a particular forte of public lecturing on Art Matters, found it difficult to speak. My address was very brief. I managed to thank all those who had been responsible for the show, who had loaned their paintings and had supported me over the years. I felt it to be a most inadequate speech — but it brought a thunderous applause. 'The best speech you've ever made,' said my old friend Peter Boon, over the din. Maybe I'd always talked too much on other occasions.

14

Melbecks

We arrived in the Lake District on July 15, 1980. Within a week we began our toil. And we *did* toil, from early in the morning until, often enough, after midnight with barely any break for entertainment. Melbecks gave us the variety of life that dispels boredom.

During our stay in Lorton we had travelled the width and depth of Lakeland looking for the ideal place.

One of the difficulties was that we were not totally sure what our ideals were — nor, in fact, were we certain that we had completely identical sets of criteria. We looked at houses everywhere from the far north of Keswick to way south of Windermere, from Kendal to the fringe of West Cumberland. There was always something not quite right with one or other of them — too modern, too phoney, too far out of the Lakes, too near the town centre, too big, too small — and above all too costly!

We found Melbecks quite early on in our search. We decided it was too big and too isolated and kept on looking. Every now and again, following disappointment after disapointment, we kept returning to Melbecks to have another look.

After a while the seven miles from Keswick didn't seem an unmanageable distance for our everyday shopping needs. And gradually we began to realise its isolation, on the five hundred foot contour on the north-west slopes of Skiddaw, overlooking the Bassenthwaite plains, the Embleton gap and the Derwent valley, was its greatest virtue. The idea was beginning to take root that what we had found, even if a few modifications were necessary, was a haven of peace.

Melbecks is really two houses standing one in front of the other. The front part facing down the valley and across the Lake is a typically Cumbrian farmhouse of Georgian style with the high ceilinged rooms. Five windows of the appropriate twelve-glass-paned design located in the front — three on the first floor and two at ground floor level, balanced symmetrically about a heavy wooden panelled door, itself surrounded by massive dressed sandstone slabs — suggest the layout of the rooms.

A wide stone staircase leads up from the entrance hall to a high ceilinged landing on either side of which are the living rooms and bedrooms.

Behind the Georgian section the old low farmhouse faces up to the higher slopes of Skiddaw and forms a protective wall, with the barns, of what would once have been a busy farmyard. Across the yard and the smaller barn a 'garth' of splendid oaks, sycamores, chestnut trees and elms shelters the yard and the house from the March gales.

We estimated, from our observations of dated buildings of similar types, that the front part of the house was probably constructed in the late eighteenth century or early nineteenth and the older part some hundred and fifty years earlier.

The 'modifications' took six months and cost far more money than either of us could have dreamt they would have cost . . .

A dreadful modern fireplace of tiles and plastic was removed and replaced by a natural stone fireplace of massive sandstone blocks. Two of these had been gateposts — six feet by one and a half feet by six inches thick. They formed the hearth and the mantelpiece. Old lino was lifted in the kitchen. Beneath it were beautiful sandstone slabs, which had to be stripped and chipped free of cement and adhesive.

In one room we discovered under the flooring material an old oak floor. We lifted it all up and found pasted underneath the floorboards old newspaper over one hundred and fifty years old. I trimmed the ancient oak slabs and got rid of all the old pieces of tin that had been used to patch up holes and relaid the floor to allow it to live, once more, as the lovely timber it is. We removed modern windows and glass doors and replaced them with those more in keeping with the character of an old Cumbrian farm house.

We farmed out the jobs to local builders, plumbers, joiners, electricians but we were still involved with every operation ourselves. Both Etsu and I discovered or developed skills hitherto unrealised.

Between two brick walls, standing in the middle of the kitchen, we found an ancient stone staircase. It didn't go anywhere, it was a relic of the original farmhouse before the front Georgian part of the building was added. We carefully removed the stone stairs and stored them in a barn. At every turn we discovered history — there was more than enough to keep us intrigued.

I would never have guessed at what is involved in doing up an old place — neither in terms of personal effort nor cost. Nor, I was to find out, was one always *totally* satisfied with what had been achieved.

There is always something that one might have done better or cheaper, to be more aesthetically pleasing, or more practical. But often it is just too late and too costly to backtrack — or one eventually becomes worn out by the constant grind, debris and apparently endless chaos. So it was with us — then after months of really hard work, we began to see a glimmer of daylight.

In the meantime Emma had started school.

I had never been involved with a small school. All fond parents want The Best for their children. The trouble often revolves round the parents themselves not knowing what the best really is!

Whatever reservations I may have had about a two-room, two-teacher country school were completely dispelled when I really began to see what it meant.

It was obvious that the children received a care and attention, together with opportunities for individual development, that may well be impossible in a large, over-crowded city school. They didn't have to study nature from books — it was all around them, in the fields, hedgerows and woods, on the fells and along stream banks. And they walked about amongst it and touched it.

Emma rapidly learned to read and made friends. School for her meant being happy . . . What more can a parent ask for his child?

After we bought Melbecks I was surprised to find that as well as owning the land in front of the house and the garth behind, we were the possessors of nearly two acres of woods. Chapel Beck, a beautiful bubbling stream, runs between high rocky banks throughout the length of the coppice. Someone said to us at the time, 'The only thing it might be good for is growing bluebells!' — a comment which has proved to be a decided understatement.

There are badgers in the wood; red squirrels anxiously pursue their daily business. One morning we startled a female red deer standing in the middle of the road that winds through the glen — when we came round the corner she skipped nimbly and gracefully away. Foxes are quite numerous. One crossed the road the other day with a blackbird in its mouth. A buzzard winters there.

We have an old mine in the wood — probably a lead mine, once; now just a hole in the ground. It's highly likely that it won't be much good for anything, except maybe to shelter a frightened animal — but, like Everest, it's there!

From our windows, between a sycamore and a tall, youngish oak, I can see the top of Skiddaw. It is a mountain which is so easy to underestimate. Only since I have got to know Skiddaw in a season of moods do I realise that there is more to the peak than its height.

Were it no higher than, say, Great Calva or Binsey (adjacent peaks amongst the Northern Fells) it would be as little visited as these two — but in its honour a broad, blazened trail winds from the car park at Applethwaite up the south east spur of the fell. This is the usual tourist route.

To me, the most delightful approach to, or descent from, Skiddaw is by way of Ullock Pike along the ridge that is thrown down to the north west of the summit. The views from the Pike are amongst the most memorable to me in the District. To the west a steep hillside falls down to Bassenthwaite and beyond the lake lies that exquisite pile of fells that comprise the Newlands, Coledale and Whinlatter massif, with Grisedale Pike lording it over the Causey ridges and the northern flanks of the Buttermere fells. To the east the Ullock Pike ridge, from its twin peaks, falls away into Southerndale. Past this the eye searches out Melbecks — and the Uldale and Caldbeck fells nestle lonely and neglected, around Whitewater Dash.

I have walked on Skiddaw on all its sides — in the sun, on the tourist route and on New Year's day, with five year old Emma, across an icy summit, where we had to take very great care that the wintry blast didn't whisk her off her feet as it had done once before on Coledale Hause and yet again on the Hopegill Head — Grisedale Pike Ridge where we lashed her onto a fifty-foot length of eight millimetre nylon between Brian Dodson and myself.

Or again, on skis, straight up from Melbecks on Christmas day with Tom Price and his two sons during the hard winter of 1981/82. On this occasion we climbed above the skiable snow and reached hard ice through which sharp pointed rocks, as vicious as shark's teeth, played havoc with the fishscales on my lightweight cross-country skis. As we skirted the western edge of the plateau that lies to the north of Skiddaw, between the summit and Melbecks I was amazed at the snow and ice architecture on the lip of the steep plunge into Barkbethdale. Huge cornices had built up — in places where I wouldn't have believed it possible. The shallow gullies, cutting up through the Skiddaw Slates from the lonely dale, were packed with long, broad ribbons of quite steep snow. True, it wouldn't have been technically hard to climb — but this was Skiddaw we were on, not the Ben. And Skiddaw is not supposed to be that sort of mountain. A soft crimson glow lit the sky down the Derwent Valley as the sun, hidden in the clouds across the Solway, bade farewell to yet another Christmas.

One late October day Chris Eilbeck and I walked up from Melbecks via Dash Falls, then, into the mist along the fence line that leads interminably, it seems, to the northern plateau beneath the summit. From here we ascended the final rise and reached the summit cairn. Disembodied voices reached us through the blanket of mist. We saw no-one. It was almost as if the Spirits of this high temple were conducting a secret ritual to cleanse it from the ravages of yet another year of pilgrims. From the southerly summit we dropped down the slaty rocks and crossed onto the top of the Ullock Pike ridge. Beyond Ullock's twin peaks the mists broke, and we

descended into a late autumn landscape. The rain kept off, but it
hung, in promise, above our heads. Back in the kitchen at Melbecks,
in front of a glowing fire, we finished a pot of tea and marvelled once
more at the ever changing face of this most pedestrian of mountains.
Those who only know Skiddaw as a backdrop to the gasometers
in Keswick are missing a great deal. Come and see it from
Bassenthwaite village — as a sleeping giant — or approach it from
the north across Uldale moor and notice how, suddenly, the
mountain has slimmed into the gracious pyramid of some far-away
Scottish peak and how the Ullock Pike ridge has, equally sharply,
been drawn out into an exciting outline of curves and rises, pinnacles
and folds.

When you have done this you will know why I paint it so often.

15

The Second Time Round

The first climbs I did on my return to England were Double Slab Climb in Newlands (I had made the first ascent of this, in April in 1948, with Bert Beck) and Gillercombe Buttress. These two climbs were done with Chris Eilbeck and Brian Crystal on the weekend of the Fell and Rock Climbing Club's Annual Dinner in October 1979. It had all happened in a curious way.

A few months before I left Australia to return to the U.K. I was given a book called *Rock Climbing in the Lake District* by Geoff Cram, Chris Eilbeck and Ian Roper. In the preface of this most admirable of selective guidebooks the authors state their aim, namely 'to describe some two hundred climbs selected from the fifteen hundred available in the Lakes' for the purpose of providing a 'balanced selection' of climbs for those climbers who are either first-time visitors or who rarely climb in the Lakes.

In their selection the writers had included fifteen of my own first ascents. Anyone, I thought, who is as discerning as this must be worth knowing. I decided to write to one of them at the address given. It was that of Chris Eilbeck. The result was that we met for the Annual Dinner and have kept up the tradition since then — climbing or walking on the Dinner Weekend at the end of October and on occasions at other times of the year.

Chris and Brian both lived in Edinburgh. Both of them were in their early thirties. Chris, who came originally from Whitehaven and from where he'd climbed a great deal on Pillar Rock, was a mathematician at Heriot-Watt University. Brian, who had studied law, was a braw Scot. They were both about my height, but much more fit, and were obviously very experienced mountaineers.

Chris's lead of Gillercombe Buttress on a very wet, cold day was a classic. As I watched his neat footwork in the utterly foul conditions we encountered I could see him easily as the young climber who, with Geoff Cram and Bill Lounds, had put up those splendid-looking routes on Pillar Rock some ten or twelve years earlier — Thanatos, Electron, Eros and (I was to find out later) a stock of others.

As winter was close upon us, no more climbing was done that year. The Dodsons joined us in our cottage in Lorton during the January of 1980 and we walked, in superb conditions — bright sunshine, a few inches of snow — around the head of Warnscale at Buttermere, and along the Forestry trails under Hobcarton and Grisedale Pike, before we returned to Australia to clear up our affairs prior to returning to Melbecks.

By the time of the next Annual Dinner (1980) our work at Melbecks was reaching some degree of finality and both Etsu and I were feeling the need of a break. I was curious also about what had happened to my contemporaries.

I had contacted Tom Price very soon after my return. It was clear that he was fit and active. His light frame and deceptive shuffling gait gobbled up the miles, I was to discover.

The one other person I wanted to meet again was Jim Birkett. How to do this? I wondered. There are three columns of Birketts in the Cumbrian 'phone book, including half a column of J. Birketts (I had forgotten that his initials were R. J.). I then had a brilliant idea. I'd just bought a copy of *Climber and Rambler,* the mountaineering periodical, and been startled by the photos of young men ascending what I would have considered to be the most improbable of places. The Editor, I thought, will know where everyone is and what they are doing — I'll ring him. I rang Walt Unsworth one morning in October. 'I'm not sure of Jim's address, but why not ring his son,' answered Walt 'he's a regular contributor to the magazine? His name is Bill Birkett — he'll tell you how to get in touch.' Which was precisely how things did turn out and I met Jim again at Bill's home in Kendal a few weeks later . . .

In the meantime Bill had contacted me again. 'I'm doing a book on a hundred years of climbing in the Lake District,' he said, 'I would like you to be in it. Could I come along and interview you?'

I was quite pleased to co-operate and equally curious about what he had in mind and how he intended to handle his theme.

At the end of the interview he said, 'Do you fancy a day on the fells?' I said, 'Yes, I certainly would!' The day on the hills turned out to be many days and they led to many exciting moments.

Top grade climbing in the Lake District (and, one supposes, anywhere else in Britain) is a very specialised activity, with its leading practitioners highly conversant with equipment, technique, standards, ethics and particularly, the competition. I suppose it has always been like this; I was certainly very curious about it in its 1980's form. If I had searched every crag in Lakeland, I doubt if I could have found anyone who would have been more switched-on to my thinking and who would have led me so carefully and knowledgeably through the overhangs and impasses associated with modern climbing than Bill Birkett. A well built lad of about thirty he was superbly fit (despite, when I first met him, the broken wrist he sported) and his loyalty to his native heath was unquestionable. He knew the fells and crags as well as anyone I'd ever met. We rapidly established a rapport . . .

With the exception of the last two years or so of my life in Australia I had virtually cut myself off from the development of rock-climbing as an activity. The methods of 1952 were still for all practical purposes the same methods that I was using twenty-five years later. The only difference being that I was using 'P.A.' friction boots instead of Woolworths' plimsolls — that is, I still used a hawser-laid nylon rope, a waist loop, piton hammer and pitons (and these very sparingly) and forged steel krabs. Modern developments such as kernmantel construction ropes, lightweight krabs, sit-harness, runners, wired-stoppers, tapes, sticht plates were still part of my future.

There was, therefore, this huge gap in my awareness of the development of climbing. True, Frank Davies had filled me in, during my visit in 1967, but I had not really followed up the lead he gave me.

With Bill Birkett, I began to discover things very rapidly.

I had returned to England, content, in my own mind, in the belief that what I wanted to climb were some of the old classic easier climbs — climbs that we used to regard as the middle of the road; Diffs and V. Diffs, I felt, would figure largely amongst these, whilst possibly, on a good day, in the bright sunshine, I might climb a Mild Severe. This grade I recalled, was the standard aimed for by the bulk of climbers in the late 'forties. Indeed, by comparison, the numbers who led anything harder were few. It would be fair to say that in the forties I virtually knew, personally, or by repute, every regular climber in the Lakes, at that time, who led at VS standard!

My re-education began early in January 1981. After a week of walking with my old friend Brian and his wife June Dodson, Etsu and Emma, I was given a conducted tour by Bill of some of the modern grounds — first my old stamping ground in Langstrath, Eagle Crag, and then White Ghyll, Dove Crag, Raven Crag, and several more. Bill pointed out the lines, discussed the difficulty, gave me some of the history.

On the last day of January, Bill, Ken Forsythe and I went to Raven Crag in Langdale and did four climbs. I couldn't remember what they were, but I seemed to get up them satisfactorily enough.

The next day we went to Shepherd's Crag. Amongst other things we did Brown Crag Wall at Hard Severe, the Direct ascent of Brown Slabs Crack, which is given as VS, and Eve which is similarly rated.

'What happened to the Mild Severes in hot sunshine?' I queried. 'It's all in the mind,' answered Bill, 'You'll be doing Hard VS before the end of the year.' As it happened I did Hard VS exactly six weeks later. I felt at the time it was outside my league — although I managed to get up. It was thought to be a new climb on Yew Crag Knotts in Honister Pass, about one hundred and thirty feet high, quite steep, and graded by Bill and Ken as HVS. They called it Eternal Spring.

From then my mountain activities in 1981 took off. I kept a rough diary of events and found by the end of the year that I had had seventy-eight days on the mountains — walking, climbing, skiing, skating. We'd had a superb week in Skye in June where Brian Dodson and I met our old mutual friend A. C. ('Ginger') Cain and Derek Price. The four of us had one of those unforgettable days on Sron na Ciche in sunshine (and if not dry rock, at least much of the water was avoidable) when amongst other things we did Cioch West and the Arrow Route on the Cioch Slab. My photo of the two parties strung out on Cioch Slab reminds me of Collins Street, Melbourne, at 5 p.m. — all heads in line, pointed in the same direction.

Throughout the year Etsu and Emma had been involved in numerous mountain trips. Little Emma, whilst still in her fifth year, had been to the top of Skiddaw, Grisedale Pike, Hopegill Head, High Street, Crinkle Crags, and many lesser peaks.

On Remembrance Day 1981 she and I walked to the top of Gable. We didn't travel very quickly and the crowds were heading back down Green Gable as we approached its top. When we arrived at the tablet on the Gable summit we were almost alone. We put on warm clothes and anoraks and Emma got into my rucksack and cuddled up to me to shelter from the wind. I tried to explain to her what the memorial plaque meant and we ate our sandwiches and drank our tea which chilled almost as it hit the plastic cup. I felt very close to this mite on the now lonely summit. We had the world, momentarily, to ourselves.

Etsu's mountain year had not been without interest either!

Brian and June Dodson had given us a copy of *The Big Walks* by Gilbert and Wilson, in which Tom Price had written the chapter on *Shap to Ravenglass*.

Early in the year we were all sitting in front of the fire at Melbecks partaking of an excellent malt when Tom said 'You wouldn't think from reading the article that I haven't done the walk in one day; not, mind you,' he hastened to add, 'that there is any necessity to do so. It can be split into any number of segments . . .' But he was too late; the seeds had been sown. We wouldn't let him forget it.

The attempt was fixed for the Second of May. The participants were to be Tom and his long-legged son, Trevor, Etsu and Matthew Harvey in the walking party with Mike Harvey and his other son,

Ben, in the back up team. Brian, June and I were to concentrate on picking up and delivering cars and generally acting as a cheer squad with bags of advice, hope and enthusiasm.

The walking party left their car near Shap at 3.15 a.m. on the chosen day. The weather, the day before, had, as it happened, not been good and indeed, on the day after, it was extremely wet and raw. Yet on the day itself it was perfect for walking — sunny but cool; not much wind; high clouds.

The walk went through Keld, up Swindale across the Old Corpse Road to the head of Mardale, where Mike Harvey met the party for a pre-breakfast snack at 6 a.m. From Mardale Head they ascended onto Riggindale Crag, to the north of Blea Water, and then up the ridge onto High Street at 2,663 feet. From High Street the track skirted the Knott and made direct for Angle Tarn, a mile beyond which it dropped down sharply to Patterdale.

They had expected to be at this point at 10 a.m. but were, in fact, well before this time. Nevertheless, Mike was there and breakfast was served near the village. The walk up Grisedale climbed some twelve hundred feet to Grisedale Tarn before crossing the col between Seat Sandal and Dollywaggon Pike from where it fell a thousand feet fairly steeply to Dunmail Raise.

At Dunmail the walking party were making excellent time, being now almost an hour in front of their schedule. Mike was there with lunch. We, the cheer squad, arrived at 12.30 p.m. — too late to talk to the walkers. We could see them high up on Steel Fell, following the fenceline directly to the summit. To the consternation of passing traffic we gave the walkers a blast on our horn and exchanged vigorous hand-wavings when they noticed us.

We, and they, knew that they were now on the longest section of the walk. We had estimated a five-hour walk from Dunmail Raise to Brotherilkeld in Eskdale. They reached the northern spur of Steel Fell at sixteen hundred feet, then skirted around the top end of Far Easedale to reach High Raise at 2,500 feet. From here the boggy marshlands around Stake Pass were traversed to Angle Tarn above Rossett Gill, then up to Ore Gap. They had walked twenty-seven miles and from here on it was all downhill — the entire fifteen miles of it. We met them five miles later at Brotherilkeld, where the track down Ling Cove Beck and Upper Eskdale meets the Hardknott Pass below the Roman Fort.

This point, we had felt, would be the occasion for champagne. My pride knew no limits; I kept telling other walkers who passed our group about what the Long Walkers had achieved. The majority didn't know what I was talking about; the rest couldn't care less! They all, I think, nominated me a 'nut case'.

The ten mile walk from Brotherilkeld to Ravenglass lay mainly along the road. We tried half-heartedly to talk them into riding the remainder. We were laughed to scorn.

Brian, June and I drove away down the valley and had a bar meal at a convenient pub.

Darkness set in as we drove into Ravenglass and the tide had already turned.

At 10.15 p.m. we drove back out of the village and in a mile or so we saw the walkers swinging briskly along. When they spotted us they broke into a trot. They jogged the last mile to the sea — straight into the gently rising tide; they arrived at 10.30 p.m. It had taken them just over nineteen hours, including meal stops; they had covered forty-two miles and ascended (and descended) eight thousand feet.

Two days later Etsu, Emma, June, Brian and I were in Mardale again. We walked up onto High Street to where Etsu thought she had left her favourite hat. And sure enough it was there.!

16

'C.B.'

If pushed into a corner and compelled to answer the question 'Which is the greatest climb in the Lake District?' the answer from the majority of those who have climbed it would, I'm pretty certain, be 'C.B.' — the great Central Buttress of Scafell.

There are scores of climbs which are harder; there are many which are as steep — even steeper, there are a number of good climbs with fine situations; there are some which are equally unique in line; there is a goodly list of fine long climbs; there are a few which are steeped in historical aura. But C.B. combines all of these — size, steepness, character, quality of climbing, difficulty and atmosphere in a way which no other climb that I have seen, or ascended in the Lake District, seems quite to have done. There are plenty of young 'hard' men who agree with me on this!

Central Buttress was climbed in April 1914 by S. W. Herford, G. S. Sansom and C. F. Holland, (with assistance from H. B. Gibson and D. G. Murray). It was the climax, as Holland wrote in the Historical Section of the 1936 Fell and Rock Climbing Club guide to Scafell, 'to what was up to that time incomparably the most brilliant example of intensive rock-climbing ever seen on British climbing grounds . . .'

The ascent, which was made after concentrated planning and complex prospecting, was Herford's farewell contribution to British climbing — he was killed less than two years later in France.

There can be few climbers who generated affection, loyalty and respect as Herford did. And there are several men who have believed or, for that matter, still believe, that the spirit of Herford stalks the fells. G. R. Speaker was one of them — before his death on the Napes in 1942 he told me that one day, sitting alone at the top of Central Buttress, a figure loomed through the mist from the direction of the finish of the climb and walked towards him. They did not speak.

Speaker was utterly convinced it was the spirit of Herford. Holland, also, held similar beliefs.

The great Central Buttress of Scafell is the huge, flat, steep, wedge-shaped cliff occupying the dominating position in the middle of the magnificent northern rampart of Scafell. To its right is Pisgah Buttress and further right again, the superb Scafell Pinnacle. To the left of C.B. the wall gradually diminishes in height until it reaches its lowest point at Mickledore ridge — the col that connects Scafell and Scafell Pike.

The climb begins at a corner some twenty yards to the left of the deep cleft of Moss Ghyll, the central break in the cliff. In roughly one hundred and fifty feet of steep climbing a fine ledge is reached below a most impressive wall. This is the Oval, and above the Oval the principal line of weakness on the wall is the spectacular Great Flake — a gigantic leaf of rock which tapers to a thin knife edge where it abuts against the smooth unrelenting wall above. The top of the flake is some seventy feet above the Oval and to gain its crest is the objective on which the greatest effort is concentrated. At this point, on the tip of the flake, one is poised in possibly the most magnificent situation in Lakeland climbing.

Above the flake the climbing is quite steep and still spectacular but the major difficulties are over. From bottom to top the entire climb is one glorious life-time experience.

My association with C.B. began in 1944. I was staying alone in Wasdale at the time, not doing very much and having no companion with whom to share the crags. In the pub at Wasdale Head I met a tall well-built chap, some ten years older than me (I estimated), and who, it transpired, was an L.A.C. in the R.A.F. Mountain Rescue Team. There being few other climbers around we fell into conversation and, as is usual enough, reference was made to this climb and that — and it gradually began to sink into my brain that here was a man who had had a quite considerable experience.

He knew Scotland very well, had climbed extensively in Wales, where he had systematically picked off the 'big' climbs — and it was apparent that he was now doing the same thing in the Lakes. His name, it transpired, was George Dwyer — his friends called him Scottie.

There are some climbers who in a long career make their reputations by the sheer weight of numbers and quality of their new climbs. There are a few who, like the French Romantic painter, Gericault, achieve an enormous reputation on the strength of only one or two major works (the name of Jim Haggas springs to mind with Hangover on Dove Crag and Gordian Knot on White Gill and, well before his time, that most transitory of climbers, F. G. Balcombe, who in June 1934 made the first ascents of Buttonhook, Engineer's Slabs, and the Direct Finish to Central Buttress on

Scafell. Did he really only come to Lakeland once? And if he did, wasn't it one hell of a successful trip?) And there are some fine climbers who seldom or never do any new climbs and, presumably as a consequence, whose names are rarely sung. Jack Carswell and Tom Price are two I immediately recall. Scottie Dwyer falls into the same category. He had, it appeared, a quiet ambition — to do every VS in the then guidebooks. So far as I could ascertain at the time, it was an ambition that was nearing complete realisation.

The one particular climb that he needed for his list was C.B., climbed without resorting to Combined Tactics on the great Flake Crack!

(As I write I have a letter from Scottie in front of me penned in 1945. He wrote: 'on May the twenty-fourth a group of us went round to Dovedale, and had two parties climbing that day. I led a pal up East Face Hangover, a damned good climb, which I think might possibly be a second ascent . . . I had a letter from my pal Dick Morsley, who lives in Capel Curig . . . Jim Birkett and Tom Hill (he says) are staying there this week. They were all round on Clogwyn du'r Arddu last Sunday and did Sunset Crack! I think Jim is out to do all the Cloggy climbs this holiday and if the weather holds for him he should manage to do them all. Sincerely, Scottie.' Thus was the grapevine kept alive) . . .

The C.B. trip was planned on the spot — for the next day. The strategy went something like this — I was to lead up to the chockstone jammed near the top of the Flake and thence get into the Slings. Scottie's mate, I. app (Yappy) Hughes, would be coming second. He would climb up and over me, and with my help would be able to gain the top of the Flake. Having got there I would then join him, thus the two of us would be in a position to help Scottie, who was lying at third on the rope, should he need it, on his attempt to climb the Flake clean. (In the event our assistance was totally unnecessary.)

At the time it was traditional that the Flake Crack be climbed by means of combined tactics at the chockstone. It is true that ascents had been made without such tactics — and in fact it became increasingly standard practice to do so.

(In August the following year I received a letter from Bruce Gilchrist, mutual friend of Arthur Dolphin and myself: 'I managed to lead the Flake Direct, but by jamming the last fifteen feet, not by laybacking it as Arthur advised. I had a talk with Jim Birkett, and he thought laybacking a bit dangerous — I should like to see it done in boots . . .' which, of course, was precisely what Jim had done it in!)

Our ascent started off without much trouble. I led up to the chockstone in the Flake and went through the laborious time-honoured (and wasting) process of threading a short piece of rope behind the chock to enable me to get into position to assist the second man up the last few feet of crack. This meant being trussed up like a turkey and dangling from the lower side of the chock whilst bracing one's legs against the wall. Theoretically, one was now in a firm, safe position to render to the second, who was now in the lead, whatever assistance one felt was necessary in order to get him up to the last few feet of the Flake. That at any rate was the theory! In actual fact what happened was that after performing the 'two legged cocoon' act one was really no higher than the top of the chockstone and whereas the chockstone was solid the cocoon was not; if the cocoon began to wilt about the legs then buckling of these members was imminent and the cocoon and its load would begin to pendulum under the chockstone. This was a possible eventuality that entertained my thinking long before Yappy reached me . . . And as it transpired my fears were totally justified. I was all right as long as he was only using my thigh as a foothold. Up onto my shoulder (he was a biggish sort of lad) and his weight began to tell. From there to the top of my head caused my centre of gravity to be not where it really ought to have been. Yappy moved up and came back again, my shoulders, head, arms, hands were being used with the greatest of friendliness. Another move and retreat to his pigeon perch — and yet again a third attempt . . . I was no Nelson! The buckling began; my neck felt as if it was about to break; a pendulum act was imminent. Scottie, down on the lush grass of the Oval, the ledge at the bottom of the Flake, was taking all this in with considerable interest and, at the first signs of my legs beginning to give, let out some fearsome cry in either obscene Welsh or canteen Gaelic (I never did ask!) and the effect was electrifying. With a miraculous heave Yappy hurled himself from the top of my head, found the upper edge of the Flake and was safely anchored in no time. My turn now came; I laboriously untangled myself from the mess of ropes which bound me to the rock, got into a standing position on the chockstone and laybacked my way to the top with very little reserve of strength to spare. Scottie came straight up without the slightest trouble — took one look at my jaded visage and offered to take the lead. I accepted with unconcealed joy. And I recall cursing to myself all the rest of the way up the climb about slings and combined tactics and tradition . . . That was the last I ever saw of Scottie. We corresponded for a little while and that too faded into memory. He was a fine climber, was Scottie, and he spoke excellent Welsh (or was it Gaelic?).

*   *   *

'Have you done C.B.?' asked Bill Birkett, early in 1981. 'Yes,' I answered and recounted the experience with Scottie Dwyer in 1944.

'D'you fancy doing it again?' was his next question. And my reply to that was totally truthful: 'I'd love to!' (a reply that had little or nothing to do with the related question of whether or not I would ever have the physical ability to climb the thing again!)

'I've never done it,' he said, which I found very surprising in a young man of such profound climbing experience. 'How about us giving it a go sometime?'

'I'll never get up the bloody thing,' was my shocked reply.

''Course you will — it's all in the mind! Within twelve months you'll be doing Hard VS.'

'Bull shit!' was the best I could do.

Summer, I thought on that cold February morning, is a long way away. The crunch will never come . . .

I didn't know Bill then as I do now — but I was soon to find out that when he said something he meant it!

Summer did come — not much of a one, mark you, but the calendar indicated that it was around somewhere, and the question was raised again. And summer slid by.

But I'd got the message and went into training. The week in Skye had been an excellent introduction to long days on the hills and distant walks to tall crags, but my arms, I felt, did not perform as well as they ought to in a potential candidate for C.B. So I rigged up a weight training system — consisting of two buckets of bricks suspended from ropes which ran over pulleys attached to one of the beams in our small barn. I went into the barn meticulously — to my small daughter's intense interest — and lugged and tugged at those two buckets in a variety of postures, trying my best between whiles to answer her question 'What are you doing, Daddy?' At the end of two weeks my right shoulder was beginning to pain slightly, after the third week I couldn't lift my arm above my head without a stab of pain in the deltoid. I abandoned the bricks.

We had fixed the second weekend in September for the assault on C.B.

Ronnie Faux was brought in as the third member of the team. Ronnie was a journalist with *The Times;* he had done much rock climbing and had even been on an Everest expedition.

Ronnie and I arrived at Wasdale Head on the Friday night around 11 p.m.; Bill was already there. We pitched our tent and solemnly avoided the cans of booze. Were we not in training? we asked of each other. We were! And as we crawled into our respective sleeping bags we tried to poo-pooh and belittle the 'pit-pat' of rain on the fly sheet.

Next morning the sun shone fairly brightly — almost everywhere! Everywhere, that is, except on the top of Scafell. Gable gleamed in the sun; Scafell Pike was clear — but Scafell, like some ancient patriarch in mourning, sat there shrouded in cloud and mystery.

But not to worry, we told each other. The rocks might be a bit damp, we said, so we'll climb in socks . . . Morale, it was obvious, was high. If only I could have lifted my right arm half as high . . .

And off we set on the long haul up to Hollow Stones, that superb combe nestling between Lingmell, Scafell Pike and the great north face of Scafell.

I took my time up the rough slog of a track known as Brown Tongue. There was no need to burst a gasket, I told myself, I would need all my energy for the Flake Crack.

From below, on Brown Tongue, Hollow Stones and the north face of Scafell are hidden. The great bulk of Shamrock, the large, rather scrappy looking buttress which protrudes from the western end of the Scafell cliff line, tends to blot out or soften the contours of the main face. One is lulled into thinking that things might not be as bad as fragile memory had suggested they would be.

I climbed up to Hollow Stones on my own. The others, far in front of me, were deep in discussion on some aspect of Environmental Preservation, I was to discover when I finally caught up to them.

As I entered Hollow Stones my eye and brain began to take in the awesome sight. It was my first visit in thirty years. Nothing had changed. Memories flooded back.

The whole vast face of Scafell crag lay before me — Central Buttress, Pisgah Buttress, the Pinnacle Face and the rocks across Deep Ghyll reared up into the dense grey mists of Scafell's cloud cap. How high were they? Did it matter? They could have been thousands of feet high. They seemed to soar for ever.

I could just define the Flake Crack on C.B., and the lower reaches of Moss Ghyll and Steep Ghyll. The rocks were black.

Slashing upwards into the mist, lighter in colour than anything else, Botterill's Slab seemed utterly holdless. And then I noticed that interspersed with the dull shades of the rocks were vast glistening black patches — dropping out of the mist like veils of tears. And I realised the rocks were weeping from end to end.

I joined the others on Rake's Progress, the footpath that skirts beneath this enormous face.

Morale, I was horrified to discover, was still high!

'Socks over P.A.'s,' said Bill. I sat down on my rucksack and ate a Mars bar.

'I'll pop along and have a look at the start,' he continued, '. . . See what it's like!'

From my rucksack seat I looked across at Scafell Pike and Pikes Crag, leaning amiably into the sun; and beneath the cloud roof, away in the distance, I could see Gable basking in the sunshine. The whole of Wasdale, with the exception of Scafell, lay blinking in the bright, warm, dry air.

Bill was away ten minutes.

There was no need to ask him what he thought. I could see the answer on his face. 'Bloody horrendous. . .' he muttered, 'The whole face is as greasy as hell. . . I think we'll have to abandon it for today.'

The judgement lifted dead weights off my morale and it too soared.

'So where to?' I queried. And then, more hopefully, 'Pikes Crag — at least it's handy?'

This suggestion was treated with total disdain.

'What about Kern Knotts — look at the sun over there!' someone said.

If it couldn't be Pikes Crag there's nothing I would like better, I thought, than Kern Knotts. And we collected up our bits and pieces and headed along Rake's Progress to Mickledore — the ridge between Scafell and Scafell Pike — every now and then throwing an upward glance into the vast greyness above us.

Once on Mickledore the clouds lifted and began to unfold slowly off Scafell Crag. Eventually the whole face lay bare and glistening. We sat a while and shared our time between the tremendous array of rocks on either side of the narrow ridge.

But if we were going to Kern Knotts we'd better be moving, we eventually agreed. And off we went, first on to the top of Scafell Pike, then down the Corridor Route to Sty Head Pass and across it to the beautiful, rough, clean, dry little outcrops of Kern Knotts where we disported ourselves for hours getting back to Wasdale Head far too late for a dinner we were supposed to attend . . .

The early summer of 1982 was like that of 1940 — one that will be remembered. For weeks we had no rain to speak of and better still, for me, I had been able to do some reasonable climbing and get into something vaguely approaching form.

Bill and I once more geared up for Wasdale — for Saturday May the twenty-second to be precise. On the Friday night there was a slight shower of rain — the first in weeks.

On Saturday morning there were a few mild showers and a low cloud ceiling. With enthusiasm running high, and a wild imagination, I impressed it upon myself that the day was 'picking up'. There was even a brightness out over West Cumbria which meant that the weather was improving in that direction. I left home at 7.30 in the morning.

By the time I'd got to Rowrah the weather showed far fewer signs of getting better; by Cleator it was 'spitting' with rain; by Egremont the rain was thundering down. The farmers were delighted. I got soaked running to a 'phone box. The C.B. trip was off again . . . Again the weather improved and I got in some more good climbing. By early June I was climbing upwards of four days a week and ignoring my experiences with the buckets of bricks, I spent two lunch-times each week in the College gymnasium.

By June there was every sign that the fine weather spell was drawing to a close — hot weather interspersed with thunderstorms being the most common forecast.

Bill and I made a date for another Saturday — three weeks after the second attempt.

We met at Wasdale Head soon after nine in the morning. Pete Moffat and his family were at Brackenclose.

'Where are you going?' they asked. 'Scafell,' we replied, 'what about you?' 'Somewhere in the sun' was what they wanted. I looked up at Scafell. Once more the cloud cap sat low on the mountain's brow; once more Gable danced in the sun. 'I don't think you'll get any sun on Scafell,' said Pete. I grunted ruefully, sorely conscious that this could well be a repeat of last September and that we too, later in the day, could be bent upon the same quest as they.

Again we took our time on the walk up onto Hollow Stones. We picked up rocks on the scree and examined them for minerals, finding garnets and serpentine aplenty. A meadow pipit flew out from under our feet at one point and we found its beautiful little nest and five purply-brown eggs nestling under a bilberry tuft alongside a sheltering boulder.

We photographed the nest and then hid it again whilst the distressed owner flitted and called between nearby stones.

And above us the rocks reared up once more into the mist. Suddenly a break occurred. With incredible sharpness the Pinnacle stood outlined against a backcloth of golden mist — then was lost again before I could dig out my camera.

On Rake's Progress we put on all the surplus clothing we had carried up. Dripping with sweat a short while before as, stripped to the waist, we flogged up through the humid atmosphere on Brown Tongue, we now began to feel the cool wind that occasionally swirled the skeins of mist across the wall above us.

Suddenly, with theatrical precision the whole of the north crag was swept clear of cloud and we met our challenge eye to eye, so to speak! There were two parties on the rocks above us — one on Moss Ghyll Grooves and one on Pisgah Buttress. There was no queue for Central Buttress off to our left.

We collected our gear — two nine-millimetre ropes and a considerable assortment of wire stoppers, runners, tapes and krabs — modern protective equipment beyond the dreams of the pioneers. 'D'you think Herford would approve?' Bill's eyes twinkled as he shook a harness full of stoppers. 'He'll be spinning in his grave like a bloody top,' I offered in answer.

At the foot of the first steep pitch I tied on to a belay and Bill set off. Almost immediately he swore. 'What's it like?' I queried, knowing perfectly well what the answer was. 'Greasy as hell,' he replied; I tightened up the slack a little on my Sticht-plate. When my turn came and my foot slid sharply off the second foothold above the deck I thought to myself 'We're going to have some fun here.' I began to work out in my mind the possible lines of evacuation, assuming we got to the Oval, the big ledge below the Flake Crack, only to find further progress too much for us on the day.

The easy slabs, so called in the guidebooks, proved to be particularly trying. Possibly because they were at an easier angle than anything else on the climb they carried more lichen and the footholds, although larger, felt as if they had been buttered. We ought to have been in socks, but we wanted to keep our feet dry and warm for events that might have to follow. 'It can't be as greasy as this higher up,' I said to myself. 'It's too flaming steep above the Oval.' As it happened I was right — speaking relatively!

We had now reached the most serious part of the climb — the magnificent Flake Crack pitch. The top of the Flake Crack, where most of the action is concentrated is two hundred feet above the start of the climb. Below the latter the eye plunges down over another hundred feet or so of steep vegetated rock onto the screes in Hollow Stones. The walls all around the Flake — to the right and to the left and above, particularly above — are smooth and flat and very, very steep. Near the top of the Flake, jutting out of the Crack some eight feet or so below the horizontal upper edge of the great flake, is a precariously wedged block. This block, on a day like ours, is a very lonely place.

After drying his P.A.'s Bill launched onto the Crack. I was well belayed onto a jammed stone and sat down on a large flat rock keeping my feet out of the mud on the ledge as far as I could.

Bill worked carefully up to the chockstone fifty feet above my head and the mists closed in on him. He was there for some little time.

The wind from Mickledore Ridge strengthened and the mist wreaths played games across the face. In one instant Bill would be out of sight, safely encased in a cottonwool world; in the next the tendrils would race upwards stripping the world bare — up to blue sky and a fantastic downward heart-stopping plunge of space. Added to this was the strange effect of the mist on the rock. The instant that the vapour folds closed in the rock felt damp and cold and distinctly less comforting. When the winds blew them away the rock immediately felt drier and handleable — to the accompaniment of a groin-tickling view beneath one's feet.

Bill made some preliminary investigations of the ferocious upper crack, then after a few moments he set off again. He quickly reached — as the guidebook puts it — the 'bold layback' position. A couple of moves upwards, with the good hold in the crack serving him well, and then he was up — a beautiful piece of climbing in circumstances which were far from ideal.

I could feel Bill's elation through the double ropes we were using. Now it was my turn to advance! Blow-by-blow instructions were called down to me — although I had seen exactly what he'd done.

I moved off up the crack, head stuffed full of good advice.

Yes! The crack was a bit disconcerting half way up. The last thing in the world I wanted was to scrabble up to the chockstone and into a layback with wet friction boots on my feet. Another twenty feet or so and I had reached the chockstone. The view below was breathtaking.

If I wanted the rocks to feel dry I got the view; if I didn't want the view, but the security of the cotton wool clouds, I got damp hands! Not that I had much choice in the matter — Hobson's or otherwise!

I made my first essay onto the chockstone. What a situation! Firstly a half-hearted attempt to go for it; then I returned to the security of the chock, hooked by a loop over its top edge whilst I rested my arms. Refreshed, I took the loop off the chock and moved up again. As I eased up I felt something pulling me back down. My heart did a back-flip until I saw what it was. The yellow rope was caught under a sharp undercut of rock and was impeding my ascent. I eased back down again and got the rope out from under the edge, then set off again, left hand searching eagerly for Bill's good hold in the crack. I couldn't find it.

And just as I was easing up into the layback position the right hand, in particular, feeling distinctly greasy, I felt myself being pulled down again. I looked down and swore loudly. Down on the chockstone amongst the welter of frayed ends and loops and coils Bill had hung a krab which I had not noticed into one of these ancient relics and fed the rope through it. The ancient sling might not have done much for him had he come off — neither was it doing much for my ascent of the top of the crack. I told him what had happened and went back down again — and recovered the offending krab.

Remarkably in all these antics my arm strength seemed to be holding out quite well. Of course, with a good strong lad above me and lashed onto two ropes that were clearly in good condition there was little harm, really, that could befall me. As Bill had said in the same place some little time before — 'the weakest muscle is in the head!'

Now, assured that all our gear had been removed from the chockstone, I made my fourth attempt on the last elusive eight feet of the Crack. I got into the layback position above the chock . . . Now for the good handhold . . . What good handhold? . . . (I went higher) . . . There's no bloody handhold here. There's just the edge of the crack and it doesn't feel at all dry and comforting.

I eased up again, still searching for that mystery hold. The loop that Bill had hung from the top of the Flake dangled invitingly near me. I could just see Bill. He knew what I was thinking. 'Don't you dare,' he yelled, 'you'll never forgive yourself!' I turned away from the invitation and eased further up the layback. Above I could see the top edge of the Flake. I let go with my left hand, hung momentarily onto a greasy right handhold and stretched up on the outer face of the rock. Nothing much in the way of foothold; right handhold definitely suspect; a glittering prize nearly within reach. A couple of inches more and the fingers of my left hand curled over the superb horizontal edge of the top of the Flake. Bill whooped with delight. My own, rather naive comment was, 'I've climbed it.' In a few seconds both my hands were on the rough comforting edge. I swung out onto the front of the Flake, worked left for a couple of feet, then heaved my right leg up and over the sharp edge into total, if rather painful, security.

The pair of us laughed like kookaburras. Bill was perched like a resting racing-pigeon on the top edge of the Flake some fifteen feet away from me, lashed onto an enormous thin leaf of rock. I sat on the edge, right leg jammed behind the Flake, left foot held by the friction of the rough clean rock on its outer face. Hundreds of feet below us Hollow Stones lay in the sun. Above us, our shoulders resting against it, the great flat wall continued to rear in relentless steepness, it seemed. It was the kind of moment that will live in a climber's memory as long as life.

I worked across the sharp edge of the crack, largely by a semi hand traverse, until I reached Bill.

'What have you done with your hand,' he asked.

I looked down. I honestly hadn't noticed my right hand. The skin had been grazed off the knuckles, probably during my contretemps with the chockstone, and blood was dripping merrily therefrom. The fingers and palm of my right hand were, in fact, quite soaked in bright red fluid — which explained the greasy handholds at the top of the Flake Crack.

On Jeffcoat's Ledge we sat and ate lunch. By now the clouds had relented; the main difficulty had been overcome; our morale and good humour had risen noticeably . . .

The rest of the climb went, largely, on clean dry rock. The crack below V-ledge was slimy but the holds were good and protection adequate. The traverses both towards and away from V-ledge were a sheer delight, delicate movements in the most superb of situations, a vast space beneath one's feet and the heart singing at every step.

The final breathtaking traverse, from V-ledge across the most wonderful face, suddenly ends on the slabs at the top of Moss Ghyll Grooves. Here the handholds felt large and polished and the angle eased, by comparison, into a gentle stroll.

We both sensed the danger of relaxing too soon and it wasn't until we were actually wandering up onto the summit blocks that we decided to take off the ropes.

As we sat there coiling them, the mists came down again and I thought of those legends of the past. Does Herford's spirit wander around here? I thought. 'Do you think we'll see him?' I asked Bill.

The evening was drawing on.

'You know,' he confessed, 'I'd never bothered much about Central Buttress — mainly because I knew it was an old climb and, I suppose, mentally underrating it . . . It's made me change my mind. And what a piece of route finding! It's almost impossible to believe it was done in 1914 . . . If Herford had survived the War, what an effect he could have had on post War climbing . . .'

What else could I do but agree with him?

We got back to our gear at the foot of the face at ten minutes to seven — and shared a sandwich, the last of our chocolate and a cup of tea.

Above us, ageless in its brooding majesty, the great Central Buttress had played host to yet two more insignificant creatures who dared to take it on. It had tested us and, I would like to think, had not found us wanting so very much.

As we traced the route, up to the Oval, up the Flake, across to Jeffcoat's, the airy traverses past the poised spike on the wall above the Flake, then up to V-ledge to cross the final space walk onto M.G.G. and up to the finish, Bill said 'Magnificent!' Words had left me — all I could do was drink it in. 'Had we really been up *there*?' I thought to myself. 'Have I really joined the "C.B." Pensioners' Club — surely one of the most exclusive clubs in the world?'

In Hollow Stones we cast our eyes back for a final glance. 'If that's "Hard VS." — I'll stick to Extremes,' was Bill's last comment.

17

Return of the Native

Early April, 1982, ushered in a most significant event for me. It came
in the form of a letter written by one David Craig, whom I'd never
met, requesting my assistance in the preparation of an article or
articles which he was proposing to write about climbers of the late
thirties and forties. What made them tick? he wondered. How did
they approach things like first ascents? What was their attitude
towards equipment, the competition, and many other matters?
Could I and would I help him to find the answers? I wrote back and
said I would be delighted to participate in his project and suggested
that on a warm pleasant day I might even be prevailed upon to join
him on one or other of the easier of the fifty or so new climbs I had
made in the Lakes between 1939 and 1951. 'Marvellous,' he replied.

We met for the first time at Melbecks in mid April.

I had in mind to visit somewhere gentle and pleasing — on warm
rough rock — where no demands, other than on memory, would
disturb my complacency. Grey Crags, up in Birkness Combe or
Round How, on some nice V. Diffs, in the sun, would be ideal, I
thought. Yes, that would be very pleasant.

The weather at the time had just embarked on one of those
remarkable warm, dry spells that do occur in the Lakes from time to
time. The early summer of 1940 had been such — I remembered it
vividly. That was the time that Bert Beck, Gordon Connor and I had
started our 'Summer Siege at Buttermere' — and which had yielded
Eagle Front, Fifth Avenue, Far East Buttress, Border Buttress and
the Girdle Traverse of Eagle Crag, amongst other things. The
weather of the following year hadn't been quite so good but it had
still given us Dexter Wall, Suaviter and Fortiter and that, for us,
most mind blowing experience, the Y Gully.

Suaviter would be nice, I thought, for a day out with David. I had
done it recently with Tom Price and Brian Dodson. We hadn't found

it difficult, it offered us a good view of Eagle Crag. I could sit in the sun and regale David all day with our tales of exploration on that splendid crag. Yes! Suaviter would be ideal!

David arrived about 9.30 in the morning. It was a perfect day and he said so! He asked what I had in mind. 'Round How,' I answered, 'or Birkness Combe. Grey Crags would be delightful in this weather.' My complacency was disturbed just a trifle when he didn't bite at this splendid suggestion.

'Would Eagle Crag be dry?' he queried. God! He's not got one of those severes in mind like Piggott's Route or Easter Buttress or Half Nelson? I wondered. As it happened he hadn't!

When I expressed the opinion that I thought the crag would be quite dry, he rolled out slowly in his Scottish burr — 'Well, it's such nice weather; maybe we won't get a dry spell like this for a while; it seems a pity to waste it on something very easy — how do you think Eagle Front would go?' Oh, the low-down cunning of the man! I opened my mouth to say something. Words failed to emerge. 'We could do Eagle Front and then while the sun is on Grey Crag go across and do something over there — maybe Dexter Wall,' he continued.

'Bloody Hell,' I thought, 'I'd better stop this man. He's planning a total re-conquest of the whole Buttermere cycle! I'm not young anymore, all those things happened forty years ago; I've got arthritis . . .' To David I said, albeit very weakly, 'All right!'

From then on I was carried along in a euphoric haze.

When we reached the foot of Eagle Crag, we found the huge northern face as dry as I'd anticipated it to be. I led off on the first pitch. It was a gesture only — then David took over.

He was a man in his late forties — who had only taken to climbing about seven years before, despite a lifetime amongst the hills. He was about my height and two stones lighter and, above all, he was superbly fit. He led up Eagle Front effortlessly; I laboured on behind. It wasn't the hardest climb I had done during the last couple of years — Bill Birkett and I had certainly done harder, but to me it was more than a climb.

Memories flooded back on every pitch. The long run-out on the second pitch where I had been able to get only one good runner on over the entire ninety feet — and *that* above all difficulty — we now found lent itself to at least five jammed nuts and wired stoppers and a piton at the foot of the difficult bit on the Gangway. At the left-hand edge of the long green traverse, before making the ascent of the steep scoop onto the wonderfully exposed bracket, we hadn't, in 1940, been able to find a belay. I had solved the problem by having Bert tie onto a small loose block embedded in the grass and to sit on it! Modern gadgetry and an insitu piton gave us real belays. Up on the bracket, with that plunging view of three hundred feet to the floor of the Combe, I had knocked in an old nail, salvaged from the pit, to tie onto. Here there were now three substantial pitons. We tied on to them all, then, scratching about in the detritus of the crack, we found the remains of two more.

'Which one of them is the nail?' David asked.

'Neither,' I answered, 'it was square in cross-section!' He rummaged more. To the left of them, to his infinite delight, he found another metal object — the remains of a small metal peg, rusted round the edges but its core revealing a perfectly square cross-section. 'What about *that*, then?' he grinned triumphantly. I had to admit it *could* be the remains of the nail. It certainly was square and it most definitely wasn't very thick. After all we hadn't intended to bequeath it to posterity . . . I am told the nail had still been there (not much good — but then it never was!) sixteen years after we put it in.

From the bracket a long airy traverse right, across the mossy slab, followed by its ascent and then the magnificent final crack and we were on the small grassy 'belvedere' at the top of the climb. I recalled vividly how Bert and I had sat together in 1940 on this tiny perch overlooking the entire climb; how we had found it difficult to say anything; how, rather self-consciously, we shook hands — maybe like Mummery and Knubel would have done in a similar situation.

On this occasion, forty-two years later, I felt exactly the same. It was an incredible personal experience. Never in my most free-flowing moments had I, in my latter years in Australia, imagined or even dared to believe that one day, again, I would climb Eagle Front. True, I hadn't led it and I hadn't climbed it terribly elegantly, nor was I in possession of that blind faith and youthful arrogance which, all those years ago, had got me up it — one of my first VS climbs! But, today, there was no denying the fact — I had, once more, climbed Eagle Front. This fact cannot mean as much to anyone as it means to me. Of course there are harder climbs, probably even steeper or longer or better climbs — but for me there is only one Eagle Front and it hasn't really got much to do with hardness, steepness or any of the other objective assessments. It is to do with a lad of twenty crawling out of a dirty hole in the ground, out of a monstrous soul-destroying existence to freedom and air and space, to grab life by the tail and to swing it round the head like a stone tied to the end of a rope.

Eagle Front was not the last time David and I climbed together. It was merely the beginning. The same day we crossed to Grey Crag and did Fortiter. It proved to be very much an anticlimax; yet I know it's a pleasant enough little climb.

A week later we went to Buckstone How and it was time to do Cleopatra (said by some to be the hardest of my new climbs though I have reservations about this opinion!) Then, week after week, often enough in perfect weather but occasionally in clouds and rain, we found ourselves in Buttermere, Newlands, Borrowdale, Ennerdale.

In the five-months period between mid April and mid September I spent fifty days climbing and did over eighty climbs. In the early weeks with David I repeated many of my old first ascents.

Besides Eagle Front and Cleopatra they included the Girdle Traverse of Miners' Crag, Jezebel, Eve, Sinister Grooves, Dale Head Pillar, Slabs West and Dexter Wall — all VS climbs and a number of less difficult items.

Elsewhere I was able to climb a large number of other routes on different crags — climbs which I had wanted to do for old times' sake — with Bill Birkett, Ronnie Faux and Chris Eilbeck; climbs like Central Buttress of Scafell, the Girdle Traverse of Pillar, North West and Gomorrah also on Pillar, Tophet Wall, Fools' Paradise and many more. I even, on one occasion, dressed up in nailed boots and with an ancient hemp rope tied round my waist, with two antique slings and two forty year old krabs, led Honister Wall. I had taken three wired stoppers with me, hidden in my jacket, and put the first one on fifteen feet from the ground. When it fell out as I moved up I threw the other ones down to David and told him to shove them in the rucksack. 'I'll do it "properly",' I said — and in fact the climb went quite comfortably in nails, and I began to wonder again, as I've wondered so much recently, whether or not we aren't missing out on something with the passing of nailed boots.

By July we seemed to be nearing the end of David's project. 'Is there anything else we've missed?' he asked me one day.

With my tongue jammed securely into my cheek I said 'We ought to do a gully! I used to like gullies.'

'I've never done one,' he mused. 'What do you suggest?'

Thinking that I could take the joke a stage further I answered 'Y Gully?' He had read about this climb as, in fact, he knew of most of the other climbs I'd done — he kept a very careful eye on the guidebook lists!

I expected him to throw up his hands in mock fear and steer me onto something reasonable, but instead he answered 'That's a thought!' and it was *I* who was wondering if we shouldn't just go for another gully which, without necessarily being mine, would give the flavour of the experience. He wasn't to be put off. He got me to tell him all about Y Gully in detail. The more I talked the more interested we both became.

Eventually, one day in late July, whilst his two sons were disporting themselves in bright, warm sunshine on some extreme on Green Crag, we, with Chris Culshaw, stood at the bottom of the Y Gully on the Haystacks. My reaction to it was immediate and totally familiar. From below it is black, rotten looking, slimy and altogether off-putting. As I'd been up before I went into the first lead and after seventy feet or so managed to get something, up the steep, rotten rock and grass, that resembled a belay. David followed and led past me to the bottom of the overhanging wall that bars progress half-way up the crag and two hundred feet above the scree. Water poured down the gully despite the dryness elsewhere. Chris came up to me, then took second place on the rope with me at the tail so that when I reached them at the foot of the barrier I could lead straight through.

The gully atmosphere began to close in on all of us. Above me I could hear Chris saying to David, 'There are salmon swimming past me!'

I joined them under the wall. It was a foul place. I tried going straight up; the overhang of the wall was a great deal more pronounced than it appeared to be from below. I went up the buttress to its right and got into exactly the same predicament as Bert recorded forty years previously.

Having made the bad move over sloping and loose rock I arrived on very steep damp hyacinth grass. In nails this would have been no problem, in P.A.'s ascending the vegetation was bordering on the ridiculous. There were no runners except a highly doubtful spike away to the right. I traversed across to it. By now nerve was beginning to wilt and 'Y Gully Atmosphere' was taking over.

I eventually got up another thirty feet to a huge block belay below an enormous overhanging wall. I had reached the stage of distrusting all rock and grass however secure it might have looked on less insecure crags. The gully bed was to our left. David led into it. Then I took over for the lower part of the final chimney — which, fortunately, is only in bad rock. David came up to me and ascended into the real problem — not only do opposing walls converge but the back wall of the chimney comes outwards. The rock was covered in green moss — wet green moss! Every foothold and handhold was suspect. A long, five-inch-thick vertical flake of rock seemed to be stuck to the right wall. Were it secure it would offer reasonable progress. Were it not secure it could come crashing down, complete with leader, onto Chris and me below.

David's feet skidded alarmingly as he inched upwards above my head. Near the top he got hold of a large outward-leaning leaf — the whole assembly absurdly shaky — and gingerly worked his way through the gap at the top of the chimney.

Chris and I wasted as little time as possible following him — we both wanted to get to hell out of the place as soon as we could. I had taken the precaution of pulling my socks over my P.A.'s and felt relative security. I came up last, thankful once again that the whole crazy structure of Y Gully had once more held together long enough to let us get up.

Y Gully is rarely climbed in summer. In winter, in the right conditions of snow and ice, it will, I'm sure, make a superb climb. At

least there won't be any loose rock, it will all be bound together with
ice, and the frozen hyacinth grass is not as likely to prove as much of a
difficulty to crampons as it does to P.A.'s.

I have now done Y Gully twice in summer conditions. I'm inclined
to hazard a guess that I am the only person ever to have done so; I
mean, after all, there *are* more sensible ways of spending a warm dry
sunny afternoon. I doubt very much if I shall do Y Gully again. One
would have to be crazy . . . but then?

At the end of July David went to the Dolomites and we didn't meet
again until September.

There was one particular crag we hadn't yet visited together —
Eagle Crag in Borrowdale. The dry summer had gone but a few clear
days persuaded us that the crag could be dry. It is a delightful walk
up Stonethwaite Beck past lovely rock pools between deeply gouged
walls to the junction of Langstrath Beck and Greenup Ghyll. Here,
crossing onto the spur that comes down between the latter, we
ascended the fellside and traversed across to the south-east passing
under the steep imposing face of Eagle Crag.

Bert Beck's appreciation of Borrowdale's Eagle Crag makes a
great deal of sense: 'The crag may be the more difficult to climb but
the approach to it is the most dangerous!'

Very steep grass and heather intermixed with loose blocks of rock
and short awkward walls guard the base of the cliff. One
well-cleaned rock ramp near the left hand end of the approach rocks
gives the most convenient access to the climbs. We came in from the
right!

For me, it was just one of those days — it may have been an
incipient cold, it may have been staleness, or it may just have been
the sheer dramatic quality of the cliff line. Whatever it was I rapidly
found myself inviting David to do the leading for the day. Sid Clark
(a fine climber and native of my own birthplace) in his Borrowdale
guidebook describes Falconer's Crack as 'a classic of the crag'. It was
the first climb ever made on the main face of the crag — we were
certain it would give us a good day. We were quickly at grips with the
main problems — a steep crack and an awkward groove led up to the
remains of a peregrine's nest — now, by the look of it, long disused.

Trouble really begins at this point — an awkward traverse across
the wall on the left leads eventually to steep ribs which are climbed
with some difficulty to a pleasant ledge. Above the ledge the rough
rock continues for another seventy feet or so to the top of the crag.

Whatever my jinx was on the day, I felt a very strong urge to
handle my descent from the top of the climb with great care and, as a
consequence, reached the bottom of the crag to where our gear had
been left without undue incident.

Putting on the shoes (joggers!) in which I had walked up to the
climb I set off back down the mountain, David following a few feet

behind. After descending through all the steep rubbish and grass at the bottom of the cliff we eventually reached the open fellside and at this point I relaxed. It was then that it happened! Everything about this side of Eagle Crag is steep — the rock of the cliff itself, the heather and rocks at the bottom of it and the grass and boulders underneath these.

I was descending the wet grass clear of all the rough ground, so I thought, chatting away to David, when suddenly both feet shot from underneath me and I slid over a rocky five-foot outcrop. Bouncing on the ledge underneath, I began to somersault down the hillside between boulders and vegetation. Rocks flashed by my line of vision as I performed my pirouettes. I tried grabbing things as I passed them but to no avail. After a spectacular plunge of some thirty feet I came to a stop over another short drop. My right thigh, knee and foot were in great pain — but I could bend my leg, which indicated, I seemed to recall, no broken bones there. The foot was another matter!

It took me a long time to hobble back to the car — but eventually, I got to it, home and to bed. Gradually my upper leg took on the colours of royalty and the dimensions of a rugby ball.

But there was nothing broken. I had merely mobilised the joint of my big toe which had been partially calcified for donkeys' years due to some arthritic condition. The poor old joint didn't like what I'd done to it and was letting me know about the fact. For the next few days I could barely walk — and even when I was able to get out onto the cliffs again I found it extremely painful to use the inside edge of the right foot and concentrated on outside edging, which, most of the time, was quite adequate for my needs although the technique I developed was probably more appropriate to pigeons . . .

A short time before the event referred to above, an article had appeared in the *Times*, written by Ronnie Faux. It was about my return to my native heath — with a few jewels of wisdom thrown in from my altitude of years. Some enthusiastic sub-Editor had given it the title *Never Fall Off, The Old Tiger's Rule*. I wondered if *that* was the jinx! It was true I hadn't fallen off the rock; I'd done worse — I'd fallen off the grass!

18

Changing Winds

There is a delusion amongst those who lay claim to advancing years (as there is with those who invent climbing history) that what they have to say is of interest/importance/relevance to the younger fraternity whose times of retrospectivity lie in the future. It is a danger that has flitted through the pages of climbing journals and magazines for decades.

In succumbing to the temptation to be counted amongst them I find justification in the fact that when I left for Australia in 1952 I left climbing in Britain at a significant period of its development. It was poised at (although this was not at the time recognised as such) the brink of a fantastic upsurge in standards . . .

When I returned, nearly thirty years later all those wonderful things — the developments of Brown, Whillans, Rock and Ice, Ross, Austin, Les Brown, Geoff Oliver, Drasdo, Soper and Livesey were history.

I walked out of the Lake District's front door, so to speak, in the time of Dolphin and Jim Birkett and sneaked back in through the rear entrance in the era of Whillance, Lamb, Pete Botterill, Cleasby and Bill Birkett and watched from a distance. It has been a marvellous experience — perhaps Lazarus or Rip Van Winkle felt the same!

After the Australian interlude it was inevitable that I would find the changing wind to have wreaked havoc on old orders and values.

At the turn of the century, for example, there was little doubt in anyone's mind that the function of the climbing centres, such as they were in Britain, was to provide the mountaineer with a training ground in which he could keep himself fit for the annual trip to the Alps.

By 1920 climbers like Kelly had changed that attitude — although rock climbing was still regarded as just one facet of mountaineering.

Twenty years later at the time when Overhanging Bastion, Eagle Front and Gordian Knot were climbed there was little doubt that rock-climbing was a separate entity although it was firmly believed that *real* climbing was only done on the major crags in the main areas of activity. These, of course, were seen as the Lakes, North Wales and Scotland with the implication that Scotland meant Glencoe, Ben Nevis and Skye.

On the whole we each climbed very much in our own mountain cells, and although there were a number of climbers, like A. B. Hargreaves, who lived in the Lakes yet did a great deal of exploration in North Wales, it is true to say that generally the Welsh or Scottish based climbers stuck to their crags and the Lakes-based to theirs, even though there were plenty of outstanding examples of a breakdown in this parochial approach — namely A. T. Hargreaves' Rubicon Wall on Nevis and Kirkus' Mickledore Grooves on Scafell East Buttress.

Even within our cells a substructure existed. The *real* climbing was to be had on the *big* classic crags — Scafell, the Napes, Gimmer, Pillar Rock and Dow Crag, so far as the Lakes were concerned.

Low lying, easily reached crags were tolerated because they either provided a training ground for beginners, or because they were on the track to the main crag (like Middlefell Buttress on the way to Gimmer) or (and possibly the greatest damnation of them all) because they were suitable for an 'off-day'. Thus were Raven Crag in Langdale, Castle Rock and Black Crag in Borrowdale regarded.

I recall quite clearly, even feeling mildly apologetic about, the 'discovering' of Buckstone How and Eagle Crag in Borrowdale and that they were not quite in the same league as the big crags, although this illusion was dispelled in my mind after we'd climbed Cleopatra on Buckstone How and I'm quite certain that Eagle Crag in Borrowdale was not regarded as a second class crag after Ross and Lockey climbed Post Mortem in 1956; but this was ten years after Falconer's Crack.

In addition to the Lakes, North Wales and Scotland there were some areas where 'outcrop' climbing was done. These were seen as very important training grounds for the big crags. Most climbers (except possibly a few people who couldn't afford the money or time to get to the Lakes or Wales) saw the outcrops as serving no other real function than to provide a training back-up to the bigger centres — and, of course, many of the climbers who went on to pick the plums from the big crags in the thirties and forties *were* gritstone-trained. Laddow, Stanage, Almscliff, Ilkley, the Roches and Helsby were the principal areas from which they came. There was little limestone climbing done and sea cliff climbing seemed to be limited in general to the Bosigran area in Cornwall. It was almost heresy to entertain the idea that anyone should *prefer* these crags to the Lakes or Welsh rocks. I doubt if anyone did! Forty years later, of course, all that has changed. Hard climbers travel all over Britain to find dry rock and the sun; they remind me of the young Australian 'surfies' in their clapped-out passion-waggons who scour the Eastern seaboard of New South Wales and Victoria chasing the Big Wave. When the new breed of climbers go to the Continent it is not necessarily to climb the big classic peaks of the Alps; more than likely it will be to visit Freyr, Boux or the Verdon Gorge — the great limestone cliffs of Western Europe.

The tremendous exploration of sea cliffs in the last twenty years — cliffs on which superb rock climbs have been made — was not even remotely considered in the forties. A leisurely development of the Cornish granite cliffs had been steadily taking shape around this time but the gigantic explosion of route-finding on cliffs like Gogarth is a more recent phenomenon. And it is a salutory indication of how far we have travelled from the 'Classic Crag' syndrome when, I recall recently that one young climber, hailed as one of the Best in Britain, was described as never having climbed north of the Thames!

Even within our own local sub-cells there have been interesting, even amusing, developments. For example in 1940, Dunnerdale and Eskdale (with the exception of Esk Buttress, which for all practical purposes may be considered as part of the Scafell massif) did not exist as climbing grounds — fine crags such as Wallabarrow and Heron Crag would appear to have just grown out of the fellside. Some crags, of course, *did* — with the help of hordes of enthusiastic excavators. The two crags in Borrowdale which never fail to amuse and impress me as I pass them are Great End (the one at the entrance to Troutdale) and Goat Crag. Forty years ago they just didn't exist — at least not in the clean lines of today. A judicious burning-off of bone dry vegetation during a period of drought and a most determined cleaning up and gardening programme by a number of dedicated local climbers produced two crags of impressive dimensions. Some of the finest and hardest climbs in the Lakes at the time were made here when Read and Adams climbed Nagasaki Grooves on Great End in 1972 and Pete Livesey put up Footless Crow on Goat Crag in 1974.

Apart from the amount of new climbing that has been done between the end of the forties and today the next and most obvious feature of the climbing scene is the standard of climbing. I do not necessarily refer only to the hard climbers of the day.

I recall (in his obituary for Colin Kirkus) the comment made by A. B. Hargreaves that around that time, i.e. the late thirties and early forties, there were little more than a handful of climbers who systematically led climbs of the hardest standard — the VS standard of the day. Again, with the Lakes in mind, this would mean May Day, Great Eastern (Yellow Slab) and Overhanging Wall on

Scafell East Buttress; Central Buttress of Scafell; the Buttonhook and the Buttress, Kern Knotts; Gomorrah and the Girdle Traverse on Pillar; Deer Bield Crack; Overhanging Bastion on Castle Rock and Eliminate A on Dow Crag. These, in 1940, were regarded as the hardest climbs in the Lakes. Certainly I cannot recall more than half a dozen leaders who would systematically or regularly be known to lead them.

Even allowing for the vast increase in numbers of people who climb today, the number who lead this grade of climb is quite considerable. Looking at the situation another way the cut off point between the average, weekend or annual climber and the hard (or would-be hard) man of the forties lay somewhere around the easier Severes. Today the same point is likely to lie between say the VS category and the HVS.

From which it follows that the greatest number of people are at home on the climbs which are now of the VS category or lower. What is the reason then for this noticeable increase in standard of the general climber? The answers, I'm certain in my own mind, lie with these: the equipment, training facilities and, related to them, a fresh attitude of mind.

By equipment I mean friction boots, harness, kernmantel construction ropes and above all, protection devices. A leader in the days prior to this kind of equipment would be equipped with a hawser laid nylon or hemp rope. He would attach himself to it by a waist loop and a bowline knot. He would carry with him on the climbs one or possibly two rope slings and krabs (I am referring to the days prior to the widespread use of pegs and the availability of slim-line slings). The slings he would use would probably be of the same diameter as the rope and the krabs would be of steel — probably army surplus. It is quite likely that he would not know the ultimate tensile strength of his rope, krabs and slings, nor indeed would possession of this knowledge be of much solace. He would climb in either nailed boots or close fitting gym shoes.

With a hemp rope, if the day was wet, or if the rope was damp from the day before, it would be stiff and swollen and would not run easily through slings or over rocks. The friction on the rope would be considerable. If the rope was dry or made of hawser laid nylon it would still be far less flexible than a kernmantel rope. Even if it *were* possible to arrange a sequence of running slings on a climb, by the time four of these had been placed the frictional resistance offered by them would require that the leader would need to stop every two or three feet and pull enough rope through to enable him to move up the pitch the same distance. The number of runners used were also limited by the availability of spikes or naturally jammed stones in cracks (known as threads) that could be found on any particular pitch. Metal chocks had not been invented and pitons, of course, were *out!*

His *protection* then was restricted. Should he fall off his waist loop would cause him great pain and be very constricting. Belaying by the second man was done by passing the rope out to the leader in his right hand from under the right armpit. It was held across the back and over the opposite shoulder by the left hand, the so called 'shoulder belay'.

The result of a leader's fall usually meant that (a) it was likely he would travel a fair distance before coming on to a krab or the second and (b) because of the method of body-belaying used (as opposed to friction plate belaying) the second would find it very difficult to stop him.

If rocks didn't intervene, the leader could expect to fall a long way if he came off and the second could expect to have his hands badly burned. We were not proud of falling off (we tended to keep it a secret) and we were frightened at the prospect of so doing. In a nutshell a fall on most occasions meant either death or serious injury to the leader. One must *not,* therefore, fall off.

This was achieved by getting to know one's ability. Most free climbers would climb to a standard which did not go beyond that point that told them they were losing control of the situation. For obvious reasons the standard a leader would elect to push for on a particular day would not generally be the ultimate standard to which he was physically capable of climbing. Some barrier between the standard to which he *would* push a climb and the ultimate to which he was capable of pushing had to be established and assessed by the leader. The width of this 'performance barrier' would be conditioned by form, the weather, the exposure (that is, space beneath the leader's feet) and length of run out.

To use present day terminology all climbs, but particularly the hard ones, were *serious* routes. The mass use of artificially inserted chockstones and pegs followed later by the considerable range of commercially produced runners used in conjunction with, ropes and tapes that would withstand severe shock loading plus the security of harnesses, which would enable them to dangle in relative comfort, should they lose contact, has enabled the leaders of today to narrow the performance barrier. In many cases it is narrowed to zero width, that is, the leader falls off — possibly several times until he has overcome the problem. Falling off is now commonplace because in the majority of cases it is relatively safe to do so. I hasten to add that I am not intending to give the impression that I think *all* falling off is safe — this is an absurdity! There are plenty of occasions when, even on today's hard climbs, the leader has to move a long way above a protection point and many of those which are inserted may, for all their number, be of little more than psychological interest. In such a case some remarkable unzipping of the protection points may take place should he come off and a serious injury or fatality may follow.

My own experiences over the last two or three years as both leader and follower have convinced me that climbing today is both easier and safer than it was — but it can *never* be totally safe; an element of danger is always there. It is this element that makes climbing the joy it is.

I have recently repeated some of my old climbs. I have in fact found some of them easier to climb. (I recall Ivan Waller saying the same thing about Mickledore Grooves.) Now it would be ludicrous to suggest that I, at sixty-odd am climbing better than I was at twenty-five or thirty. The old body is not built that way. I may have a lot of the balance left but the flexibility and finger strength have taken a hammering over the years. Why then should I be able to say that some climbs are easier? The answer is that my attitude of mind has changed. I recall recently leading an airy traverse over considerable space. When I did the first ascent many years ago I felt as if I were indulging in a death defying act. Now, on this recent occasion when the going got hot I popped another nut into the crack and ran my rope through the krab. Immediately I felt relaxed. I could savour the situation and search for the most appealing sequence of moves. The climb wasn't hard — it was Eve on Shepherds Crag, a mild VS — but how much more difficult and worrying it would have felt if I'd had to do the entire fifty foot traverse without any protection over what is a quite pronounced drop. As it was I enjoyed, and was relaxed on, every move. My attitude of mind had been conditioned by the security I felt in my footwear and safety gear.

Next there is access and training. There is no doubt that with today's motorways and the availability of transport, most climbers have access, with relative ease, to large areas of Britain. There is no need to bury oneself in a nearby dirty wet gully when the weather is bad. In two or three hours driving one can often be in another drier area, with enough climbing around to keep one happy for years.

Again, for much the same reasons climbers can and do train several times a week — on small crags which offer enough variety and difficulty to maintain suppleness and arm strength. And of course there are the climbing walls — walls which have been custom built for the purpose. There is, certainly in England and Wales, a considerable future for training indoors in a constant, pleasant atmosphere — and already I have heard the philosophy expounded that 'Crags are training grounds for climbing walls.'

19

The Gentle Evening

The winter of 82/83 was an indeterminate affair — sometimes quite mild, at other times the bringer of scrappy snow and poor ice. It was not really a good winter for anything except, possibly, water pipes.

Etsu and I managed to ski from Applethwaite, via Skiddaw House to Melbecks but the snow was poor and rocks like fangs, in black ice, spoiled much of our downhill running. Ice in the gullies was little better; there were no great winter ascents to keep us glowing.

Winter gave way to spring but in terms of weather one didn't notice very much of a change.

Occasionally the sun shone sweetly. We had such a day in March when a visit to White Ghyll yielded amongst other things an ascent of Slip Knot, an early climb of Jim Birkett's and a minor classic on the crag. There was deep snow on the high central fells and a sharp wind from this quarter hustled up the Ghyll. Out of the wind we were into summer; in it we plummeted back to winter.

We had almost the same experience on Raven Crag in Thirlmere on Whillan's Raven Traverse, where we'd left the foot of the crag in bright warm sunshine and our sweaters in the rucksacks. High up on the traverse a bitterly cold wind attacked us and we retreated off the top of Communist Convert, the fine Dolphin route on the crag.

The year was getting off to a scrappy start. Had last year been the experience of a lifetime I wondered to myself? Am I going to pay for it now with raw wet days and inferior climbs until arthritis and rheumatism take their inevitable tolls?

The A.G.M. and Dinner of the B.M.C. were held in Llanberis in April. Tom Price and I drove down on the Friday. For a year now Tom had been the President of the British Mountaineering Council; Joe Walmesley, Dave Roberts and I were the Vice Presidents. At the Victoria Hotel we met up with Dennis Gray, the B.M.C.'s incredibly hard working General Secretary and decided that on the morrow we should visit Tremadoc. This we did.

The entire cliff, to me a kind of super Shepherd's Crag, was alive with climbers as Dennis led off up 'One Step in the Clouds'. I climbed second on the rope sporting my favourite leather hat (large numbers of people think it's Australian and want to know why there are no longer any corks hanging from the brim; others think it's Tyrolean and expect me to yodel — actually, I bought it in Middlesbrough!). Tom was wearing his cloth cap.

Just as we all assembled at the ledge below the superb top pitch another party, in modern drag, emerged on a hard climb to our left. The leader knew Dennis and they exchanged greetings. Then his eyes fell on Tom and me. 'Christ, Dennis, what have you got there' he exclaimed 'the Youth Group of Nineteen Fifty?'

All three of us fell against the wall laughing. I said, between giggles, 'You're ten years out mate.'

Early in May Tom and I were invited to attend the International Free Climbing Meet in Geneva organised by the Geneva Section of the Swiss Alpine Club, whose President was André Roch. The B.M.C. were sending a team of young hard climbers and André had asked Tom to go along as his guest. Tom and André had been good friends for nearly thirty years, since first they had met at a Club Dinner meet in the Lakes where André was the guest of honour and Tom had been nominated to take him climbing. André is one of the great names in mountaineering — with numerous major climbs to his credit such as the second ascent of the North Face of the Matterhorn, the first descent of the North Face of the Dru, and first ascent of the North Face of the Triolet. He was on several Himalayan expeditions and, with Raymond Lambert and others forced the ascent of the spur (to be known from thence onwards as the Geneva Spur) which leads to the South Col on Everest.

The invitation to stay with André and his family was extended to me also and on May 18 we flew to Geneva. Bill Birkett, Chris Hamper and Ian Parsons were the hard team. Tom and I described ourselves as 'observers'.

The International meet was very well organised and splendidly successful. A list of teams included those sent from Britain, Austria, Poland, Jugoslavia, Greece, Holland, Belgium and of course there were representatives from Switzerland and France.

All the climbing was done on the Saléve, a series of very steep limestone faces up to five hundred feet high rising in terraces above each other over a front of a mile or so. The climbing on the main faces of the major massif, Le Coin, was steep and hard and, for me, extremely exciting.

Whilst the young tigers disported themselves on the major lines André, Tom and I explored the whole massif by a splendid tourist route which traversed across intervening cirques and ledges to make a most spectacular circular tour of the Saléve group. Many excellent climbs were made by the teams and a remarkable camaraderie revealed itself. A show of slides and a discussion of modern climbing ethics (carried out in English) occupied the one wet day. On the last day Ian Parsons, one of the British team, asked me if I would like to join him on one of the routes on Le Coin. I had noticed a huge flake several hundred feet high had split off the north west face of the great cliff. The right hand edge of this is known as the Grande Arête and begins at the Rampe de la Grande Arête. We elected to climb this and to finish off from near the top of it by a route known as Le Paturage — which Pete Livesey had recommended in his book on French limestone climbing. These two routes strung together, preceded by a steep little climb, Dumont Jaune, of two hundred feet or so on the wall below the Rampe of the Grande Arête gave us a continuous ascent of very steep rock for something like seven hundred feet.

As he started off up the lower wall I said to Ian 'I used to be a fair climber, *once* — with the emphasis on the "once". Look after an old geriatric like me, won't you.' He grinned and away he went. The climbing (apart from the almost, for me, appallingly slippery nature of the limestone on one or two early moves) was sheer magic. The one really hard move I found was where the Paturage climb left the security of the Grande Aréte and we had to work across, then up, the great steep wall to its right, when we had ascended something like five hundred feet. Ian climbed the crux beautifully. 'How do you rate it?' I asked. 'Probably E1,' he answered. I grimaced. E1 standard after several hundred feet of VS climbing with the odd bit of HVS and a lot of work on the arms might be pushing my luck a bit too much I thought to myself. I made a decision. 'Remember what I said about my old age?' I reminded Ian, 'I don't think there's going to be much point in arse-ing about trying to do this fancifully. I'm going for it and when I do — pull like hell!' He grinned, 'O.K.' And he was as good as his word. I went for it and got a comforting heave from Ian and in moments was up beside him on his magnificently airy stance. Hundreds of feet below we could see the car park and the tennis court and it was just possible to make out André and Tom sitting at a table near the chalet and watching our efforts with obvious interest. I waved and got an answering signal. I was very tired by now. My arms ached, but the years had slipped away from me. Elation carried me forward. There was another hard little section above a further long run out, but, somehow, it didn't seem to matter. Gradually the angle eased and we reached a superb tree growing out of the cliff — then in a hundred feet more we were there. 'That's it,' said Ian, 'we're up!' To someone like him who had climbed the big routes in the Yosemite and in the Verdon Gorge and on scores of other major crags in Europe and Britain our climb may not have appeared to be anything more than a good quality run-of-the-mill sort of expedition. It meant far more than that to me — I felt at last I'd got into the nineteen eighties. I was tired, but very, very happy.

That night the Club gave us all a farewell party in a magnificent château some way out of Geneva. Here amongst some of the great names of Alpinism (including Loulou Boulaz and Yvette Vaucher, two of the greatest women climbers of all time) we ate and drank and talked and laughed the remaining hours away.

It was a magnificent occasion.

The day after I returned to Bassenthwaite I was on Shepherd's Crag with a group of students. The rock felt amiable and rough and very cosy.

And the good weather arrived . . .

In his catamaran 'Pocketee' Alan Aldred and I sailed up to the Western Isles calling in on Arran on the way. Here we spent a fabulous day on Cir Mhor — hot sun, a gentle breeze, a long walk from Brodick and an ascent of the incredible rough granite of Sou-Wester Slabs and Rosa Pinnacle. A few days later we were in Plockton and Ginger Cain and I drove out along the road to Applecross to the splendid roadside crags on the Western face of Sgurr a' Chaorochain. Here on superb Torridonian sandstone, no more than five minutes from the road at the top of the Bealach na Ba, we climbed a Tom Patey special — called Sword of Gideon. We soloed the first hundred and fifty feet and roped up at the foot of the steep crux wall — a hundred and thirty feet of firm rounded sandstone. We were up in just over an hour. 'What do you think of that?' asked Ginger. 'Terrific,' I answered. 'How would you like to have soloed the wall as well?' he went on.

'I wouldn't.'

'Patey did!'

Back in the Lakes a week later I had to meet Bill Birkett to discuss a project we were working on together.

'Where shall we meet?'

'Let's make it the Golden Rule in Ambleside — we might do a climb.'

We went up to White Ghyll.

The evening was still very warm when we reached the Ghyll.

I had been thinking all the way up of the things I would like to do. There was White Ghyll Wall, a splendid Mild VS, first climbed by Bill's dad in 1946. Or there was Gordian Knot, a major breakthrough on the main crag by Jim Haggas in 1940 — and also rated Mild VS, or if we felt like pushing the boat out a little bit further there was Haste Not, a little bit harder and also, like the other two, a climb of superb quality — and all on the *Upper* Crag.

We stopped at the sycamore, the centre of activities for the *Lower* Crag. It stands in the gully bed just below Slip Knot.

'I've done Slip Knot a couple of times recently,' I said to Bill, getting my oar in first.

'I wasn't thinking of that,' he answered. I looked up the crag to the right of Slip Knot and saw the groove and roof of Joe Brown's climb, Laugh Not. It's HVS. 'You mean we should try Laugh Not?' I queried.

'No! I wasn't thinking of that, either.'

I followed his gaze back up the crag to the 'slim, overhung groove' to the right of it.

'You don't mean Man of Straw? It's Extreme!' I wailed.

'Is it?' he answered with feigned naivete, knowing perfectly well that it is, and then, as an afterthought, 'It's just your kind of climbing.'

We soloed up to the start of the groove proper and roped up. Bill cruised up the climb giving a running commentary all the way. 'Look,' he said after he'd pulled out to the left from under the roof, 'a big ledge!' and he began to demonstrate the truth of this by standing on one foot and waving both arms about. Even from where I was standing at the foot of the groove I knew the 'big ledge' couldn't be any more than two inches long by one inch wide. But everything, I suppose, is relative.

When he'd finished the pitch and tied on to the peg belay he yelled down, 'Have you tried using chalk?' I was prepared to use anything to get me up that slim groove.

From his stance he dropped the chalk bag. It fell perfectly into my hands at the foot of the groove then I tightened up my P.A.s and began to climb. Maybe it was the chalk, maybe it *was* my kind of climbing, maybe I was climbing better, maybe it was Bill's explicit instructions, maybe it was a hangover from the Saléve — or, more likely, maybe it was a little of all of them — be that as it may the groove, though very smooth, particularly for the left foot, and the handhold on the arête felt quite adequate. The pull out from under the roof onto Bill's 'ledge' beneath a steep and very smooth slab went without too much trouble. From the foothold I could see it was necessary to make a rising two step movement up and to the right to the arête above the roof from under which I'd recently emerged. 'Handholds?' I questioned. 'You don't need them, balance up on the footholds'. I levitated on the ridiculous footholds on the wall and made for what appeared to be a good hold out on the arête. When I pounced on it I felt it shake. 'The bloody thing rattles,' I cried. 'Don't be bothered about things like that,' he grinned, 'you've made it.' And so I had — I'd climbed my first guide-book rated Extreme.

A couple of days later David Craig and I were walking in the evening light across the spur of Brandreth after having done that magnificent climb on the north crag of Gable — Engineers Slabs.

The dying sun was beginning to sneak round onto the big face, lighting the arêtes and ribs in a soft glow.

Below us, in Ennerdale, an evening mist had descended. Pillar had gone, lost in the soft greys of the fellside behind. Away to our right Buttermere and Crummock fused into a delicate haze. I thought of another recent occasion when a similar magic had invested the hills.

Two of us had been climbing all day in Birkness Combe. The sun warmed the wonderful rough rock. Despite my bad foot the climbing was all air and balance — every move a joy. As we finished the last climb of the day a loony wind sprang up and a soft, semi-transparent veil of mist descended on the crags.

It was six o'clock before we began to descend into the bed of the Combe. Above us the slabs and walls of the different buttresses had taken on strange proportions in the eerie grey light. Across the scree a grim Eagle Crag seemed gigantic, even Grey Wall appeared enormous. As we stood at the first stream of cool water, a peregrine floated above our heads, making for Chockstone Buttress. Up on the scree to the east of Eagle Crag a Herdwick, invisible in the haze, disturbed a small stone which tinkled uncannily as it fell to join its former neighbours.

Before we crossed the ancient terminal moraines of the long-gone glacier we stood transfixed in wonder, staring back into the upper reaches of the Combe. Ridge after mysterious ridge seemed to have been thrown down from both sides of the valley, each ridge, every buttress, clearly outlined, and yet firmly painted in its own particular vertical shade of grey.

Nothing moved. Even the sheep were hushed. No peregrine or indeed any other winged creature stirred.

Strange grey boulders, never seen before, stood clearly etched against an equally clean edged backcloth of paler grey. It was as if the scene was set for another race, a race of spirits, which danced and laughed silently amongst the folds of rock, happy once more to be alone again, away from the prying eyes of those who had recently intruded into their secret, silent world.

We turned away from the scene, both of us deep in our own private thoughts.

Below us the Lake was still, its shoreline faintly visible. A white shape beyond Hassness Point revealed itself as the guest house. At the head of the valley Gatesgarth farm lay silently in its pastures — and the wind sprang up again as we came out of the Combe. It was warm. We had been wearing anoraks for the last half hour; now the air was almost stultifying. Fleetwith Pike and the craggy rounded summits of the Haystacks were just visible in the haze.

By the time we reached the foot of Scarth Gap the air was clammy. Crossing the bridge we turned down towards the Lake and went in. The water was bitterly cold. Frozen fingers raked down one's spine and gripped one's stomach muscles. Emerging we dried on our spare clothing and, putting on shorts and T-shirts, sat on the lake shore — the warm wind sighing through the elms behind us.

The valley was a symphony of greys. 'I love this place' I realised again, and memory drifted backwards in time.

It was near to here that my journey had begun — early in the morning in the bright sunshine. And I thought with long, sad, and happy memories of those who had passed this way with me — of the Connor twins, of Bert Beck and George Rushworth and our campsite after Central Chimney just a few yards away; of Austin Barton and Elwyn Banner Mendus. I thought of Speaker, and how over forty years ago he had taken a raw beginner up his first Severe and of Stan Dirkin and the two Brians — Dodson and Blake. Then came that long curve in my journey and along its way the many friends in Australia who, had they known these places as I know them, would have felt as I felt . . .

Under the elms a magpie chattered — breaking into the song of the east wind. Without words we picked up our gear and walked back across the rush-grown field feeling strangely clean — and the grey began to deepen into dusk as we headed for home.

20

'1984'

My 1984 was not Orwell's. If '82 had, for me, been memorable for climbing and '83 for painting, my most enjoyable recollections of the following year are of people.

Of course, with attending various B.M.C. and Fell and Rock meetings I had met many people whom I had known of, hitherto, only by name. I had also received invitations to be guest speaker at various club dinners. That of the Pinnacle Club in 1982 is one I remember with particular pleasure. Angela Soper was in the Chair and I met Gwen Moffat again after many years.

The young lady whose job it was to introduce the guest speaker had done her homework very well. It seemed as if she had poked into every odd cranny and under every carpet of my life. With scintillating wit she had me wilting in mock dismay whilst her fellow members rocked with delight as each skeleton was disinterred. I was reminded, and they were informed, of things long and best forgotten; one did not have to be Sexton Blake to realise that Tom Price was the Mole. Only he would recollect that, away back in 1949, he and Stan Dirkin had borne me Gatesgarth Barn-wards on their shoulders and laid me gently to rest in the hay after I'd been speaking at just such another function.

In the years I'd been away many bright stars had risen — some still on the ascent, others on the wane. I took a delight in meeting them.

Early in the year the headline over the B.M.C. columns in the *Climber and Rambler* ran 'Bonatti for Buxton'. The International Mountaineering Conference organised by the B.M.C. is where, ultimately, all climbers meet. The 1984 event was one that few will forget; I certainly won't.

Walter Bonatti, probably the greatest name in Alpine Climbing history, was the principal guest. A man of great sincerity, quiet charm and gentle voice, we talked, over breakfast, of the long gone years — of Loulou Boulaz and Claude Kogan and Benuzzi of Mount Kenya fame (and how I'd met the latter in Australia in 1952).

There were a number of others from overseas. But our own special guest was Wanda Rutkiewicz. In several respects there was a marked similarity between her and Bonatti. She, the first western woman on Everest and argued by many as the greatest woman mountaineer in Europe ('and America,' some would say!), has the same steady eye, quiet voice and shy, almost retiring manner. Her deeds have to be prised from her and evaluated in proper context against the backcloth of her vast mountaineering experience. Such expeditions as her 1968 ascent of the mile high rock face Troll Wall in Norway, the all women ascent of the Eiger North Pillar in 1973, the all woman ascent of the North Face of the Matterhorn in winter 1978, Pik Lenin, the first ascent of Gasherbrun III in 1975 and her ascent of Everest in 1978, were talked of as modestly as if they were little more than an ascent of the Pig Track on Snowdon.

Wanda stayed with Etsu and I at Melbecks for a week or so. Winter still hung around and so, with Bill Birkett, we went for low level rock and high snow gullies. Her attempt with Bill on an ascent of Moss Ghyll (where there was too much soft snow and the ice was too fragile) whilst I soloed an easy Pike's Crag gully was a memorable day. We returned that evening to one of Etsu's special dinners and talked long into the night.

She told us that within a few days after leaving us she would be leading a party of four Polish women climbers in an attempt on K2, second highest mountain in the world. 'Are you taking Kendal Mint Cake?' I asked her in mock seriousness. 'What is Candal Mint Cake?' she queried. 'Ah!' I replied 'Britain's secret weapon.' The morning of her departure from Carlisle we gave her four small parcels delicately wrapped and re-ribboned by Etsu. 'What! . . . Not Candal Mint Cake?' she cried. 'Yes,' I answered solemnly, 'no mountain can withstand the combined onslaught of four Polish women climbers AND Kendal Mint Cake!' A few weeks later I received a note from her '. . . The Candal Mint Cake is on its way to K2. My colleagues are delighted with it.' But not even Kendal Mint could do the trick. Her next note said 'The weather was against us . . .'

It was at the conference that I first met the legendary Don Whillans.

I had talked to Don before, but never really met him. It had been in Sydney, Australia, where he was giving a lecture; I rang him from my home fifty miles away.

'Is that Don Whillans?'

'Aye!'

'This is Bill Peascod.'

'Oh, Aye!', pause, 'The Bill Peascod of Buttermere?'

'Aye.' (It was easy to slip back into Cumbrian dialect.)

'Bloody Hell, I thowt you were dead.'

I told him I was not, but was coming back to England, hoping to do some climbing and maybe have a beer with him some day (I don't know why I knew he would like a beer).

That evening in Buxton I caught up with him and Tony Greenbank, a journalist from Ambleside with a vast enthusiasm for living and climbing. After the first pint we had another and then, as it happened, several more. Bill Birkett joined us — our combined experiences spanned nearly fifty years of British rock climbing. We had a grand time.

'You know,' said Don, 'there's a climb I've never done and I've wanted to do it since I was fifteen.'

'What's that?' I queried.

'Your Eagle Front.'

'We'll do it!' said umpteen pints of beer, confidently. Greenbank, characteristically slapping his thigh with glee, was shouting 'When? When?'

Prudence overcame beer courage. 'Who's going to lead it?' I countered.

'We'll git up t'bugger somehow,' answered Don — 'but' as an afterthought, 'no sneaky training, mind. Only training allowed is ten pints of beer the night before.' Some weeks later I got a card from Norway. It said

> . . . Am up here in the frozen North getting 'frosnip' in the 'cobblers' . . . Beer prices here turned me teetotal, and fags are £2.50 a packet. I haven't forgotten Eagle Front. Keep Tony on his toes. Cheers the noo, Don.

My exhibition of painting at Kendal's Abbot Hall Gallery in 1983 led to some pleasing developments. As a result of the show I had begun to exhibit in the Thackeray Gallery, just off Kensington Square in London. Its Director, Priscilla Andersen, was thoroughly experienced and professional and, what is just as important, was on my wavelength where the paintings were concerned. Early in the year we had discussed the possibility of a one-man show. She rang me up to say that there was a vacancy in late October — would I be interested? I was — and work began! It was to continue for some months.

In between whiles, when I'd reached exhaustion point with painting I slipped off into the fells.

Chris Bonington lives nearby and even though we were both under similar sorts of time restrictions we managed to sneak off for an odd afternoon or evening on the crags. I like climbing with Chris. He is good to be out with. He has a fund of stories of other places and people and (which ought to be apparent from his tremendous climbing history) is really a very fine rock climber. Most people, one imagines, see him as the Himalayan man. Fewer seem to realise that, like many other great mountaineers (Doug Scott, Don Whillans, Al Rouse) Bonington is also very good on rock. His is not the highly technical expertise of the modern generation, many of whom are, fundamentally, rock climbers. Bonington is a mountaineer. He is a thoughtful climber on rock. His moves always seem to be carefully assessed before he makes them and when he goes for them they happen smoothly and with certainty. He is a climber who 'looks' and is, one feels, safe on rock — not through lashings of protective equipment, but from long experience and understanding of his own capabilities.

Add to this the two other factors, namely his deep affection for the Lake District and his unquestionable joy in being on rock and you have something of the personality that makes him such a good companion on Lakeland hills.

One early summer afternoon Chris picked me up at Melbecks for a day on the crags. As we drove along the Lake side he said, 'I've been asked to do a series on climbing in the Lakes. Border TV will be shooting it. This is what I have in mind . . '

And he set out the broad details of the project. The programmes were to cover a sort of climbing history beginning in 1940. Each decade would be represented by one climb and hopefully would include the climber or climbers involved in the first ascent. A helicopter would be used to get climbers, film crew and gear up the mountain . . . would I be interested in doing the 1940's segment — climbing Eagle Front with him?

I was very interested — particularly in the helicopter bit. I'd long had a penchant for 'heli-climbing'! I was also interested in who was in the segment on the next decade — he hoped to get Brown and Whillans for Dovedale Grooves he told me, a ferocious climb for its day on Dove Crag, up from Patterdale. As it happened Brown was out of action with an injury to his ankle but Whillans was available. This all looked like being great fun!

Then Chris said 'Will you lead Eagle Front — and would you be prepared to do some of it wearing the gear of the forties?' This meant gym shoes, hemp rope, very few slings (two only in fact) and no stoppers or chocks. I pondered this one a while and said 'Yes, if it's dry and if there's a bottle of champagne at the top,' I added with a grin.

After his return from his Karakorum Expedition with Al Rouse we all assembled at Wasdale Head. It had been a glorious summer, but by now the good weather was history. The chopper couldn't even get over Black Sail Pass! When we finally got up to Eagle Crag in Birkness Combe my worst fears were realised. Eagle Crag was wet — in places very wet — and sections of it, that had to be climbed through, were covered in a rich slime.

We pondered the situation and decided to start off in the old gear until such time as the conditions demanded we should change into modern drag — as it happened this was at the top of the first easy pitch. Long before I got there I ran into a slimy groove and had to climb in socks. On the ledge above I changed into my climbing harness and pulled socks over my rubber-soled climbing boots. Life began to take on a rosier hue . . .

I was amazed how much work is involved in making a climbing documentary. One camera crew shot us from below; another crew, Tony Riley and Mo Anthoine, together with the director Paul Berriff 'jumared' (that is, climbed up fixed ropes using metal friction clips attached to the ropes) alongside us.

It is fairly obvious that for filming projects such as ours the cliff face experience is not just limited to the climbers. Tony and Mo were both very competent climbers. Mo, who is also an equipment manufacturer in Llanberis had, in fact, climbed extensively throughout the world. All of this made for good companionship, a relaxed atmosphere and a cheerful banter between the filmers and the filmed.

Pete Whillance, a young hard climber from Carlisle and one of the most brilliant of his generation, was taking care of security, supported by a team of other highly experienced climbers — Murray Hamilton, Al Rouse and Ray Parker. Nothing missed Pete's shrewd eye. I realised again, as I'd noticed with Bill Birkett, that climbers like him seem to be a product of the rock itself — to them it is almost home. I pondered ruefully to myself 'Once, a long time ago, I might have been like that.' Now, at sixty-four, I wasn't leaping about as I used to — but then I wasn't normally on Eagle Front when it was in the 'cruddy' state it was in now!

We came to the crux, a bulge, at the start of the third pitch — an awkward enough move when dry; now it was a 'river of shit' and I said so. Far down below us, from the sound recording base, a gale of laughter swept up the crag and I realised I'd done it again — forgotten that under our shirts were the microphones that were recording everything we said. Ah well, climbers tended to a certain verbal richness when things got a bit difficult I reasoned — and I got on with the problem of the bulge. 'Chris,' I announced, 'only one way for it! In the old days, when in trouble it was combined tactics . . . and I'm in trouble now!' I climbed onto his shoulders. I no longer weigh only ten stones. He winced and said something that brought another laugh from the valley. As he straightened up I launched from his shoulders onto the bulge and, praying that my socks would stick to the greasy rock teetered up slowly out of trouble. It was several days later that we got back onto the face. By now the exposed upper traverse across the so-called Waterworn Slab, from what had become known as Nail Ledge, was very greasy indeed — but it 'went', as did the big upper crack and it was with considerable satisfaction that we knew the climbing bit was 'in the can'. Now all we had to do was a finale and an introductory sequence which I was told would involve riding a bike down Newlands Pass amongst other things.

Chris led up the last few feet of the easy rock at the top of the climb and I was told to rest my bones until he called. When I arrived at the top of the cliff I found him wreathed in a broad grin and sitting on a gently sloping slab. As the cameras trained on us he suddenly leapt into high theatrical action, rushed across to a boulder and pulled out from behind it — a bottle of champagne. I had completely forgotten my crack about leading it only if there was champagne at the finish. But we were not going to be left in peace to enjoy it — apart from anything else there were the covetous eyes of the film crew on us. I noticed Mo Anthoine smack his lips.

The procedure dictated to us was that Chris and I would share the initial sips of the champagne after which the chopper, presently sitting on the main High Crag — High Stile ridge a few hundred feet away would take off. Carrying a film crew, it would circle us then back off over the cliff. As Chris and I receded in the camera lens the full height of the face up which we had laboured would come into view and dwarf us. It would make a marvellous fade-out, it was said. We broached the bottle and did the initial sipping. The champagne tasted marvellous — then a small problem! The weather and the up draughts on the face, unnoticed by us, rendered the chopper segment somewhat difficult. This move, it was announced, had to be called off — at least for the moment. Within seconds of this pronouncement the vultures had homed in on the bottle!

But the 'backing-off' bit by the helicopter still seemed like a good idea. So a couple of days later we were back again at Gatesgarth. Now nearing the end of the shooting — all that remained (and this had to be structured to meet the logistics of the weather) was an initial early morning walk up to the Combe to be filmed, then we'd be lifted by the chopper to the top of the crag for the champagne segment and the final shots, on Newlands Pass, which would follow immediately afterwards.

Everything went well.

By three o'clock Chris and I were sitting once again on the top of Eagle Crag. Our instructions were explicit. The chopper would first of all circle us, we would uncork the bottle and sip. The chopper would then back off over the Combe. 'Don't look up at the chopper, O.K.?'

'O.K.!'

We were delighted to find that the new bottle was real, not a backroom prop. The chopper circled us; we uncorked and sipped.

The chopper receded over the top of the crag. We had emptied a third of the bottle. Then . . .

'It's coming round again! Ah, Well!'

Dutifully we sipped again. The chopper repeated its routine. By now we'd got through the second third of the bottle.

'Shit, he's coming round again!' . . . We emptied the bottle.

The chopper landed on the ridge above us. Paul came running down to us . . . 'You haven't drunk it all?' We had! 'The last circuit was to attract your attention and tell you to leave some.'

'You told us not to look at the camera.' We had been most dutiful in carrying out instructions. Within minutes we were back at Gatesgarth Farm, with preparations being made for the Newlands episode.

I felt at peace with the world.

A short time later we gathered at the top of the pass. All traffic had been stopped; the chopper was in the air above me. I set off on my ride down to Buttermere. The bike was old but in good condition. The brakes had been thoroughly checked. As I skimmed easily downhill I became blasé. This, I thought, is easy. I'll try it with one hand — and did. The front wheel began to wobble. Something unscripted was imminent. I had two options if I were to come off, I reasoned (and suddenly I realised I would!). Either the big drop on the right and a spectacular catapult into space or the grass, wall and odd rock on the left. I headed for the grass and rock on the left. Gracefully, I believe, the bike and I parted company.

From the chopper the word flashed to the control van at the top of the hill 'Bill's come off the bleeding bike.' And Mo added, 'He's pissed!'

When the van reached me only seconds later, it seemed, I was busy putting the chain, which had come off during my disembarkation, back onto its drive sprocket. We tried again; within minutes I was on my way, this time with two hands firmly clasped on the handlebars and whistling 'Begin the Beguine' to the swish of the tyres on the tarmacadam. It was really a very enjoyable experience . . .

A few days later I was doing a repair job on a barn door when a huge motorbike roared into the yard and the rider, a short little fellow of unmistakable proportions, dismounted. We were delighted to see him.

'Etsu, this is Don Whillans.' The pair of them hit it off immediately. Don's dry humour and his shrewd thinking on mountain matters and people, his vast experience that merely trickled, rather than forced its way into a conversation were a delight to her. As everyone who's had much to do with him knows, Don is a stickler for time. If he says six o'clock he means precisely that (or preferably just a little earlier). Etsu knows that when I say six o'clock it means any time from seven onwards. His precision was exceedingly refreshing to her.

He told us the film segment on Dovedale Grooves was being shot at some time during the following week. He had come up early to do a little bit of walking, he said. His 'little bit of walking' turned out to be several fairly hefty hikes. I was inundated with work for my exhibition in London and pleaded forgiveness. The arrangements worked very well.

On the Tuesday before his departure for filming I said to him 'Look, I've *had* bloody work, what about we go and do a little climb somewhere tomorrow?' It was agreed — but first he would like to call on a mate of his, who used to be a plumber and ran a trout farm, and then he would like to visit Michael Moon's bookshop in Whitehaven.

The pair of us mounted the Honda and departed. Someone once said to me 'Don doesn't drive very fast.' Whoever it was, has never been with him on a long straight road. Mounted on that powerful beast, the '500', the wind drag almost ripping me off the pillion, I clung on desperately to the grab bar and crouched as low as possible (which isn't really terribly effective when the driver in front of you is four inches shorter) to reduce the wind resistance. I won't say I was worried, but I did recall how thirty-odd years before Stan Dirkin and I (actually travelling along the same road, not far away) in mid winter struck an ice patch. On that occasion the bike suddenly shot from underneath us. I landed on the rucksack I was carrying and skidded merrily along on the ice behind Stan and the bike which, somehow, had managed to reverse the order of things — now the bike was on top of Stan! The entire episode was so funny, I recall, that I began laughing like a drain — until I noticed the 'presence' behind me. It was an ancient saloon car that hadn't been travelling too slowly either. When we came off, its driver had jammed on his brakes. The car spun through ninety degrees and it too was gliding happily down the ice, broadside on. There was every possibility that I was about to become the meat in a motorbike/saloon car sandwich. My laughter evaporated. Thankfully we all slid to a halt without further complications — although I felt extremely sorry for the elderly couple who got out of the car in an obviously high state of shock! That was a long time ago and, anyway, there's no ice on the road, I consoled myself. Don and I got to the trout farm at a more amiable speed through the narrow lanes of West Cumbria. His friend wasn't in. So we went to Michael Moon's at Whitehaven. It was closed. 'Never mind,' I said, 'We'll go to Beckermet — he's got another shop there.'

So we drove on to Beckermet, south of Egremont.

'He doesn't run it here any more,' we were told by a lady in the village.

'We're not doing very well, are we?' commented Don drily, as we remounted the bike and pointed it towards Buttermere.

It was a lovely day at the top of Honister. When we got to Buckstone How the sun had swung round onto the main face, where the rock after recent rain was drying out quite well.

'What about Honister Wall?' I said.

'Aye! It looks all right,' he replied, surveying the first pitch. 'Where does it go?'

I pointed out the direction as we roped up.

'Who's leading?'

I suggested we alternate.

'Right, I'll give it first go — what do we need?' I said he'd get a sling on a knob about half way up the seventy feet pitch.

I had become so used to seeing climbers bedecked with masses of 'protection' that it came as a breath of fresh air to see him set off with no more than two slings. 'Aye! That's enough — it should be aw reet,' and away he went. In no time he was at the belay and I, who knew every move on the climb was not long after him.

'I'll run the next two pitches into one,' I commented, 'it'll save time — and we can get to the Scafell for a pint and a sandwich.'

Having picked up the habit from him, I didn't waste time looking for anchor points for wire stoppers and such like and did the next two pitches with only a couple of runners in situ.

It seemed that in no time at all we were both standing on the comfortable ledge at the foot of Black Wall, about half way up the three hundred feet climb. This is technically the most difficult pitch on the route — it was Don's turn!

'Where does it go?'

I pointed out the traverse and where the hidden hold could be found.

Don Whillans, as I've said, is short and carried a lot of weight. He has remarkably solid shoulders and the most powerful looking wrists I have seen on any climber; they remind me of the fetlocks of a horse. It is equally apparent that he possesses in those shoulders and arms an enormous strength — but what I hadn't quite bargained on was his remarkable agility. He didn't climb Black Wall — he leapt up it. I know it's not hard, but it's steep and the sequence of moves is awkward on first acquaintance. Don went across that wall like a tarantula in top gear.

'Give me a handhold,' he quipped, 'and I'll show you the fancy footwork.'

In one moment of sparkling revelation I saw a hint of the man that many see as probably the finest mountaineer this country has ever produced and undeniably one of its greatest rock climbers.

I saw him rise, first of all a few feet delicately on small holds then leap for a high up knob. A massive fist curled over the handhold and his body (weight of no consequence) swung up to a distant foothold.

All the secret holds were rejected. He didn't need them! He was up the wall in a flash, effortlessly and without the slightest of bother.

('Dovedale Grooves,' I said to myself, 'you've had it!' And I was absolutely convinced that this little powerful climbing machine would have no trouble on that very hard climb which, first ascended by him and Joe Brown thirty-odd years before, had had to wait ten years before anyone else was able to get up it. As it happened, despite the horseplay, I was right!)

The rest of Honister Wall went easily and we sat in the sun for a few minutes. I have done the climb many times. I usually estimate a couple of hours for the ascent. Whillans and I had done it in just over the hour, and we hadn't really been pushing it — just climbing and joking along.

From the summit we rattled down the side of the cliff and recovered our rucksacks and boots. 'Nice time to get to the Scafell in Borrowdale,' I said. We got to the pub just after two o'clock. Bar lunches were off.

'Any sandwiches?'

'The last one's just gone!'

We settled for a couple of packets of crisps.

'We're not doing real well today, are we,' was Don's comment, dry as ever!

I worked hard and consistently on the paintings during the summer.

An occasional day on the hills with Chris Bonington, David Craig or the Prices and a commitment to attend a meet of the Association of British Members of the Swiss Alpine Club in Saas Fee (at which Alpine centre an ascent of the South-South West Ridge of the Egginer, involving a late start, atrocious weather and a descent in the dark of some five and a half thousand feet from the summit to Saas Almagell, developed, for George Watkins and me, into a mini-epic) were the main diversions from the studio.

After each I returned, batteries re-charged, to my painting. In preparing a large exhibition I have always found that I work best when the pressure is on. If I'm working sporadically on an odd painting I tend to find myself fiddling with ideas and don't get round to bringing the work to fruition. With a large number of paintings I find I develop a coherence, some ideas generate others. After a while the longed-for rapport with the canvas is attained and the paintings begin to work. I invariably destroy the ones that come early in the sequence — either by painting them out completely and re-starting or by eliminating unnecessary detail to develop a nuance that had remained unrealised in the first version. All of this, the customary progression, was being gone through — but slowly I was getting somewhere. Then, quite suddenly I realised the exhibition was completed. At the end of September the paintings went to the framers . . . The heat was off!

A postcard arrived from Don, from Bod Hyfryd in Penmaenmawr. 'Am at home now. We'll expect you sometimes in October . . .' I phoned him back.

'We'll be down next weekend and we might do a bit . . .'

'Champion,' replied the Little Chap. 'I'll get my boots out.'

At Bod Hyfryd we met Don's wife, Audrey — quietly unruffled, taking climbing talk in her stride, she welcomed us warmly.

Our visit coincided with much rain in the Pass and with the Climbers' Club's Annual Dinner. We turned up at the Victoria in Llanberis 'for a few jars and a crack' and had plenty of both.

I was surprised how many climbers I knew there. Four years ago I didn't know any of them. Now I was being greeted like some antiquated Prodigal Son — the Camaraderie of the Crags is a grand feeling. In a way it reminds me of the pre-war miners — humour and rivalry within the ranks, but a solid barrier against those who are not of them and who wish to do them down.

On the Sunday morning it seemed that the whole of North Wales was under low cloud — except for Penmaenmawr. Here, in warm sun the two of us walked on the hills behind the town. The Carnedds, to the south, were now bathed in warm light; to the north, in Conwy Bay, a small yacht battled through choppy seas. We talked of times past — of the pre-war years, of the Golden Age of the Himalayas, of climbing in the forties and fifties, of the Rock and Ice, of the lads that had gone and those of today.

In the afternoon we drove out to Anglesey with Audrey, Etsu and Emma and walked along the sea cliffs. A fast current ran in a great arc outside Gogarth Bay. Within the shelter of the stupendous coastal cliffs the water was strangely calm and, like the rocks, deserted. Above the cliffs the heather had turned a soft golden brown.

'Next year,' said Don, 'as soon as the nice weather gets here, and when it's still quiet, come down for a couple of weeks and we'll have a good look round. We'll nip down to Pembroke and maybe Cornwall; it's grand there — and we'll go up to Cloggy and see what's going on . . .'

'Right,' I answered 'and I fancy the Dolomites or maybe even Japan.'

'Aye, Ah fancy Japan myself,' he mused, 'And there's still Eagle Front.'

Back at Melbecks next morning the invitations for my show in the Thackeray Gallery arrived, then a ring from my framer to say that all the work was ready. Suddenly I felt a great elation — an excitement I hadn't known for years; there was so much to do and see and feel — the air seemed charged with life and the end of my journey out of the dawn light seemed as far away as ever it had been.